2000 Years of Social Wisdom

Catholic Social Teaching from the Papacy

2000 Years of Social Wisdom, 1st ed.

©2016 by Christopher Jay

This work is available free of charge at www.whywesingatmass.org

This work is available under the terms of the free GNU Documentation license: http://www.gnu.org/licenses/fdl-1.3.en.html. This work may be distributed for free, so long as the content is not modified.

Composed by Christopher Jay.

Please contact music@whywesingatmass.org

Ad Majorem Dei Gloriam.

> "Blessed is the man who walks not in the counsel of the wicked, nor stands in the way of sinners, nor sits in the seat of scoffers. But his delight is in the law of the LORD, and on His law he meditates day and night."
>
> *Psalm 1*

Table of Contents
Note: See end of the book for an alphabetized Table of Contents.

Prelude viii

1. Life & Human Nature 1
- -Life- 1
- -Contraception, Sterilization, & Abortion- 5
- -Elderly & Disabled- 8
- -Euthanasia- 9
- -Ethics- 10
- -Bioethics- 11
- -Pornography & Drugs- 12
- -Capital Punishment- 12
- -Human Trafficking- 13

2. Family, Community, and Government 14
- -Family- 14
- -Divorce- 17
- -Marriage- 17
- -Adoption- 19
- -Inheritance- 19
- -Private Property - 19
- -Proportional Ownership for All –or – Promotion of Ownership- ... 24
- -Role of the State- 28
- -Anarchy- 36
- -Principle of Subsidiarity- 37
- -Role of the Church in Society & Politics- 38
- -Role of Catholics in Public Activity- 45

- Politics & Public Activity - 46
- Catholic Social Teaching- 48
- Separation of Church and State or Church and Public Life- 48
- Progress & Reform- 51
- Legislation & Practical Application of Social Principles- 56
- Regulation- 60
- Welfare & State Subsidies- 61
- Healthcare- 64
- Taxes & Tax Evasion- 65
- Class Warfare- 66
- Freedom of Press & Freedom of Speech- 66
- Media, Social Media, & the News- 67
- Propaganda- 70
- Advertising & Consumerism- 70
- Consumers- 71
- Public versus Private- 72
- Education- 74
- Youth- 78
- Utopias & Ideologies- 79
- Evangelization- 81
- Dialogue & Differences in Opinion - 81
- Women & Women in the Workplace- 86
- Racism- 87
- Minorities- 87
- Discrimination- 87
- Form of Government- 88
- Democracy- 88

-Public Authority- 89
-Peace- 90
-War- 92
-Global and Foreign Relationships- 93
-Foreign Policy- 94
-Culture - 95
-Urbanization- 96
-Atheism- 98
-Terrorism- 100
-Patriotism- 100
-Voting- 100
-Tourism- 101

3. Rights & Responsibilities 102
-Charity (Caritas)- 102
-Rights- 103
-Right to Life- 106
-Freedom- 106
-Freedom of Religion and Conscience- 108

4. Poor and Vulnerable 111
-Poor- 111
-Foreign Aid- 112
-Volunteer Aid- 116
-Development- 116
-Liberation Theology- 121
-Non-Violent Resistance- 122

5. Work & the Economy 123
-Economics- 123

-Labor- 127

-The Market- 130

-Free Market –or- *Laissez Faire* Market- 131

-Free Consent- 138

-Contracts- 139

-Production- 139

-Obligations of Workers to Employers- 141

-Strikes- 141

-Obligations of Employers to Workers- 141

-Wages & Profit- 143

-Workplace- 149

-Rest & Sunday Worship- 150

-Unemployment- 151

-Unions & Non-Government Organizations- 151

-Liberalism- 155

-Capitalism- 156

-Socialism- 161

-Communism & Marxism- 164

-Capitalism v. Socialism- 165

-Reform- 170

-Foreign Markets- 171

-Investments & Investing- 172

-Finance- 174

-Small Businesses & Co-operatives- 175

-Outsourcing- 175

-Tariffs- 177

-Monopolies- 177

-International Trade- 178

-World Fund & International Debt- 179

6. One Human Body (Solidarity) 181

-Solidarity & Human Dignity- 181

-Equality & Inequality- 183

-Immigration & Emigration- 185

-Revolution- 187

-The Arms Race & Disarmament- 188

-Global Cooperation & Foreign Policy- 189

-United Nations- 196

-Population Expansion- 197

7. Creation, Ecological Issues, and the Environment 200

-Science & Technology- 200

-Ecological & Environmental Concerns- 206

-Energy- 213

-Agriculture- 214

INDEX OF PAPAL DOCUMENTS 218

Prelude

To all Men of Goodwill

"The principles [The Church] gives are of universal application…We call, not only Our own sons and brothers scattered throughout the world, but also men of goodwill everywhere." *Mater et Magistra, 1961.*

I begin this work by humbly asking the reader to read this prelude, so as to easier read and understand the entire contents.

<u>This work is a collection of papal quotes on a spectrum of issues, with minimal commentary; for the most part it is not my personal take on Catholic Social teaching but rather a collection of direct quotes from papal encyclicals.</u> As such, I do not consider myself to have "authored," but rather, to have "composed."

I compose this work to those of goodwill – where "goodwill" is a fearless commitment to the Truth, even when it demands we change. Without this disposition of goodwill, no reasonable discourse can be had. Such a disposition could be framed hypothetically as, "<u>If</u> I realize that this is true and that I am in error – would I change?" If not, there is no goodwill, and further discourse is pointless. Truth cannot be shared, happiness cannot be reached, without basic goodwill; and it is to all those who possess this goodwill that I give this work.

This book is meant first and foremost as a discovery of what the Catholic Church has <u>actually</u> taught for the past 2000 years in regards to "social teaching," as laid out by teachings from the past 150 years (i.e. addressed to the modern world). As the Catholic Church is not *exclusively* anchored in any particular time or place, so too the teaching is not allegiant to any political party or country. I have also constructed this work to be as simple as possible: these few pages cannot delineate all of Catholic Social teaching, rather it is intended to build a foundation. There is much more to find in these teachings than I have laid out here; this is a curated selection based on topics that I have found either critical or confusing to many, especially since most topics are polarized (i.e. public vs. private, capitalism vs. socialism, etc.) with the Church taking either the difficult middle ground or a totally different stance than any given popular polarized ideology.

I believe that discussions like this require candid openness, and this is why I lay out my motive for composing this. There are many existing works on

Catholic Social teaching, notably the Pontifical *Justitia et Pax* Council's *Compendium of the Social Doctrine of the Church* which lays out a broad summary of the Catholic Church's Social teachings. There are also numerous documents from Bishops, as well as works of private authors. In my experience, however, people are suspicious of the above: apprehensive – often, unfortunately rightly - that the latter sometimes does not reflect the official teachings of the Church. Preaching that sounds more like partisan persuasion than teaching, reports of the USCCB (United States Conference of Catholic Bishops) accepting millions from politically-motivated sources, or even bare distortion of Catholic Social Teaching etc., lend an unfortunate but concrete credence to these fears. Sadly, much trust has been betrayed in this area, especially in the area of education. Therefore, I mean here to give access to the most common teaching authority of the Church: the Papal encyclicals and the Popes themselves. Certainly, disputes will arise. However, if a discussion arises about a certain teaching, I recommend using the references and the internet to find the original document and context.

With regard to discussing current politics and Catholic Social Teaching, one must be cautious to represent Catholic Teaching with sources, not assumptions. This work will help in that regard. However, even Jesus's words can be abused and taken out of context - papal teachings are no exception. Ergo, I strongly recommend that (1) one interested in the Church's stance on a specific issue read the entire section here, and (2) look up the actual encyclical online to assess it in context. Although I have done my best to make sure that quotes were not presented out of context here, the distinction between what the Popes *are saying* and what they are *not saying* is crucial: jumping to conclusions by failing to contextualize will destroy a proper understanding of these encyclicals.

> "The Church, which has long experience in human affairs and has no desire to be involved in the political activities of any nation, 'seeks but one goal: to carry forward the work of Christ under the lead of the befriending Spirit. And Christ entered this world to give witness to the truth; to save, not to judge; to serve, not to be served.' Founded to build the kingdom of heaven on earth rather than to acquire temporal power, the Church openly avows that the two powers—Church and State—are distinct from one another; that each is supreme in its own sphere of competency."
> *Populorum Progresso*, 1967.

Isaiah 55:8: "'For my thoughts are not your thoughts, nor are your ways my ways,' declares the LORD." I must again stress that there may be many teachings which surprise even educated and practicing Catholics, especially American Catholics. Always there is continuity in regards to official teachings on *faith and morals,* while customs and structural configurations may change throughout the years. That being said, I humbly ask the reader to approach the papal teachings in the spirit of Isaiah, remembering that God's ways are not our ways, possibly even the ways we have come to think of as comfortable, conservative, and traditional. As Pope Paul VI points out in *Humane Vitae*, the Pope, as representing the Church, is not the arbiter or author of Truth, only the caretaker and interpreter. This is, I believe, another sign that the Church's teachings are of God, namely, that like the prophet Jeremiah they make us <u>all</u> uncomfortable with our complacencies, while offering us the way that is better than what we had thought.

Recalling that we are the branches, and Christ is the vine (John 15:5), we know as Catholics that in order to receive the life that is Truth, we must adhere to the vine. Christ instituted His Church on earth to be the pillar and foundation of Truth (1 Timothy 3:15); we cannot call ourselves Catholic and disregard the authority of that same Church in any matter. Regardless of whether the issue is one of faith and morals, when the Church speaks *authoritatively*, any Catholic is bound.

I must also stress again that, in reading these teachings, one must be <u>very</u> careful to hear both what the Popes are saying, and what they are **not** saying. So too, the subjects, though categorized separately, are inseparably connected: reading all of them in reference to one another gives the fullest picture.

I must preface this work by defining and explaining a few key elements: Catholic Social Teaching, Encyclicals (and the character of Church teaching), Liberalism, Capitalism, and Socialism.

-**Catholic Social Teaching** is the application of Catholic principles in a social setting, from the local to the global. It has developed, not so much as new teachings per se, but newly formulated teachings out of existing doctrine that concern specific modern phenomena that have sprung up in the last 300 or so years. The Catholic Church has always applied Christ's mission to all areas of life – scientific, political, social, etc. -, but Pope Leo XIII's teaching (ca. 1880) is recognized as the impetus that formalized Catholic Social Teaching as contained here, with the encyclical *Rerum Novarum* – "Of New Things" or "Of Revolutionary Things". "On the basis of the long period of experience, it cannot be rash to say that [*Rerum Novarum*] has proved itself the Magna Charta upon which all Christian activity in the social field ought to be based, as on a foundation." (*Quadragesimo Anno*, 1931).

Let it be also said, bolded, underscored, and emphasized, that the Catholic Church teaches, and has always taught, that the external life of actions *must* come from, and be preserved by, the more important inner and contemplative life. Luke 10:41. Matthew 7:21. Without a core of prayer and silence – i.e. love of God - productive activity, including profit, elections, and even evangelization, is a meaningless, short-term noise. 1 Corinthians 13:1. "May these warning words of the divine Master ever sound in men's ears: "For what doth it profit a man, if he gain the whole world and suffer the loss of his own soul? Or what exchange shall a man give for his soul?" (*Mater et Magistra*, 1961).

-**Encyclicals** are the common "teaching letters" of the Church.

Before I go further, however, let me delineate the character of Church authority that has developed, which is so often misunderstood by non-Catholics and serious Catholics alike.

Catholics understand that the Pope, *when explicitly in his teaching capacity*, is infallible in the areas of Faith and Morals. This does not mean that everything the Pope utters is infallible, nor that encyclicals are infallible. For instance, the Pope could privately - say, at a dinner party - teach error; likewise, he could publicly – say, a Wednesday audience - teach error. Similarly, he – and the Church as a whole – does not claim to be correct about scientific or empirical fact. The latter claim would be absurd given the Church's primary mission as an Apostolic vehicle of Salvation.

Explicit annunciation (i.e. saying "We hereby declare…" etc.) and repeated teaching statements over time (i.e. by successive Popes) denote a pronunciation of infallibility in regards to teachings on Faith and Morals. This work attempts to illustrate and trace said chronological lines; however, this work's primary focus is not to trace the *infallibility* of a given teaching, but rather, its *authority*.

Authority is not an "on-off" switch: there are various levels of authority, both in the Church and everywhere. This means that the Pope has different teaching tools available at his disposal, which he will purposefully choose. In order of importance, the common instruments are the Papal Bull (highest), Encyclical, Apostolic Exhortation or Letter, Wednesday Audience, and daily homily (lower). Note that there is a purposefulness involved: a "Tweet" or an off-the-cuff remark is not teaching authority. Every document in this collection, except Blessed Pope Paul VI's *Octogessima Adveniens* and Pope Francis' *Evangelii Gaudium*, is an Encyclical, which is the penultimate teaching instrument of the Church. While specific <u>doctrines</u> can be developed infallibly <u>within</u> encyclicals (especially where successors re-iterate teaching), encyclicals are indeed <u>authoritative</u> and binding on all Catholics, and are Church teaching.

<u>The fact that authority is not an "either-or," however, means that a teaching can be binding to Catholics even if not infallible, and even if not regarding Faith and Morals.</u> This point is often misunderstood by Catholics, who tend to think that if a teaching is not infallible, they can disregard it. If a Pope speaks officially, and <u>especially if multiple Popes declare on the same issue</u> (as they have on many issues, beginning from Pope Leo XIII and currently with Pope Francis) a practicing Catholic <u>must</u> adhere to those teachings: if not agree with them, certainly respect them utterly. (cf. Code of Canon Law, Book 3, 747-755; cf. Catechism of the Catholic Church, par. 888). Especially in our under-educated and over-broadcasted day and age, it is a temptation to think that we are qualified to publicly and frivolously dissent. To put it in perspective, formal dissent by a Catholic of encycicalic teaching, where the disagreement is fundamental and serious, should involve personal discourse with the Vatican. Again, as a Catholic, merely because an issue is not clear-cut infallible does not mean it cannot be binding – it may be a temporary (as in, for this century) Apostolic decree, but it is an exercise of Peter's keys and ergo cannot be taken lightly.

Too, papal teachings are not without context: certain statements (say, about a scientific fact, Unions, or a diagnosis of a current issue) are necessarily contextual and not necessarily pronouncements that bind since they are clearly, in context, not meant to be so. Again, the Church does not seek to adjudicate on empirical debates. For example, what may be true of Unions now may not be true of Unions 100 years ago. The actual teaching, the principle behind the empirical diagnosis, however, is authoritative.

The opposite imbalance to disregarding Papal authority is "Ultramontinism," which essentially means recklessly regarding every statement of the Popes as 100% authoritative and true. This too is not a Catholic understanding of Magisterial authority: one is not called to believe as doctrine what has not been promulgated as doctrine, or act immorally if an authority demands it. Popes are sinners, and have both spoken and acted in error. If the Pope speaks error against established teaching, he is indeed wrong: he is only protected by the Holy Spirit (i.e. infallible), when teaching on faith and morals, and only then *ex Cathedra* (i.e. officially acting with full teaching authority). However, as with all authority - but especially so with the Chair of Peter - any disagreement must made with true respect, not just lip-service to respect.

The distinction between "being right" and "being obedient" is crucial: sometimes, we may have better ideas than Peter about how to run the Church, but for some reason, the Holy Spirit hasn't yet put us in charge. John Henry Newman explained it thus:

> I say with Cardinal Bellarmine whether the Pope be infallible or not in any pronouncement, anyhow he is to be obeyed. No good can come from disobedience. His facts and his warnings may be all wrong; his deliberations may have been biased. He may have been misled. Imperiousness and craft, tyranny and cruelty, may be patent in the conduct of his advisers and instruments. But when he speaks formally and authoritatively he speaks as our Lord would have him speak, and all those imperfections and sins of individuals are overruled for that result which our Lord intends… and therefore the Pope's word stands, and a blessing goes with obedience to it, and no blessing with disobedience. JHN, *Letter to Lady Simeon*, 1867.

Towards non-Catholics, though the Papal teachings have a different relevance, I would invite serious examination: the Popes come from a 2,000 year old institution responsible for founding much of the world we live in, ergo their words should at very least be pondered in a spirit of goodwill.

To reiterate: this work is a collection primarily of Papal Encyclicals, which in certain contexts are possibly infallible when referring to doctrines, and are almost certainly authoritative to each and every person who calls themselves Catholic. Generally speaking, it is the definition of a Catholic that he or she, to the best of their knowledge, accepts the authority and the teaching of the Catholic Church.

So much for an explanation of Encyclicals. Three more terms must also be touched upon before Catholic Social Teaching is discussed:

Liberalism, Capitalism, and Socialism are movements of the modern world that have influenced us more than we realize. Like many others I fear, I often used these terms without understanding their origin, relationships, and essences of each, and hence I have been obligated to step back and study them so as to be able to summarize them here, as a general understanding of them is *essential* to understanding the modern world and a discussion of Catholic Social Teaching.

Liberalism is a movement which grew up in the 1700s; a social philosophy that grew out of and through the Enlightenment. It is vital to appreciate the historical context: after the Protestant revolt and subsequent religious wars and ever-splintering denominations, several movements grew up that sought to create a self-contained system which was wholly non-religious. Liberalism became the most popular, at least in the Americas. Liberalism taught that religion could be adhered to privately, but public relationships would be strictly assessed only by economic standards. Traditionally, Christendom had understood that government and society were essentially good things, and their objective was to allow people to pursue virtue – and therefore happiness-, both personally and collectively. Liberalism radically departed from this understanding. In short, Liberalism taught that (1) the goal of society is maximum production of goods (and government would only "referee" by that standard), and (2) that free choice of the individual to enter into personal or social contract was paramount (hence the name "Liberalism"). "Toleration" was the crowning virtue for the Liberal. (See Locke's *Two Treatises on Government*). Ergo, "Liberation" means material security, without a public recognition of man's spiritual nature.

There were two corollaries that followed from these premises: (1) the government was a necessary evil, since intervention by the government created artificial economic flows (since arguably, by definition, government cannot create wealth); therefore, government was to be minimized to maximize production. (2) The public sphere was to be strictly separate from religion – religion and God could only be present as a personal belief or preference (hence the popular term nowadays: "values" – which denotes a preferential <u>taste</u> rather than an adherence to objective reality). Put differently, free choice of association and dealing for one's perceived benefit is the one and only foundation of society. Liberalism was – and still is – an attempt to establish an "objective," non-spiritual, non-religious, non-traditional structure of society: society is to function on the basis of material trade and consent. Thinkers such as John Locke, Voltaire, Rousseau, etc. are figureheads of this movement.

In sum, the direction of society, according to Liberalism, should be determined by whatever structure allows for the greatest production of material goods, as determined by individual self-interest. Religion and virtue are good things, but cannot be central to the functioning of society; hence, toleration and separation of Church and State are emphasized.

Capitalism is the economic offspring of Liberalism. Capitalism can be thought of as a system of economics, production, and social structure (one or all of these) in which efficient production is emphasized. Thus government and/or regulatory influences are minimized or removed to aid production. In its purest form, all contracts are validated exclusively by the free choice of those involved (hence, "laissez faire," which is French for "allow to do").

Capitalism, being the implementation of the philosophy of Liberalism, has many forms and faces. Each form can refer to a certain facet that may or not represent the whole (i.e. "Industrialization" refers merely to a structure of production, not necessarily other elements that "Capitalism" connotes). Since this partitioning is especially true of Capitalism, one often finds partial elements of Capitalism without the whole philosophy being fully implemented; hence, it could be said the term "Capitalism" is often used equivocally.

However, understood as a social philosophy, the core of Capitalism could essentially be summed up thus: each individual looks out for his own desires, and what is good for himself will ultimately benefit society (i.e. sometimes called "trickle-down" effect; not necessarily the same as "trickle-down" tax policies which lower taxes to stimulate growth). Thus, autonomous choice (as long as it does not infringe on other's rights) and self-interest are the lynch-pin of society, and the measurement of success is material production. Adam Smith's *Wealth of Nations* is seen as the cornerstone of Capitalism, with later figures like Friedrich Hayek and Ayn Rand's *Atlas Shrugged* embodying Capitalist thought – "Greed is good." The Austrian School of economics (Historical relatives of the so-called "Manchester Liberals") is an example of a modern branch of "pure" capitalism: for example, Dickens' pre-conversion Scrooge is often defended by these Libertarians as rightly exercising his self-interest and uncompromising efficiency (google "Mises + Scrooge). Figures such as Michael Novak (*Spirit of Democratic Capitalism*) represent an attempt to maintain the identity of Capitalism – Christ is "kept out of the marketplace" and societal success is measured in terms of production – while specifically attempting to establish compatibility between Capitalism and Christianity. It is noteworthy that the latter author professes to be at odds with elements of traditional Catholic social teaching, characterizing it as outdated, unrealistic, or too influenced by Socialism or Theocracy.

In Capitalism, government and society are thought to balance the marketplace; however, since harnessing the power of government is the most effective means of acquiring profit for an individual (again, the objective of Capitalist Society), historically, Capitalistic societies tend to evolve into a government-business: i.e. Socialism.

Socialism is any system in which all rights to personal property are repudiated, usually in an effort to promote a more fair society and greater shared wealth. Generally, all rights to property are ultimately owned and dispensed by a central authority – the state – and the society is considered one single unit, as opposed to a unit of individuals. Since the State is the smallest unit of society, it follows that the family, or any other formal hierarchy separate from the state, is either assimilated into the state or removed. Early proponents are often associated with the French Revolution, or around that time. Early socialists did also spring from the colonial American and German thinkers as well. Charles Fourier, Thomas Pain, and Henri de Saint-Simon are names that are associated with early Socialism. Since then, many other names such as Lenin, Stalin, Castro, George Orwell, Albert Einstein, Saul Alinski, and possibly Martin Luther King Jr. are identified with socialism. Current American politician Bernie Sanders self-identifies as a Democratic Socialist.

I must also note: Socialism is <u>not</u> the idea that property may be held in common, or that ownership has a hierarchical universal dimension. Holding property in common is not Socialism if it is voluntary; similarly, traditional Catholic thought right from the beginning has held that God owns everything – He grants us the right to private property, and that right is not ultimate. Rather, Socialism is the comprehensive repudiation of private property, the melding of all societal units into one. The distinction is crucial: Acts 2 is <u>not</u> Socialism.

Communism is a "brand" of Socialism that involves revolution – essentially, a violent implementation of Socialist principles based on the teachings of Marx, Engels, Lenin, etc. Nearly everyone is aware, to some extent, of *The Communist Manifesto* and the Bolshevik Revolution. There are other notable socialist expressions, such as the German National Socialist Party (Nazi), and many others.

If the latter entities are a violent implementation of Socialist Principles, Fabian Socialism is the opposite: implementation through covert means: education (especially early education), media, films, clubs, government policies, etc. Although the Fabian Society of London itself has taken on somewhat mythical proportions, it is well known that names like George Bernard Shaw, H.G. Wells, and recently, Tony Blair, are associated with it.

I would like to conclude with two objections that I commonly encounter whenever Catholic Social Teaching is brought up, in the hopes that I can allay them right here.

First: "The Pope (or Church) is a spiritual authority – and doesn't know how to practically handle real-world social (or economic, or policy) situations (or – 'should stay out of politics/science/personal relationships/etc.')."

I reply that the above claim is simply false. "The Church makes a moral judgment about economic and social matters, 'when the fundamental rights of the person or the salvation of souls requires it.'" (CCC par 2420). What *is* true is that the Popes usually have a different aim than most politicians or economists – thank God. The Pope is the visible head of the Church on earth – just as we individuals have a spiritual and visible dimension. Matthew 16:16. He *is* the head of a State – a small, but independent State. The Pope comes from one of the oldest lines of authorities in the world, and sees events in a framework that is not exclusively bound by politics, ideology, profit, or time and place. The Church values empirical scientists, economic or political, but possesses a view that is far more comprehensive than mere big data can give. Science can tell us how hard the hammer is swinging; it cannot tell us if it is ok to hit someone on the head with that hammer. Economics can tell us if a business is efficient; it cannot tell us if a financial system is immoral and therefore destructive. Though profits are a firm requirement of business, the measure of business morality is not profit.

It is inherently obvious, too, that self-identified Catholics are bound to accept the teachings of the Church, in regards to Social Teaching, and all other doctrines. As mentioned above, merely because the "infallible" switch may or may not be fully "on" – so to speak – the doctrines may still be binding; certainly, they are worthy of loyal respect. Again, Church teaching is not a set of arbitrary restrictions on "freedom"; rather, it is more like a blueprint that will keep the house from caving in; thus, we listen not as legalistic nit-picks, but out of love and gratitude for illumination. Otherwise, we are merely in our own little bubble-church unto ourselves. (Cf. 1 Corinthians 12; cf. John 15:5).

"For it must not be forgotten that the Church has the right and duty not only to safeguard her teaching on faith and morals, but also to exercise her authority over her sons by intervening in their external affairs whenever a judgment has to be made concerning the practical application of this teaching." *Pacem in Terris*, 1963.

In my experience, the Catholics that have argued that the Popes should leave economics to the economists are generally miscasting the Pope's words, taking one or two quotes out of context. Hence this work.

Second: "The Popes contradict each other."

I reply: sometimes, they do. However, Popes do not contradict each other in regards to infallibly taught doctrines. Popes may differ, as I have said above, on policies, Canon Law, or diagnoses (i.e. Insurance? Road-building? Unions?). Or, more commonly, they emphasize the urgency of certain topics as required by current, contextual occasions. More often than not however, this "contradiction" is a misinterpretation of the Pope's *meaning*. I stress: this is a work of curated quotes.

It is crucial to remember that empirical data, whether it be dinosaur fossils, climate research, or demographic data, is there to underline the principles which the Church is concerned with. Science can tell us how to construct a car; Science cannot tell us if running people over with the car is immoral. The Gallup poll cannot tell us if something is right or wrong; it merely informs us if something is popular or not.

Too often disagreement with papal teaching comes about by either misunderstanding or "reading into" the text: keep reading or look up the original document, keeping in mind what the pope is NOT saying. The Pope must speak with sharp intellectual distinctions that clumsy – or, God forbid, crooked – interpretation can easily muddle. Anybody can be taken out of context, as the current Holy Father's words show: "POPE FRANCIS TEACHES CATS GO TO HEAVEN"… not quite. For example, saying "we must work together" does not mean syncretism; saying "property has a universal dimension" does not mean socialism – although both latter statements *can* be misunderstood, imputing meaning that is not there is often dangerous or downright deceptive, especially since Popes often "baptize" terms which others have loaded with disreputable implications. ("seamless garment" for example, in *Laudato Si*).

Finally, I conclude with the reflection that God, in His mercy, does not necessarily demand that we make the right choice in each and every situation in life – we cannot. Saints are not perfect; they are penitents. What He does ask is that even if we cannot make the objectively best decision in our shortsightedness, we always make the decision out of love for Him, and we always *think* about the decisions that we make, discern them, through His view, not ours. (1 Peter 3:15). The best system in the world is empty and destructive without love through a strong contemplative prayer life. Catholic Social teaching could be summed up in one sentence as: Pray, then work accordingly. "Faith without works is dead." (James 2:20).

"It must be admitted that men very often find themselves in a sad state because they do not give enough thought and consideration to these things. So We call upon men of deep thought and wisdom—Catholics and Christians, believers in God and devotees of truth and justice, all men of good will—to take as their own Christ's injunction, "Seek and you shall find." Blaze the trails to mutual cooperation among men, to deeper knowledge and more widespread charity, to a way of life marked by true brotherhood, to a human society based on mutual harmony."

Populorum Progresso, 1967.

Christopher Jay, 2016

Note: hereafter, any <u>underlined emphasis</u> in the text is mine, while [brackets] denote a summary or reference for brevity's sake. Italics are from the original text.

1. Life & Human Nature

-Life-

"We must solemnly proclaim that human life is transmitted by means of the family, and the family is based upon a marriage which is one and indissoluble and, with respect to Christians, raised to the dignity of a sacrament. The transmission of human life is the result of a personal and conscious act, and, as such, is subject to the all-holy, inviolable and immutable laws of God, which no man may ignore or disobey. He is not therefore permitted to use certain ways and means which are allowable in the propagation of plant and animal life. Human life is sacred—all men must recognize that fact. From its very inception it reveals the creating hand of God. Those who violate His laws not only offend the divine majesty and degrade themselves and humanity, they also sap the vitality of the political community of which they are members." (*Mater et Magistra*, 1961, par.193-194)

"Genesis relates how God gave two commandments to our first parents: to transmit human life—"Increase and mutliply" —and to bring nature into their service—"Fill the earth, and subdue it." These two commandments are complementary...
...A provident God grants sufficient means to the human race to find a dignified solution to the problems attendant upon the transmission of human life." (*Mater et Magistra*, 1961, par.196-198)

"Furthermore, whatever is opposed to life itself, such as any type of murder, genocide, abortion, euthanasia or wilful self-destruction, whatever violates the integrity of the human person, such as mutilation, torments inflicted on body or mind, attempts to coerce the will itself; whatever insults human dignity, such as subhuman living conditions, arbitrary imprisonment, deportation, slavery, prostitution, the selling of women and children; as well as disgraceful working conditions, where men are treated as mere tools for profit, rather than as free and responsible persons; all these things and others of their like are infamies indeed. They poison human society, but they do more harm to those who practice them than those who suffer from the injury. Moreover, they are supreme dishonor to the Creator." (*Gaudium et Spes*, 1965, par. 27)

-This condemnation includes torture, even, as elsewhere noted, as means to a good end, or on an international stage.

"The Second Vatican Council, in a passage which retains all its relevance today, forcefully condemned a number of crimes and attacks against human life. Thirty years later, taking up the words of the Council and with the same forcefulness I repeat that condemnation <u>in the name of the whole Church,</u> certain that I am interpreting the genuine sentiment of every upright conscience: [See preceding quote from *Gaudium et Spes.*]". (*Evangelium Vitae*, 1995, par. 3)

"It is impossible to catalogue completely the vast array of threats to human life, so many are the forms, whether explicit or hidden, in which they appear today! … <u>It is not only that in generalized opinion these attacks tend no longer to be considered as "crimes"; paradoxically they assume the nature of "rights", to the point that the State is called upon to give them legal recognition and to make them available through the free services of health-care personnel.</u>" (*Evangelium Vitae*, 1995, par.10-11)

-In America, for instance, this is especially relevant in light of recent healthcare conflicts.

"On a more general level, there exists in contemporary culture a certain Promethean attitude which leads people to think that they can control life and death by taking the decisions about them into their own hands." (*Evangelium Vitae*, 1995, par.15)

"Life is always a good." (*Evangelium Vitae*, 1995, par.34)

"The deliberate decision to deprive an innocent human being of his life is always morally evil and can never be licit either as an end in itself or as a means to a good end… Nothing and no one can in any way permit the killing of an innocent human being, whether a fetus or an embryo, an infant or an adult, an old person, or one suffering from an incurable disease, or a person who is dying. Furthermore, no one is permitted to ask for this act of killing, either for himself or herself or for another person entrusted to his or her care, nor can he or she consent to it, either explicitly or implicitly. <u>Nor can any authority legitimately recommend or permit such an action</u>"."(*Evangelium Vitae*, 1995, par.58)

"Sometimes it is feared that the child to be born would live in such conditions that it would be better if the birth did not take place. Nevertheless, these reasons and others like them, however serious and tragic, can never justify the deliberate killing of an innocent human being.
As well as the mother, there are often other people too who decide upon the death of the child in the womb…Sometimes the woman is subjected to such strong pressure that she feels psychologically forced to have an abortion: <u>certainly in this case moral responsibility lies particularly with those who have directly or indirectly obliged her to have an abortion. Doctors and nurses are also responsible, when they place at the service of death skills which were acquired for promoting life.</u>
<u>But responsibility likewise falls on the legislators who have promoted and approved abortion laws</u>…" (*Evangelium Vitae*, 1995, par.39)

"Human life is sacred and inviolable at every moment of existence, including the initial phase which precedes birth." (*Evangelium Vitae*, 1995, par.61)

"Among the Latin authors, Tertullian affirms: "It is anticipated murder to prevent someone from being born; it makes little difference whether one kills a soul already born or puts it to death at birth. He who will one day be a man is a man already".
Throughout Christianity's two thousand year history, this same doctrine has been constantly taught by the Fathers of the Church and by her Pastors and Doctors.
… <u>The 1917 Code of Canon Law punished abortion with excommunication</u>… The excommunication affects all those who commit this crime with knowledge of the penalty attached, and thus includes those accomplices without whose help the crime would not have been committed…. In the Church the purpose of the penalty of excommunication is to make an individual fully aware of the gravity of a certain sin and then to foster genuine conversion and repentance."
(*Evangelium Vitae*, 1995, par.61-62)

"Not only must human life not be taken, but it must be protected with loving concern… Love also gives meaning to suffering and death; despite the mystery which surrounds them, they can become saving events." (*Evangelium Vitae*, 1995, par.81)

"What is urgently called for is a general mobilization of consciences and a united ethical effort to activate a great campaign in support of life." (*Evangelium Vitae*, 1995, par.95)

"I would now like to say a special word to women who have had an abortion. The Church is aware of the many factors which may have influenced your decision, and she does not doubt that in many cases it was a painful and even shattering decision. The wound in your heart may not yet have healed. Certainly what happened was and remains terribly wrong. But do not give in to discouragement and do not lose hope. Try rather to understand what happened and face it honestly. If you have not already done so, give yourselves over with humility and trust to repentance. The Father of mercies is ready to give you his forgiveness and his peace in the Sacrament of Reconciliation…. Through your commitment to life, whether by accepting the birth of other children or by welcoming and caring for those most in need of someone to be close to them, you will become promoters of a new way of looking at human life." (*Evangelium Vitae*, 1995, par.99)

"The Gospel of life is not for believers alone: it is for everyone." (*Evangelium Vitae*, 1995, par.101)

"Among the vulnerable for whom the Church wishes to care with particular love and concern are unborn children, the most defenceless and innocent among us. Nowadays efforts are made to deny them their human dignity and to do with them whatever one pleases, taking their lives and passing laws preventing anyone from standing in the way of this… Yet this defence of unborn life is closely linked to the defence of each and every other human right. … Precisely because this involves the internal consistency of our message about the value of the human person, the Church cannot be expected to change her position on this question… This is not something subject to alleged reforms or "modernizations." It is not "progressive" to try to resolve problems by eliminating a human life." (*Evangelii Gaudium*, 2013, par.213-214)

"When we fail to acknowledge as part of reality the worth of a poor person, a human embryo, a person with disabilities – to offer just a few examples – it becomes difficult to hear the cry of nature itself; everything is connected." (*Laudato Si*, 2015, par 117)

-Contraception, Sterilization, & Abortion-

-Although it may be argued that these three topics are completely separate subjects, the logically analysis of their underlying principle shows them to be inseparably linked with one another – justify one, justify all. See Evangelium Vitae *par. 13 (below).*

"The <u>question of human procreation</u>, like every other question which touches human life, involves more than the limited aspects specific to such disciplines as biology, psychology, demography or sociology. It is the whole man…"
(*Humanae Vitae*,1968, par.7)

"With regard to physical, economic, psychological and social conditions, responsible parenthood is exercised by those who prudently and generously decide to have more children, and by those who, for serious reasons and with due respect to moral precepts, decide not to have additional children for either a certain or an indefinite period of time.
… Responsible parenthood… requires that husband and wife, keeping a right order of priorities, recognize their own duties toward God, themselves, their families and human society.
<u>From this it follows that they are not free to act as they choose in the service of transmitting life, as if it were wholly up to them to decide what is the right course to follow. On the contrary, they are bound to ensure that what they do corresponds to the will of God the Creator.</u> The very nature of marriage and its use makes His will clear…" (*Humanae Vitae*,1968, par.10)

"The sexual activity, in which husband and wife are intimately and chastely united with one another, through which human life is transmitted, is, as the recent Council recalled, "<u>noble and worthy</u>." It does <u>not, moreover, cease to be legitimate even when, for reasons independent of their will, it is foreseen to be infertile</u>… The Church, nevertheless, in urging men to the observance of the precepts of the natural law, which it interprets by its constant doctrine, <u>teaches that each and every marital act must of necessity retain its intrinsic relationship to the procreation of human life.</u>
… [All men] must also recognize that an act of mutual love which impairs the capacity to transmit life which God the Creator, through specific laws, has built into it, frustrates His design which constitutes the norm of marriage, and contradicts the will of the Author of life. Hence <u>to use this divine gift while depriving it, even if only partially, of its meaning and purpose, is equally</u>

repugnant to the nature of man and of woman, and is consequently in opposition to the plan of God and His holy will.

… Therefore We base Our words on the first principles of a human and Christian doctrine of marriage when We are obliged once more to declare that the direct interruption of the generative process already begun and, above all, all direct abortion, even for therapeutic reasons, are to be absolutely excluded as lawful means of regulating the number of children. Equally to be condemned, as the magisterium of the Church has affirmed on many occasions, is direct sterilization, whether of the man or of the woman, whether permanent or temporary.

Similarly excluded is any action which either before, at the moment of, or after sexual intercourse, is specifically intended to prevent procreation—whether as an end or as a means.

Neither is it valid to argue, as a justification for sexual intercourse which is deliberately contraceptive, that a lesser evil is to be preferred to a greater one, or that such intercourse would merge with procreative acts of past and future to form a single entity, and so be qualified by exactly the same moral goodness as these. Though it is true that sometimes it is lawful to tolerate a lesser moral evil in order to avoid a greater evil or in order to promote a greater good," it is never lawful, even for the gravest reasons, to do evil that good may come of it" (*Humanae Vitae*,1968, par.11-14)

"On the other hand, the Church does not consider at all illicit the use of those therapeutic means necessary to cure bodily diseases, even if a foreseeable impediment to procreation should result there from—provided such impediment is not directly intended for any motive whatsoever." (*Humanae Vitae*,1968, par.15)

"the Church teaches that married people may then take advantage of the natural cycles immanent in the reproductive system and engage in marital intercourse only during those times that are infertile, thus controlling birth in a way which does not in the least offend the moral principles which We have just explained." (*Humanae Vitae*,1968, par.16)

-Known as "NFP" or "Natural Family Planning." Note that this is not the "rhythm method," nor is it "Catholic contraception." NFP can still be morally unacceptable if practiced out of a "contraceptive mentality," i.e. not being open to life or avoiding children without discerning a serious reason.

"Finally, careful consideration should be given to the danger of this power passing into the hands of those public authorities who care little for the precepts of the moral law. …Who will prevent public authorities from favoring those contraceptive methods which they consider more effective? Should they regard this as necessary, they may even impose their use on everyone."
(*Humanae Vitae*,1968, par.17)

"It is to be anticipated that perhaps not everyone will easily accept this particular teaching. There is too much clamorous outcry against the voice of the Church, and this is intensified by modern means of communication… She does not, because of this, evade the duty imposed on her of proclaiming humbly but firmly the entire moral law, both natural and evangelical.
Since the Church did not make either of these laws, she cannot be their arbiter—only their guardian and interpreter. It could never be right for her to declare lawful what is in fact unlawful, since that, by its very nature, is always opposed to the true good of man." (*Humanae Vitae*,1968, par.18)

"Human ingenuity seems to be directed more towards limiting, suppressing or destroying the sources of life — including recourse to abortion, which unfortunately is so widespread in the world — than towards defending and opening up the possibilities of life. The Encyclical *Sollicitudo rei socialis* denounced systematic anti-childbearing campaigns which, on the basis of a distorted view of the demographic problem and in a climate of "absolute lack of respect for the freedom of choice of the parties involved", often subject them "to intolerable pressures ... in order to force them to submit to this new form of oppression". These policies are extending their field of action by the use of new techniques, to the point of poisoning the lives of millions of defenceless human beings, as if in a form of "chemical warfare"." (*Centesimus annus*, 1991, par. 39)

"But despite their differences of nature and moral gravity, contraception and abortion are often closely connected, as fruits of the same tree." (*Evangelium Vitae*, 1995, par.13)

"On the other hand, it is troubling that, when some ecological movements defend the integrity of the environment, rightly demanding that certain limits be imposed on scientific research, they sometimes fail to apply those same principles to human life. There is a tendency to justify transgressing all boundaries when experimentation is carried out on living human embryos. We forget that the inalienable worth of a human being transcends his or her degree of development." (*Laudato Si*, 2015, par 136)

-Elderly & Disabled-

"Man has the right to live. He has the right to bodily integrity and to the means necessary for the proper development of life, particularly food, clothing, shelter, medical care, rest, and, finally, the necessary social services. In consequence, he has the right to be looked after in the event of illhealth; disability stemming from his work; widowhood; old age; enforced unemployment; or whenever through no fault of his own he is deprived of the means of livelihood." (*Pacem in Terris*, 1963, par.11)

"…care must be taken that sufficient and suitable work and the possibility of the appropriate technical and professional formation are furnished. The livelihood and the human dignity especially of those who are in very difficult conditions because of illness or old age must be guaranteed." (*Gaudium et Spes*, 1965, par.66)

"The Church directs her attention to those new "poor" - the handicapped and the maladjusted, the old, different groups of those on the fringe of society, and so on - in order to recognize them, help them; defend their place and dignity in a society hardened by competition and the attraction of success." (*Octogesima Adveniens*, 1971, par.16)

"Recently, national communities and international organizations have turned their attention to another question connected with work, one full of implications: the question of disabled people. They too are fully human subjects with corresponding innate, sacred and inviolable rights, and, in spite of the limitations and sufferings affecting their bodies and faculties, they point up more clearly the dignity and greatness of man. … It would be radically unworthy of man, and a denial of our common humanity, to admit to the life of the community, and thus admit to work, only those who are fully functional. *To do so would be to practice a serious form of discrimination*, that of the strong and healthy against the weak and sick. Work in the objective sense should be subordinated, in this circumstance too, to the dignity of man, to the subject of work and not to economic advantage.

… Many practical problems arise at this point, as well as legal and economic ones; but the community, that is to say, the public authorities, associations and intermediate groups, business enterprises and the disabled themselves should pool their ideas and resources so as to attain this goal that must not be shirked: *that disabled people may be offered work according to their capabilities*, for this is demanded by their dignity as persons and as subjects of work." (*Laborem Exercens*, 1981, par. 22)

"Without hiding the fact that this is a complex and difficult task, it is to be hoped that <u>a correct concept of labour in the subjective sense</u> will produce a situation which will make it possible for disabled people to feel that they are not cut off from the working world or dependent upon society, but that they are full-scale subjects of work, useful, respected for their human dignity and called to contribute to the progress and welfare of their families and of the community according to their particular capacities." (*Laborem Exercens*, 1981, par. 22)

-this keeping in mind that the "subject" of work is <u>man</u>, not mere production.

"The Church is close to those married couples who, with great anguish and suffering, willingly accept gravely handicapped children. She is also grateful to all those families which, through adoption, welcome children abandoned by their parents because of disabilities or illnesses." (*Evangelium Vitae*, 1995, par.63)

"<u>Special attention must be given to the elderly</u>. While in some cultures older people remain a part of the family with an important and active role, in others the elderly are regarded as a useless burden and are left to themselves. Here the temptation to resort to euthanasia can more easily arise.
Neglect of the elderly or their outright rejection are intolerable." (*Evangelium Vitae*, 1995, par.94)

-Euthanasia-

"<u>No one, however, can arbitrarily choose whether to live or die; the absolute master of such a decision is the Creator alone, in whom "we live and move and have our being"</u> (Acts 17:28)." (*Evangelium Vitae*, 1995, par.47)

"Euthanasia in the strict sense is understood to be an action or omission which of itself and by intention causes death, with the purpose of eliminating all suffering.

... Euthanasia must be distinguished from the decision to forego so-called "aggressive medical treatment", in other words, medical procedures which no longer correspond to the real situation of the patient, either because they are by now disproportionate to any expected results or because they impose an excessive burden on the patient and his family. In such situations, when death is clearly imminent and inevitable, one can in conscience "refuse forms of treatment that would only secure a precarious and burdensome prolongation of life, so long as the normal care due to the sick person in similar cases is not interrupted"... To forego extraordinary or disproportionate means is not the equivalent of suicide or euthanasia; it rather expresses acceptance of the human condition in the face of death.

... Taking into account these distinctions, in harmony with the Magisterium of my Predecessors and in communion with the Bishops of the Catholic Church, I confirm that euthanasia is a grave violation of the law of God, since it is the deliberate and morally unacceptable killing of a human person.

... Suicide is always as morally objectionable as murder.

... True "compassion" leads to sharing another's pain; it does not kill the person whose suffering we cannot bear." (*Evangelium Vitae*, 1995, par.65-66)

-Ethics-

"*The economy needs ethics in order to function correctly*— not any ethics whatsoever, but an ethics which is people-centred. Today we hear much talk of ethics in the world of economy, finance and business... These processes are praiseworthy and deserve much support... It would be advisable, however, to develop a sound criterion of discernment, since the adjective "ethical" can be abused.

... Among other things, [the term "ethical"] risks being used to justify the financing of projects that are in reality unethical. The word "ethical", then, should not be used to make ideological distinctions, as if to suggest that initiatives not formally so designated would not be ethical. Efforts are needed — and it is essential to say this — not only to create "ethical" sectors or segments of the economy or the world of finance, but to ensure that the whole economy — the whole of finance — is ethical, not merely by virtue of an external label, but by its respect for requirements intrinsic to its very nature." (*Caritas in Veritatae*, 2009, par.45)

"Behind this attitude [of the endless thirst for power and increased profits] lurks a rejection of ethics and a rejection of God. Ethics has come to be viewed with a certain scornful derision. It is seen as counterproductive, too human, because it makes money and power relative. It is felt to be a threat, since it condemns the manipulation and debasement of the person. In effect, ethics leads to a God who calls for a committed response which is outside the categories of the marketplace." (*Evangelii Gaudium*, 2013, par.57)

-Bioethics-

"A particularly crucial battleground in today's cultural struggle between the supremacy of technology and human moral responsibility is the field of *bioethics*…It is no coincidence that closing the door to transcendence brings one up short against a difficulty: how could being emerge from nothing, how could intelligence be born from chance? <u>Faced with these dramatic questions, reason and faith can come to each other's assistance. Only together will they save man.</u> *Entranced by an exclusive reliance on technology, reason without faith is doomed to flounder in an illusion of its own omnipotence. Faith without reason risks being cut off from everyday life.* … *In vitro* fertilization, embryo research, the possibility of manufacturing clones and human hybrids: all this is now emerging and being promoted in today's highly disillusioned culture, which believes it has mastered every mystery, because the origin of life is now within our grasp… In this type of culture, the conscience is simply invited to take note of technological possibilities. Yet we must not underestimate the disturbing scenarios that threaten our future, or the powerful new instruments that the "culture of death" has at its disposal. To the tragic and widespread scourge of abortion we may well have to add in the future — indeed it is already surreptitiously present — <u>the systematic eugenic programming of births</u>. At the other end of the spectrum, a pro-euthanasia mindset is making inroads as an equally damaging assertion of control over life that under certain circumstances is deemed no longer worth living. Underlying these scenarios are cultural viewpoints that deny human dignity." (*Caritas in Veritatae*, 2009, par.75)

-Even a surface examination of the history of Eugenics (including compulsory sterilization programs that operate in the U.S. <u>even today</u>, the origins of Planned Parenthood and the American Eugenics movement which subsequently influenced the Nazi party, etc.) will validate the words of the Popes on this subject.

-Pornography & Drugs-

-See "Advertising" (chapter 2) for related references.

"A striking example of artificial consumption contrary to the health and dignity of the human person, and certainly not easy to control, is the use of drugs. Widespread drug use is a sign of a serious malfunction in the social system; it also implies a materialistic and, in a certain sense, destructive "reading" of human needs. In this way the innovative capacity of a free economy is brought to a one-sided and inadequate conclusion. Drugs, as well as pornography and other forms of consumerism which exploit the frailty of the weak, tend to fill the resulting spiritual void." (*Centesimus annus*, 1991, par. 36)

"The new forms of slavery to drugs and the lack of hope into which so many people fall can be explained not only in sociological and psychological terms but also in essentially spiritual terms." (*Caritas in Veritatae*, 2009, par.76)

-Capital Punishment-

"[as a sign of hope] there is evidence of a growing public opposition to the death penalty, even when such a penalty is seen as a kind of "legitimate defence" on the part of society. Modern society in fact has the means of effectively suppressing crime by rendering criminals harmless without definitively denying them the chance to reform." (*Evangelium Vitae*, 1995, par.28)

The Church more and more regards Capital Punishment as a collective form of self-defense. Just as self-defense is only justified when there is no other alternative – the life of the aggressor or one's own life - only when there is no other way to defend society can a criminal be executed.

"There are in fact situations in which values proposed by God's Law seem to involve a genuine paradox. This happens for example in the case of legitimate defense, in which the right to protect one's own life and the duty not to harm someone else's life are difficult to reconcile in practice.
… Moreover, "legitimate defense can be not only a right but a grave duty for someone responsible for another's life, the common good of the family or of the State". Unfortunately it happens that the need to render the aggressor incapable of causing harm sometimes involves taking his life.

... This is the context in which to place the problem of the death penalty. On this matter there is a growing tendency, both in the Church and in civil society, to demand that it be applied in a very limited way or even that it be abolished completely... Public authority must redress the violation of personal and social rights by imposing on the offender an adequate punishment for the crime, as a condition for the offender to regain the exercise of his or her freedom. In this way authority also fulfils the purpose of defending public order and ensuring people's safety, while at the same time offering the offender an incentive and help to change his or her behavior and be rehabilitated.

It is clear that, for these purposes to be achieved, the nature and extent of the punishment must be carefully evaluated and decided upon, and ought not go to the extreme of executing the offender except in cases of absolute necessity: in other words, when it would not be possible otherwise to defend society. <u>Today however, as a result of steady improvements in the organization of the penal system, such cases are very rare, if not practically non-existent.</u>" (*Evangelium Vitae*, 1995, par.55-56)

-Human Trafficking-

"I have always been distressed at the lot of those who are victims of various kinds of human trafficking. How I wish that all of us would hear God's cry: "Where is your brother?" (Gen 4:9)." (*Evangelii Gaudium*, 2013, par.211)

2. Family, Community, and Government

-Family-

"<u>Hence we have the family, the "society" of a man's house - a society very small, one must admit, but none the less a true society, and one older than any State. Consequently, it has rights and duties peculiar to itself which are quite independent of the State.</u>" (*Rerum Novarum*, 1891, par.12)

"A family, no less than a State, is, as We have said, a true society, governed by an authority peculiar to itself, that is to say, by the authority of the father. Provided, therefore, the limits… the family has at least equal rights with the State in the choice and pursuit of the things needful to its preservation and its just liberty." (*Rerum Novarum*, 1891, par.13)

"<u>The contention, then, that the civil government should at its option intrude into and exercise intimate control over the family and the household is a great and pernicious error</u>. True, if a family finds itself in exceeding distress… it is right that extreme necessity be met by public aid... But the rulers of the commonwealth must go no further; here, nature bids them stop. Paternal authority can be neither abolished nor absorbed by the State; for it has the same source as human life itself." (*Rerum Novarum*, 1891, par.14)

See "Inheritance" for related references.

"Mothers, concentrating on household duties, should work primarily in the home or in its immediate vicinity. It is an intolerable abuse, and to be abolished at all cost, for mothers on account of the father's low wage to be forced to engage in gainful occupations outside the home to the neglect of their proper cares and duties, especially the training of children." (*Quadragesimo Anno*, 1931, par 71)

"But however extensive and far-reaching the influence of the State on the economy may be, it must never be exerted to the extent of depriving the individual citizen of his freedom of action. It must rather <u>augment</u> his freedom while effectively guaranteeing the protection of his essential personal rights.

Among these is a man's right and duty to be primarily responsible for his own upkeep and that of his family." (*Mater et Magistra*, 1961, par.55)

"The family, founded upon marriage freely contracted, one and indissoluble, must be regarded as the natural, primary cell of human society." (*Pacem in Terris*, 1963, par.16)

-the family, as opposed to the mere individual, is properly the stable "unit" of society.

"Nevertheless it remains each man's duty to retain an understanding of the whole human person in which the values of intellect, will, conscience and fraternity are preeminent… The family is, as it were, the primary mother and nurse of this education." (*Gaudium et Spes*, 1965, par.61)

"The family's influence may have been excessive at some periods of history and in some places, to the extent that it was exercised to the detriment of the fundamental rights of the individual. … The natural family, stable and monogamous—as fashioned by God and sanctified by Christianity—"in which different generations live together, helping each other to acquire greater wisdom and to harmonize personal rights with other social needs, is the basis of society"" (*Populorum Progresso*, 1967, par.36)

"The first and fundamental structure for "human ecology" is the family, in which man receives his first formative ideas about truth and goodness, and learns what it means to love and to be loved, and thus what it actually means to be a person. Here we mean the *family* founded on marriage, in which the mutual gift of self by husband and wife creates an environment in which children can be born and develop their potentialities, become aware of their dignity and prepare to face their unique and individual destiny. But it often happens that people are discouraged from creating the proper conditions for human reproduction and are led to consider themselves and their lives as a series of sensations to be experienced rather than as a work to be accomplished. The result is a lack of freedom, which causes a person to reject a commitment to enter into a stable relationship with another person and to bring children into the world, or which leads people to consider children as one of the many "things" which an individual can have or not have, according to taste, and which compete with other possibilities.

It is necessary to go back to seeing the family as the *sanctuary of life*…In the face of the so-called culture of death, the family is the heart of the culture of life." (*Centesimus annus*, 1991, par. 39)

"It can happen, however, that when a family does decide to live up fully to its vocation, it finds itself without the necessary support from the State and without sufficient resources. It is urgent therefore to promote not only family policies, but also those social policies which have the family as their principle object, policies which assist the family by providing adequate resources and efficient means of support, both for bringing up children and for looking after the elderly, so as to avoid distancing the latter from the family unit and in order to strengthen relations between generations." (*Centesimus annus*, 1991, par. 49)

"States are called to enact policies promoting the centrality and the integrity of the family founded on marriage between a man and a woman, the primary vital cell of society, and to assume responsibility for its economic and fiscal needs, while respecting its essentially relational character." (*Caritas in Veritatae*, 2009, par.44)

"The family is experiencing a profound cultural crisis, as are all communities and social bonds. In the case of the family, the weakening of these bonds is particularly serious because the family is the fundamental cell of society, where we learn to live with others despite our differences and to belong to one another; it is also the place where parents pass on the faith to their children. Marriage now tends to be viewed as a form of mere emotional satisfaction that can be constructed in any way or modified at will." (*Evangelii Gaudium*, 2013, par.66)

"Pope Benedict XVI spoke of an "ecology of man", based on the fact that "man too has a nature that he must respect and that he cannot manipulate at will"… thinking that we enjoy absolute power over our own bodies turns, often subtly, into thinking that we enjoy absolute power over creation. Learning to accept our body, to care for it and to respect its fullest meaning, is an essential element of any genuine human ecology. Also, valuing one's own body in its femininity or masculinity is necessary if I am going to be able to recognize myself in an encounter with someone who is different… It is not a healthy attitude which would seek 'to cancel out sexual difference because it no longer knows how to confront it'. [quoting a Wednesday audience]" (*Laudato Si*, 2015, par 155)

"Outstanding among [societal groups] is the family, as the basic cell of society." (*Laudato Si*, 2015, par 157)

"[quoting St. John Paul II *Centessimus Annus*] 'In the face of the so-called culture of death, the family is the heart of the culture of life'. In the family we first learn how to show love and respect for life; we are taught the proper use of things, order and cleanliness, respect for the local ecosystem and care for all creatures." (*Laudato Si*, 2015, par 213)

-Divorce-

"Married love is also faithful and exclusive of all other, and this until death." (*Humanae Vitae*,1968, par.9)

-Marriage-

"Thus a man and a woman, who by their compact of conjugal love "are no longer two, but one flesh" (Matt. 19:6)…As a mutual gift of two persons, this intimate union and the good of the children impose total fidelity on the spouses and argue for an unbreakable oneness between them." (*Gaudium et Spes*, 1965, par.48)

"<u>Marriage and conjugal love are by their nature ordained toward the begetting and educating of children. Children are really the supreme gift of marriage and contribute very substantially to the welfare of their parents.</u>
… <u>[Parents] should realize that they are thereby cooperators with the love of God the Creator</u>… But in their manner of acting, spouses should be aware that they cannot proceed arbitrarily, but must always be governed according to a conscience dutifully conformed to the divine law itself, and should be submissive toward the Church's teaching office, which authentically interprets that law in the light of the Gospel.
… <u>Marriage to be sure is not instituted solely for procreation</u>; rather, its very nature as an unbreakable compact between persons, and the welfare of the children, both demand that the mutual love of the spouses be embodied in a rightly ordered manner, that it grow and ripen. Therefore, marriage persists as a whole manner and communion of life, and maintains its value and indissolubility, even when despite the often intense desire of the couple, offspring are lacking.

... This council realizes that [couples often] find themselves in circumstances where at least temporarily the size of their families should not be increased. As a result, the faithful exercise of love and the full intimacy of their lives is hard to maintain. But where the intimacy of married life is broken off, its faithfulness can sometimes be imperiled and its quality of fruitfulness ruined, for then the upbringing of the children and the courage to accept new ones are both endangered.
To these problems there are those who presume to offer dishonorable solutions indeed; they do not recoil even from the taking of life.
... Therefore from the moment of its conception life must be guarded with the greatest care while abortion and infanticide are unspeakable crimes.
... Relying on these principles, sons of the Church may not undertake methods of birth control which are found blameworthy by the teaching authority of the Church in its unfolding of the divine law.
<u>All should be persuaded that human life and the task of transmitting it are not realities bound up with this world alone. Hence they cannot be measured or perceived only in terms of it, but always have a bearing on the eternal destiny of men.</u>
... Parents or guardians should by prudent advice provide guidance to their young with respect to founding a family, and the young ought to listen gladly. <u>At the same time no pressure, direct or indirect, should be put on the young to make them enter marriage or choose a specific partner.</u>
... Public authority should regard it as a sacred duty to recognize, protect and promote their authentic nature, to shield public morality and to favor the prosperity of home life. The right of parents to beget and educate their children in the bosom of the family must be safeguarded. Children too who unhappily lack the blessing of a family should be protected by prudent legislation and various undertakings and assisted by the help they need." (*Gaudium et Spes*, 1965, par.51-52)

"For We invite all [the Bishops], We implore you, to give a lead to your priests who assist you in the sacred ministry, and to the faithful of your dioceses, and to devote yourselves with all zeal and without delay to safeguarding the holiness of marriage, in order to guide married life to its full human and Christian perfection. Consider this mission as one of your most urgent responsibilities at the present time." (*Humanae Vitae*,1968, par.30)

-Adoption-

"A particularly significant expression of solidarity between families is a willingness to adopt or take in children abandoned by their parents or in situations of serious hardship. True parental love is ready to go beyond the bonds of flesh and blood in order to accept children from other families, offering them whatever is necessary for their well-being and full development." (*Evangelium Vitae*, 1995, par.93)

-Inheritance-

"It is a most sacred law of nature that a father should provide food and all necessaries for those whom he has begotten… Now, in no other way can a father effect this except by the ownership of productive property, which he can transmit to his children by inheritance." (*Rerum Novarum*, 1891, par.13)

-Private Property -

"For, every man has by nature the right to possess property as his own." (*Rerum Novarum*, 1891, par.6)

"Hence, man not only should possess the fruits of the earth, but also the very soil, inasmuch as from the produce of the earth he has to lay by provision for the future. …Man precedes the State, and possesses, prior to the formation of any State, the right of providing for the substance of his body." (*Rerum Novarum*, 1891, par.7)

"Therefore, those whom fortune favors are warned that riches do not bring freedom from sorrow and are of no avail for eternal happiness, but rather are obstacles …a most strict account must be given to the Supreme Judge for all we possess… It rests on the principle that it is one thing to have a right to the possession of money and another to have a right to use money as one wills. … But if the question be asked: How must one's possessions be used? - the Church replies without hesitation in the words of [St. Thomas Aquinas]: "Man should not consider his material possessions as his own, but as common to all, so as to share them without hesitation when others are in need.' … True, no one is commanded to distribute to others that which is required for his own needs and those of his household; nor even to give away what is reasonably required to keep up becomingly his condition in life… But, when what necessity demands has been supplied, and one's standing fairly taken thought for, it becomes a duty to give to the indigent out of what remains over. "Of that which remaineth, give alms." It is a duty, not of justice (save in extreme cases), but of Christian charity - a duty not enforced by human law". (*Rerum Novarum*, 1891, par.22)

"Neither must it be supposed that the solicitude of the Church is so preoccupied with the spiritual concerns of her children as to neglect their temporal and earthly interests… Christian morality, when adequately and completely practiced, leads of itself to temporal prosperity, for it merits the blessing of that God who is the source of all blessings; it powerfully restrains the greed of possession and the thirst for pleasure - twin plagues, which too often make a man who is void of self-restraint miserable in the midst of abundance; it makes men supply for the lack of means through economy, teaching them to be content with frugal living, and further, keeping them out of the reach of those vices which devour not small incomes merely, but large fortunes, and dissipate many a goodly inheritance." (*Rerum Novarum*, 1891, par.28)

"Secondly, private ownership of property, including that of productive goods, is a natural right which the State cannot suppress. But it naturally entails a social obligation as well. It is a right which must be exercised not only for one's own personal benefit but also for the benefit of others." (*Mater et Magistra*, 1961, par.19)

"…it would be quite useless to insist on free and personal initiative in the economic field, while at the same time withdrawing man's right to dispose freely of the means indispensable to the achievement of such initiative." (*Mater et Magistra*, 1961, par.109)

"But it is not enough to assert that the right to own private property and the means of production is inherent in human nature. We must also insist on the extension of this right in practice to all classes of citizens." (*Mater et Magistra*, 1961, par.113)

"Our predecessors have insisted time and again on the social function inherent in the right of private ownership, for it cannot be denied that in the plan of the

Creator all of this world's goods are primarily intended for the worthy support of the entire human race." (*Mater et Magistra*, 1961, par.119)

"…the right of private ownership is clearly sanctioned by the Gospel. Yet at the same time, the divine Master frequently extends to the rich the insistent invitation to convert their material goods into spiritual ones by conferring them on the poor. "Lay not up to yourselves treasures on earth; where the rust and moth consume and where thieves break through and steal. But lay up to yourselves treasures in heaven; where neither the rust nor moth doth consume, and where thieves do not break through nor steal."" (*Mater et Magistra*, 1961, par.121)

"In using them, therefore, man should regard the external things that he legitimately possesses not only as his own but also as common in the sense that they should be able to benefit not only him but also others. On the other hand, the right of having a share of earthly goods sufficient for oneself and one's family belongs to everyone. The Fathers and Doctors of the Church held this opinion, teaching that men are obliged to come to the relief of the poor and to do so not merely out of their superfluous goods." (*Gaudium et Spes*, 1965, par.69)

"Private property or some ownership of external goods confers on everyone a sphere wholly necessary for the autonomy of the person and the family, and it should be regarded as an extension of human freedom. Lastly, since it adds incentives for carrying on one's function and charge, it constitutes one of the conditions for civil liberties.
… Goods can be transferred to the public domain only by the competent authority, according to the demands and within the limits of the common good, and with fair compensation. Furthermore, it is the right of public authority to prevent anyone from abusing his private property to the detriment of the common good.
… In many underdeveloped regions there are large or even extensive rural estates which are only slightly cultivated or lie completely idle for the sake of profit, while the majority of the people either are without land or have only very small fields, and, on the other hand, it is evidently urgent to increase the productivity of the fields… [these cases] should be distributed to those who can make these lands fruitful; in this case, the necessary things and means, especially educational aids and the right facilities for cooperative organization, must be supplied. Whenever, nevertheless, the common good requires expropriation,

compensation must be reckoned in equity after all the circumstances have been weighed." (*Gaudium et Spes*, 1965, par.71)

-In context: in countries or even areas that are struggling economically, speculators are not justified in claiming the "trickle-down effect," or by claiming that "the whole economy" benefits at the detriment of those affected by their speculation. This is simple utilitarian moral relativism – i.e. justifying an unjust rape of resources or labor by comparing it to an aggregate good or some worse prior evil. Note too that "legal" does not necessarily equal "just." When capital comes to an area, it is immoral that some starve while others live in overflowing luxury, as the wealthy have a new-found responsibility to help those around them; not through the dependency of welfare, but by providing arrangements that enable achieving ownership. See "Proportional Ownership for All" for related references.

"The pursuit of life's necessities is quite legitimate; hence we are duty-bound to do the work which enables us to obtain them: "If anyone is unwilling to work, do not let him eat." But the acquisition of worldly goods can lead men to greed, to the unrelenting desire for more, to the pursuit of greater personal power. Rich and poor alike—be they individuals, families or nations—can fall prey to avarice and soulstifling materialism." (*Populorum Progresso*, 1967, par.18)

"Everyone knows that the Fathers of the Church laid down the duty of the rich toward the poor in no uncertain terms. As St. Ambrose put it: "You are not making a gift of what is yours to the poor man, but you are giving him back what is his. You have been appropriating things that are meant to be for the common use of everyone. The earth belongs to everyone, not to the rich." These words indicate that the right to private property is not absolute and unconditional.
No one may appropriate surplus goods solely for his own private use when others lack the bare necessities of life. In short, "as the Fathers of the Church and other eminent theologians tell us, the right of private property may never be exercised to the detriment of the common good." When "private gain and basic community needs conflict with one another," it is for the public authorities "to seek a solution to these questions, with the active involvement of individual citizens and social groups."
If certain landed estates impede the general prosperity because they are extensive, unused or poorly used, or because they bring hardship to peoples or are detrimental to the interests of the country, the common good sometimes demands their expropriation.

Vatican II affirms this emphatically. At the same time it clearly teaches that income thus derived is not for man's capricious use, and that <u>the exclusive pursuit of personal gain is prohibited</u>." (*Populorum Progresso*, 1967, par.22-24)

"It is necessary to state once more the characteristic principle of Christian social doctrine: <u>the goods of this world are originally meant for all. The right to private property is valid and necessary</u>, but it does not nullify the value of this principle. Private property, in fact, is under a "social mortgage," which means that it has an intrinsically social function, based upon and justified precisely by the principle of the universal destination of goods. Likewise, in this concern for the poor, one must not overlook that special form of poverty which consists in being deprived of fundamental human rights, in particular the right to religious freedom and also the right to freedom of economic initiative." (*Sollilicitudo Rei Socialis*, 1987, par.42)

"<u>The Pope [St. John Paul II] is well aware that private property is not an absolute value, nor does he fail to proclaim the necessary complementary principles, such as the universal destination of the earth's goods</u>.
On the other hand, it is certainly true that the type of private property which Leo XIII mainly considers is land ownership. But this does not mean that the reasons adduced to safeguard private property or to affirm the right to possess the things necessary for one's personal development and the development of one's family, whatever the concrete form which that right may assume, are not still valid today." (*Centesimus annus*, 1991, par. 6)

"While the Pope proclaimed the right to private ownership, he affirmed with equal clarity that the "use" of goods, while marked by freedom, is subordinated to their original common destination as created goods, as well as to the will of Jesus Christ as expressed in the Gospel.
… <u>The Successors of Leo XIII have repeated this twofold affirmation: the necessity and therefore the legitimacy of private ownership, as well as the limits which are imposed on it</u>." (*Centesimus annus*, 1991, par. 30)

"In our time, in particular, there exists another form of ownership which is becoming no less important than land: the possession of know-how, technology and skill. The wealth of the industrialized nations is based much more on this kind of ownership than on natural resources." (*Centesimus annus*, 1991, par. 32)

"The private ownership of goods is justified by the need to protect and increase them, so that they can better serve the common good; for this reason, solidarity must be lived as the decision to restore to the poor what belongs to them." (*Evangelii Gaudium*, 2013, par.189)

"Sadly, even human rights can be used as a justification for an inordinate defense of individual rights or the rights of the richer peoples… It must be reiterated that "the more fortunate should renounce some of their rights so as to place their goods more generously at the service of others". To speak properly of our own rights, we need to broaden our perspective and to hear the plea of other peoples and other regions than those of our own country." (*Evangelii Gaudium*, 2013, par.190)

"The principle of the subordination of private property to the universal destination of goods, and thus the right of everyone to their use, is a golden rule of social conduct and 'the first principle of the whole ethical and social order'. [quoting St. John Paul II's *Laborem Exercens*] The Christian tradition has never recognized the right to private property as absolute or inviolable, and has stressed the social purpose of all forms of private property… [St. John Paul II] clearly explained that 'the Church does indeed defend the legitimate right to private property, but she also teaches no less clearly that there is always a social mortgage on all private property, in order that goods may serve the general purpose that God gave them.'" (*Laudato Si*, 2015, par 93)

-Proportional Ownership for All-

-or-

-Promotion of Ownership-

-Note: it is essential to understand Catholic teaching on property to understand Proportional Ownership. See following references for further explanation of what proportional ownership is and is not. It is not re-distribution of property, nor is it that being wealthy is bad. Rather, it is that when a wealthy person or people have ample means of sustenance, and those around them do not to the point of massive disparity (especially if the low end of that disparity is grinding poverty), those who are wealthy have a responsibility to help those around them help themselves, to offset the discrepancy. Although direct monetary support could be one way – it is perhaps the most temporary, dangerous, and least effective - technical education, real-value work (as opposed to meaningless state-sponsored "kickstand" employment), infrastructure, and other such structures are a more viable, long-term solution. Actual ownership especially of

land, as much as possible, should be promoted. In short, each unit of society should have sufficient property to enable them to live a noble life, not merely base survival, but prosperity even. New prosperity incurs new responsibility: if one were to find a cure for cancer, for example, and bury it, this would be evil for the same principles above.

"<u>The law, therefore, should favor ownership, and its policy should be to induce as many as possible of the people to become owners</u>. Many excellent results will follow from this; and, first of all, property will certainly become more equitably divided. For, the result of civil change and revolution has been to divide cities into two classes separated by a wide chasm... <u>Men always work harder and more readily when they work on that which belongs to them</u>." (*Rerum Novarum*, 1891, par.47)

-Note: there is a right and a wrong way to accomplish this – not through permanent welfare, which is simply a form of slavery created through dependency, but through opportunities to help others help themselves. While there are certain singular contexts in which it becomes necessary to expropriate private ownership, this cannot be recklessly misconstrued as wholesale redistribution by, say, a government – such would be Communism. See Private Property *and* Welfare *for references.*

"<u>Accordingly, twin rocks of shipwreck must be carefully avoided</u>. For, as one is wrecked upon, or comes close to, what is known as "<u>individualism</u>" by denying or minimizing the social and public character of the right of property, so by rejecting or minimizing the private and individual character of this same right, one inevitably runs into "<u>collectivism</u>" or at least closely approaches its tenets." (*Quadragesimo Anno*, 1931, par.46)

"The right of property is distinct from its use. That justice called <u>commutative</u> commands sacred respect for the division of possessions and forbids invasion of others' rights through the exceeding of the limits of one's own property; but the duty of owners to use their property only in a right way does not come under this type of justice, but under other virtues, obligations of which "<u>cannot be enforced by legal action</u>." <u>Therefore, they are in error who assert that ownership and its right use are limited by the same boundaries</u>; and it is much farther still from the truth to hold that a right to property is destroyed or lost by reason of abuse or non-use." (*Quadragesimo Anno*, 1931, par.47)

-Note: It is a fine line what Pope Pius XI is and is not saying: he is not saying necessarily that abuse of property is acceptable, but rather, that civil or communal action resulting from abuse of private property would have to have an extreme effect on the common good. This is of course the author's commentary – a close reading of the full text is necessarily to prudently apply the above principles, so as to avoid the "twin rocks of shipwreck."

"Furthermore, <u>a person's superfluous income</u>, that is, income which he does not need to sustain life fittingly and with dignity, <u>is not left wholly to his own free determination</u>. Rather the Sacred Scriptures and the Fathers of the Church constantly declare in the most explicit language that the rich are <u>bound by a very grave precept</u> to practice almsgiving, beneficence, and munificence. Expending larger incomes so that opportunity for gainful work may be abundant, provided, however, that this work is applied to <u>producing really useful goods</u>, ought to be considered, as We deduce from the principles of the [St. Thomas Aquinas], an outstanding exemplification of the virtue of munificence and one particularly suited to the needs of the times." (*Quadragesimo Anno*, 1931, par 50-51)

"To each, therefore, <u>must</u> be given his own share of goods, and the distribution of created goods, which, as every discerning person knows, is laboring today under the gravest evils due to the huge disparity between the few exceedingly rich and the unnumbered property-less, must be effectively called back to and brought into conformity with the norms of the common good, that is, social justice." (*Quadragesimo Anno*, 1931, par 58)

-It is worth noting again: this is <u>not</u> re-distribution, in the sense of a government confiscation and re-distribution of property. In context, Pope Pius XI – as are his popes before and after him- is referring to distribution via equitable and honorable sharing of production by employers, as opposed to the greed that creates "huge disparity." Again, the Popes have and still do, call for not a legislated, forced re-distribution, but an organic distribution of property via equitable and generous wages and opportunities <u>to work towards ownership</u>. See Wages *and* Welfare.

"…the immense multitude of the non-owning workers on the one hand and the enormous riches of certain very wealthy men on the other establish an <u>unanswerable argument</u> that the riches which are so abundantly produced in our age of "industrialism," as it is called, <u>are not rightly distributed and equitably</u>

made available to the various classes of the people." (*Quadragesimo Anno*, 1931, par 60)

"Because these [large companies, who are self-financing] are financing replacement and plant expansion out of their own profits, they grow at a very rapid rate. In such cases We believe that the workers should be allocated shares in the firms for which they work, especially when they are paid no more than a minimum wage." (*Mater et Magistra*, 1961, par.75)

-i.e. ownership for the employees – maximizing ownership*, especially of land and businesses, as opposed to mere leasing, or mere contractual employment.*

"[proper enterprise demands that] parties co-operate actively and loyally in the common enterprise, not so much for what they can get out of it for themselves, but as discharging a duty and rendering a service to their fellow men." (*Mater et Magistra*, 1961, par.92)

"All this implies that the workers have their say in, and make their own contribution to, the efficient running and development of the enterprise. … All this serves to create an environment in which workers are encouraged to assume greater responsibility in their own sphere of employment." (*Mater et Magistra*, 1961, par.92-96)

"The disproportionate distribution of wealth and poverty and the existence of some countries and continents that are developed and of others that are not, call for a levelling out and for a search for ways to ensure just development for all." (*Laborem Exercens*, 1981, par. 3)

"In the light of the [Official Catholic Teachings on Property], the many proposals put forward by experts in Catholic social teaching and by the highest Magisterium of the Church take on special significance: proposals for joint ownership of the means of work, sharing by the workers in the management and/or profits of businesses, so-called shareholding by labour, etc. Whether these various proposals can or cannot be applied concretely, it is clear that recognition of the proper position of labour and the worker in the production process demands various adaptations in the sphere of the right to ownership of the means of production." (*Laborem Exercens*, 1981, par. 14)

-The concrete application is another challenging issue altogether; the principle, however, is necessary and universal. In practice, it has again and again been found successful.

"Therefore, while the position of "rigid" capitalism must undergo continual revision, in order to be reformed from the point of view of human rights, both human rights in the widest sense and those linked with man's work, it must be stated that, from the same point of view, these many deeply desired reforms cannot be achieved by an *a priori elimination of private ownership of the means of production*." (*Laborem Exercens*, 1981, par. 15)

"<u>We are therefore faced with a serious problem of unequal distribution of the means of subsistence originally meant for everybody, and thus also an unequal distribution of the benefits deriving from them</u>." (*Sollilicitudo Rei Socialis*, 1987, par.9)

-Role of the State-

"Now a State chiefly prospers and thrives through moral rule, well-regulated family life, respect for religion and justice, the moderation and fair imposing of public taxes, the progress of the arts and of trade, the abundant yield of the land-through everything, in fact, which makes the citizens better and happier. Hereby, then, it lies in the power of a ruler to benefit every class in the State, and amongst the rest to promote to the utmost the interests of the poor; and this in virtue of his office, and without being open to suspicion of undue interference…" (*Rerum Novarum*, 1891, par.32)

-In context: the State has a critical role in the public sphere, but where possible, non-governmental bodies must achieve the desired ends. See Principle of Subsidiarity. *The Role of the State could be said to be fulfilling those roles, and <u>only</u> those roles, which private enterprise cannot properly fill (i.e. the "Common Good")— often this is a fluid thing, depending on the virtue, freedom, and initiative of a society.*

"Whenever the general interest or any particular class suffers, or is threatened with harm, which can in no other way be met or prevented, the public authority must step in to deal with it...
… if circumstances were such as that among the working class the ties of family life were relaxed; if religion were found to suffer through the workers not having time and opportunity afforded them to practice its duties; if in

workshops and factories there were danger to morals through the mixing of the sexes or from other harmful occasions of evil; or if employers laid burdens upon their workmen which were unjust, or degraded them with conditions repugnant to their dignity as human beings... - in such cases, there can be no question but that, <u>within certain limits, it would be right to invoke the aid and authority of the law</u>." (*Rerum Novarum*, 1891, par.36)

"With regard to civil authority, Leo XIII, boldly breaking through the confines imposed by Liberalism, fearlessly taught that <u>government must not be thought a mere guardian of law and of good order</u>, but rather must put forth every effort so that "through the entire scheme of laws and institutions . . . both public and individual well-being may develop spontaneously out of the very structure and administration of the State." <u>Just freedom of action must, of course, be left both to individual citizens and to families, yet only on condition that the common good be preserved and wrong to any individual be abolished</u>. The function of the rulers of the State, moreover, is to watch over the community and its parts; but in protecting private individuals in their rights, chief consideration ought to be given to the weak and the poor." (*Quadragesimo Anno*, 1931, par. 25)

"When we speak of the reform of institutions, the State comes chiefly to mind, not as if universal well-being were to be expected from its activity, but because things have come to such a pass through the evil of what we have termed "individualism" that, following upon the overthrow and near extinction of that rich social life which was once highly developed through associations of various kinds, there remain virtually only individuals and the State...
Still, that most weighty principle, which cannot be set aside or changed, remains fixed and unshaken in social philosophy: Just as it is gravely wrong to take from individuals what they can accomplish by their own initiative and industry and give it to the community, so also it is an injustice and at the same time a grave evil and disturbance of right order to assign to a greater and higher association what lesser and subordinate organizations can do… <u>The supreme authority of the State ought, therefore, to let subordinate groups handle matters and concerns of lesser importance, which would otherwise dissipate its efforts greatly</u>." (*Quadragesimo Anno*, 1931, par. 78-80)

-*The above is otherwise known as* Principle of Subsidiarity.

"The social policy of the State, therefore, must devote itself to the re-establishment of the Industries and Professions." (*Quadragesimo Anno*, 1931, par. 82)

"As for the State, its whole *raison d'etre* [reason for existence] is the realization of the common good in the temporal order. It cannot, therefore, hold aloof from economic matters. On the contrary, it must do all in its power to promote the production of a sufficient supply of material goods, "the use of which is necessary for the practice of virtue." It has also the duty to protect the rights of all its people, and particularly of its weaker members, the workers, women and children. It can never be right for the State to shirk its obligation of working actively for the betterment of the condition of the workingman." (*Mater et Magistra*, 1961, par.20)

"This development in the social life of man is at once a symptom and a cause of the growing intervention of the State, even in matters which are of intimate concern to the individual, hence of great importance and not devoid of risk. We might cite as examples such matters as health and education, the choice of a career, and the care and rehabilitation of the physically and mentally handicapped.
… Clearly, this sort of development in social relationships brings many advantages in its train.
… At the same time, however, this… brings with it a multiplicity of restrictive laws and regulations in many departments of human life. As a consequence, it narrows the sphere of a person's freedom of action. The means often used… all conspire to make it difficult for a person to think independently of outside influences, to act on his own initiative, exercise his responsibility and express and fulfil his own personality. What then? Must we conclude that these increased social relationships necessarily reduce men to the condition of being mere automatons? By no means." (*Mater et Magistra*, 1961, par.62)

-In order to properly understand the role of the State, it is necessary to examine The Principle of Subsidiarity.

"State and public ownership of property is very much on the increase today [due to the demands of the common good]… But here, too, the "principle of subsidiary function" must be observed. The State and other agencies of public law must not extend their ownership beyond what is clearly required by considerations of the common good properly understood, and even then there must be safeguards.

… <u>Furthermore, a strict check should constantly be kept upon [the State's economic] activity, so as to avoid any possibility of the concentration of undue economic power in the hands of a few State officials, to the detriment of the best interests of the community.</u>

… Tragic situations and urgent problems of an intimate and personal nature are continually arising which the State with all its machinery is unable to remedy or assist. There will always remain, therefore, a vast field for the exercise of human sympathy and the Christian charity of individuals. <u>We would observe, finally, that the efforts of individuals, or of groups of private citizens, are definitely more effective in promoting spiritual values than is the activity of public authority.</u>" (*Mater et Magistra*, 1961, par.117)

"Private enterprise too must contribute to an economic and social balance in the different areas of the same political community. <u>Indeed, in accordance with "the principle of subsidiary function," public authority must encourage and assist private enterprise, entrusting to it, wherever possible, the continuation of economic development.</u>" (*Mater et Magistra*, 1961, par.152)

"Hence it is from [God] that State officials derive their dignity, for they share to some extent in the authority of God Himself.

… representatives of the State have no power to bind men in conscience, unless their own authority is tied to God's authority, and is a participation in it.

… Their obedience to civil authorities is never an obedience paid to them as men. It is in reality an act of homage paid to God… <u>Consequently, laws and decrees passed in contravention of the moral order, and hence of the divine will, can have no binding force in conscience…</u>" (*Pacem in Terris*, 1963, par.49-50)

"[Because they must contribute to the Common Welfare, Men] must harmonize their own interests with the needs of others, and offer their goods and services as their rulers shall direct—assuming, of course, that justice is maintained and the authorities are acting within the limits of their competence.

… The attainment of the common good is the sole reason for the existence of civil authorities." (*Pacem in Terris*, 1963, par. 53-54)

"In addition, heads of States must make a positive contribution to the creation of an overall climate in which the individual can both safeguard his own rights and fulfill his duties, and can do so readily… political, economic and cultural inequities among citizens become more and more widespread when public authorities fail to take appropriate action in these spheres.
…Such services [that public administration should care for and develop] include road-building, transportation, communications, drinking-water, housing, medical care, ample facilities for the practice of religion, and aids to recreation. The government must also see to the provision of insurance facilities…
.. [also provide] opportunities for suitable employment… It must make sure that working men are paid a just and equitable wage… It must facilitate the formation of intermediate groups… And finally, it must ensure that everyone has the means and opportunity of sharing as far as possible in cultural benefits." (*Pacem in Terris*, 1963, par.63-64)

-In context: the above does not, in context, necessarily mean that the State should always and exclusively by the one in charge of these items… wherever possible (herein lies the challenge), a private body must direct them. The State's role is to always to care for them, but not necessarily exclusively control them.

"The common welfare further demands that in their efforts to co-ordinate and protect, and their efforts to promote, the rights of citizens, the civil authorities preserve a delicate balance. An excessive concern for the rights of any particular individuals or groups might well result in the principal advantages of the State being in effect monopolized by these citizens. Or again, the absurd situation can arise where the civil authorities, while taking measures to protect the rights of citizens, themselves stand in the way of the full exercise of these rights." (*Pacem in Terris*, 1963, par.65)

"We must, however, reject the view that the will of the [governing body] is the primary and only source of a citizen's rights and duties, and of the binding force of political constitutions and the government's authority." (*Pacem in Terris*, 1963, par.78)

-Civil Rights follow those granted by God through Divine Law and Nature: the judgment of the Nuremberg trials, however one views them, recognizes this inescapable fact – duty as a human being precedes duty as a statesman.

"And just as individual men may not pursue their own private interests in a way that is unfair and detrimental to others, so too it would be criminal in a State to aim at improving itself by the use of methods which involve other nations in injury and unjust oppression. ... 'Take away justice, and what are kingdoms but mighty bands of robbers'" (*Pacem in Terris*, 1963, par.92)

"Now, if one considers carefully the inner significance of the common good on the one hand, and the nature and function of public authority on the other, one cannot fail to see that there is an intrinsic connection between them. ... Consequently the moral order itself demands the establishment of some such general form of public authority." (*Pacem in Terris*, 1963, par.136-137)

"Rulers must be careful not to hamper the development of family, social or cultural groups, nor that of intermediate bodies or organizations, and not to deprive them of opportunities for legitimate and constructive activity; they should willingly seek rather to promote the orderly pursuit of such activity. Citizens, for their part, either individually or collectively, must be careful not to attribute excessive power to public authority, not to make exaggerated and untimely demands upon it in their own interests, lessening in this way the responsible role of persons, families and social groups.
The complex circumstances of our day make it necessary for public authority to intervene more often in social, economic and cultural matters in order to bring about favorable conditions which will give more effective help to citizens and groups in their free pursuit of man's total well-being.
... But when the exercise of rights is restricted temporarily for the common good, freedom should be restored immediately upon change of circumstances. Moreover, it is inhuman for public authority to fall back on dictatorial systems or totalitarian methods which violate the rights of the person or social groups." (*Gaudium et Spes*, 1965, par. 75)

"If Pope Leo XIII calls upon the State to remedy the condition of the poor in accordance with justice, he does so because of his timely awareness that the State has the duty of watching over the common good and of ensuring that every sector of social life, not excluding the economic one, contributes to achieving that good, while respecting the rightful autonomy of each sector. This should not however lead us to think that Pope Leo expected the State to solve every social problem. On the contrary, he frequently insists on necessary limits to the State's intervention and on its instrumental character, inasmuch as the individual, the family and society are prior to the State, and inasmuch as the State exists in order to protect their rights and not stifle them." (*Centesimus annus*, 1991, par. 11)

-The State is not the primary care holder of our well-being: we are.

"<u>Rerum novarum is opposed to State control of the means of production, which would reduce every citizen to being a "cog" in the State machine. It is no less forceful in criticizing a concept of the State which completely excludes the economic sector from the State's range of interest and action</u>. There is certainly a legitimate sphere of autonomy in economic life which the State should not enter. The State, however, has the <u>task of determining</u> the juridical framework within which economic affairs are to be conducted, and thus of safeguarding the prerequisites of <u>a free economy, which presumes a certain equality between the parties,</u> such that one party would not be so powerful as practically to reduce the other to subservience." (*Centesimus annus*, 1991, par. 14)

-While generally optimal in theory, any sense of a "free market" can only exist when there is a comparable parity of power between the interacting parties. A free market is the most efficient structure for production; yet efficiency does not always equal moral. Trains at Auschwitz were efficient.

"The State must contribute to the achievement of these goals both directly and indirectly. Indirectly and according to the principle of subsidiarity, by creating favorable conditions for the free exercise of economic activity, which will lead to abundant opportunities for employment and sources of wealth. <u>Directly and according to the principle of solidarity, by defending the weakest, by placing certain limits on the autonomy of the parties who determine working conditions, and by ensuring in every case the necessary minimum support for the unemployed worker</u>." (*Centesimus annus*, 1991, par. 15)

"It is the task of the State to provide for the defence and preservation of common goods such as the natural and human environments, <u>which cannot be safeguarded simply by market forces</u>." (*Centesimus annus*, 1991, par. 40)

-See Ecological & Environmental Concerns *for related references.*

"Pope Leo XIII was aware of the need for a sound theory of the State in order to ensure the normal development of man's spiritual and temporal activities, both of which are indispensable… To that end, it is preferable that each power be balanced by other powers and by other spheres of responsibility which keep it within proper bounds. This is the principle of the "rule of law", in which the law is sovereign, and not the arbitrary will of individuals." (*Centesimus annus*, 1991, par. 44)

"Another task of the State is that of overseeing and directing the exercise of human rights in the economic sector. However, primary responsibility in this area belongs not to the State but to individuals and to the various groups and associations which make up society. The State could not directly ensure the right to work for all its citizens unless it controlled every aspect of economic life and restricted the free initiative of individuals. This does not mean, however, that the State has no competence in this domain, as was claimed by those who argued against any rules in the economic sphere." (*Centesimus annus*, 1991, par. 48)

"Love—caritas—will always prove necessary, even in the most just society. There is no ordering of the State so just that it can eliminate the need for a service of love. Whoever wants to eliminate love is preparing to eliminate man as such. There will always be suffering which cries out for consolation and help. There will always be loneliness. There will always be situations of material need where help in the form of concrete love of neighbor is indispensable. The State which would provide everything, absorbing everything into itself, would ultimately become a mere bureaucracy incapable of guaranteeing the very thing which the suffering person—every person—needs: namely, loving personal concern. We do not need a State which regulates and controls everything, but a State which, in accordance with the principle of subsidiarity, generously acknowledges and supports initiatives arising from the different social forces and combines spontaneity with closeness to those in need. The Church is one of those living forces: she is alive with the love enkindled by the Spirit of Christ. This love does not simply offer people material help, but refreshment and care for their souls, something which often is even more necessary than material support." (*Deus Caritas Est*, 2005, par.28)

-*Simply Beautiful.*

"When both the logic of the market and the logic of the State come to an agreement that each will continue to exercise a monopoly over its respective area of influence, in the long term much is lost: solidarity in relations between citizens, participation and adherence, actions of gratuitousness, all of which stand in contrast with *giving in order to acquire* (the logic of exchange) and giving through duty (the logic of public obligation, imposed by State law). In order to defeat underdevelopment, action is required not only on improving exchange-based transactions and implanting public welfare structures, but above all on gradually *increasing openness, in a world context, to forms of economic activity marked by quotas of gratuitousness and communion.* The exclusively binary model of market-plus-State is corrosive of society, while economic forms based on solidarity, which find their natural home in civil society without being restricted to it, build up society. The market of gratuitousness does not exist, and attitudes of gratuitousness cannot be established by law. Yet both the market and politics need individuals who are open to reciprocal gift." (*Caritas in Veritatae*, 2009, par.20)

"Civil authorities have the right and duty to adopt clear and firm measures in support of small producers and differentiated production… To claim economic freedom while real conditions bar many people from actual access to it, and while possibilities for employment continue to shrink, is to practise a doublespeak which brings politics into disrepute." (*Laudato Si*, 2015, par 129)

"Honesty and truth are needed in scientific and political discussions; these should not be limited to the issue of whether or not a particular project is permitted by law." (*Laudato Si*, 2015, par 183)
"Legal" does not necessarily equal moral, ethical, or acceptable.

"If in a given region the state does not carry out its responsibilities, some business groups can come forward in the guise of benefactors, wield real power, and consider themselves exempt from certain rules, to the point of tolerating different forms of organized crime, human trafficking, the drug trade and violence, all of which become very difficult to eradicate. If politics shows itself incapable of breaking such a perverse logic, and remains caught up in inconsequential discussions, we will continue to avoid facing the major problems of humanity." (*Laudato Si*, 2015, par 197)

-Anarchy-

-*See* Role of the State

-Principle of Subsidiarity-

The Catholic teaching of the "Principle of Subsidiarity" is quite simple. Summed up it is: No higher or larger power should do what a lower or more local power is capable of doing; similarly, if it is possible that a local body can accomplish something (as opposed to a larger centralized power) then it should be the agent of action. While this applies to any hierarchy: Global states, governments, families, organizations, etc., there are certain situations (i.e. government versus a hobby club etc.) in which the consequences of implementing the principles are —or are not - more urgent and more serious. Although not definitely termed "principle of subsidiarity" until the mid-20th century, the principle of organization is clearly delineated in Rerum Novarum *and following social encycicals.*

"The good order of society also requires that individuals and subsidiary groups within the State be effectively protected by law in the affirmation of their rights and the performance of their duties, both in their relations with each other and with government officials." (*Pacem in Terris*, 1963, par.69)

"The same principle of subsidiarity which governs the relations between public authorities and individuals, families and intermediate societies in a single State, must also apply to the relations between the public authority of the world community and the public authorities of each political community." (*Pacem in Terris*, 1963, par.140)

"…Here again the *principle of subsidiarity* must be respected: a community of a higher order should not interfere in the internal life of a community of a lower order, depriving the latter of its functions, but rather should support it in case of need and help to coordinate its activity with the activities of the rest of society, always with a view to the common good." (*Centesimus annus*, 1991, par. 48)

"Subsidiarity is first and foremost a form of assistance to the human person via the autonomy of intermediate bodies… By considering reciprocity as the heart of what it is to be a human being, subsidiarity is the most effective antidote against any form of all-encompassing welfare state." (*Caritas in Veritatae*, 2009, par.57)

"The principle of subsidiarity must remain closely linked to the principle of solidarity and vice versa... [Both individual and International] aid, whatever the donors' intentions, can sometimes lock people into a state of dependence and even foster situations of localized oppression and exploitation in the receiving country. Economic aid, in order to be true to its purpose, must not pursue secondary objectives. It must be distributed with the involvement not only of the governments of receiving countries, but also local economic agents and the bearers of culture within civil society, including local Churches. Aid programmes must increasingly acquire the characteristics of participation and completion from the grass roots... Too often in the past, aid has served to create only fringe markets for the products of these donor countries." (*Caritas in Veritatae*, 2009, par.58)

"In some places, cooperatives are being developed to exploit renewable sources of energy which ensure local self-sufficiency and even the sale of surplus energy... Because the enforcement of laws is at times inadequate due to corruption, public pressure has to be exerted in order to bring about decisive political action. Society, through non-governmental organizations and intermediate groups, must put pressure on governments to develop more rigorous regulations, procedures and controls. Unless citizens control political power – national, regional and municipal – it will not be possible to control damage to the environment." (*Laudato Si*, 2015, par 179)

-Role of the Church in Society & Politics-

"….there are men, who, although professing to be Catholics, are almost completely unmindful of that sublime law of justice and charity that binds us not only to render to everyone what is his but to succor brothers in need as Christ the Lord Himself, and - what is worse - out of greed for gain do not scruple to exploit the workers. Even more, there are men who abuse religion itself, and under its name try to hide their unjust exactions in order to protect themselves from the manifestly just demands of the workers. For they are the reason why the Church could, even though undeservedly, have the appearance of and be charged with taking the part of the rich and with being quite unmoved by the necessities and hardships of those who have been deprived, as it were, of their natural inheritance." (*Quadragesimo Anno*, 1931, par 125)

"Hence, though the Church's first care must be for souls, how she can sanctify them and make them share in the gifts of heaven, she concerns herself too with the exigencies of man's daily life, with his livelihood and education, and his general, temporal welfare and prosperity." (*Mater et Magistra*, 1961, par.3)

"Now, in bringing people to Christ, the Church has invariably—both now and in the past—brought them many social and economical advantages. <u>For true Christians cannot help feeling obliged to improve their own temporal institutions and environment.</u>
…. Moreover, in becoming as it were the life-blood of these people, the Church is not, nor does she consider herself to be, a foreign body in their midst.
… <u>The Church aims at unity… she does not aim at a uniformity…</u>" (*Mater et Magistra*, 1961, par.178-181)

"For it must not be forgotten that the Church has the right and duty not only to safeguard her teaching on faith and morals, <u>but also to exercise her authority over her sons by intervening in their external affairs</u> whenever a judgment has to be made concerning the practical application of this teaching." (*Pacem in Terris*, 1963, par.162)

"The permanent validity of the Catholic Church's social teaching admits of no doubt.
This teaching rests on one basic principle: individual human beings are the foundation, the cause and the end of every social institution.
… The principles she gives are of universal application, for they take human nature into account, and the varying conditions in which man's life is lived. They also take into account the principal characteristics of contemporary society, and are thus acceptable to all.
… First, <u>We must reaffirm most strongly that this Catholic social doctrine is an integral part of the Christian conception of life. It is therefore Our urgent desire that this doctrine be studied more and more. First of all it should be taught as part of the daily curriculum in Catholic schools of every kind, particularly seminaries</u>…
… It is not enough merely to formulate a social doctrine. It must be translated into reality." (*Mater et Magistra*, 1961, par.218-226)

"<u>To search for spiritual perfection and eternal salvation in the conduct of human affairs and institutions is not to rob these of the power to achieve their immediate, specific ends, but to enhance this power.</u>" (*Mater et Magistra*, 1961, par.257)

"By no human law can the personal dignity and liberty of man be so aptly safeguarded as by the Gospel of Christ which has been entrusted to the Church." (*Gaudium et Spes*, 1965, par.41)

"Christ, to be sure, gave His Church no proper mission in the political, economic or social order. The purpose which He set before her is a religious one. But out of this religious mission itself come a function, a light and an energy which can serve to structure and consolidate the human community according to the divine law.
… <u>She has no fiercer desire than that in pursuit of the welfare of all she may be able to develop herself freely under any kind of government which grants recognition to the basic rights of person and family, to the demands of the common good and to the free exercise of her own mission.</u>" (*Gaudium et Spes*, 1965, par.42)

-The Church's role is never to be seen as primarily a political one; an organization of this World. Its role as Guardian of Truth, however, demands that it illuminate bearing on temporal affairs. John 18:36. See Separation of Church and State.

"[The Church] has used the discoveries of different cultures so that in her preaching she might spread and explain the message of Christ to all nations, that she might examine it and more deeply understand it, that she might give it better expression in liturgical celebration and in the varied life of the community of the faithful.
But at the same time, <u>the Church, sent to all peoples of every time and place, is not bound exclusively and indissolubly to any race or nation, any particular way of life or any customary way of life recent or ancient.</u>" (*Gaudium et Spes*, 1965, par.58)

"In the face of such widely varying situations it is difficult for us to utter a unified message and to put forward a solution which has universal validity. Such is not our ambition, nor is it our mission. It is up to the Christian communities to analyze with objectivity the situation which is proper to their own country, to shed on it the light of the Gospel's unalterable words and to draw principles of reflection, norms of judgment and directives for action from the social teaching of the Church." (*Octogesima Adveniens*, 1971, par.4)

"It is with all its dynamism that the social teaching of the Church accompanies men in their search. If it does not intervene to authenticate a given structure or to propose a ready-made model, it does not thereby limit itself to recalling general principles." (*Octogesima Adveniens*, 1971, par.42)

"In the social sphere, the Church has always wished to assume a double function: first to enlighten minds in order to assist them to discover the truth and to find the right path to follow amid the different teachings that call for their attention; and secondly to take part in action and to spread, with a real care for service and effectiveness, the energies of the Gospel." (*Octogesima Adveniens*, 1971, par.48)

"The Church considers it her duty to speak out on work from the viewpoint of its human value and of the moral order to which it belongs, and she sees this as one of her important tasks within the service that she renders to the evangelical message as a whole." (*Laborem Exercens*, 1981, par. 24)

"This twofold dimension is typical of [the Church's] teaching in the social sphere. On the one hand it is constant, for it remains identical in its fundamental inspiration, in its "principles of reflection," in its "criteria of judgment," in its basic "directives for action," and above all in its vital link with the Gospel of the Lord. On the other hand, it is ever new, because it is subject to the necessary and opportune adaptations suggested by the changes in historical conditions and by the unceasing flow of the events which are the setting of the life of people and society." (*Sollilicitudo Rei Socialis*, 1987, par.3)

"Faced by cases of need, one cannot ignore them in favor of superfluous church ornaments and costly furnishings for divine worship; on the contrary it could be obligatory to sell these goods in order to provide food, drink, clothing and shelter for those who lack these things. As has been already noted, here we are shown a "hierarchy of values" [i.e. "being" over "having"]" (*Sollilicitudo Rei Socialis*, 1987, par.31)

-It is not to be misunderstood that this refers to extreme need. Nor are we to follow the example of Judas in John 12:5. Oftentimes, the ornaments and riches of the Church, in the form of ornaments and furnishings of divine worship, are the only treasures the poor have. There must be a balance: legend has it that a pope once quipped to St. Thomas Aquinas,

"The Church can no longer say, 'silver and gold I have none.' Replied St. Thomas: "True Holy Father, but neither can she say 'rise and walk.'" Cf. Acts 3:6.

"<u>The Church does not have technical revolutions to offer for the problem of underdevelopment as such, as Pope Paul VI already affirmed in his Encyclical.</u> For the Church does not propose economic and political systems or programs, nor does she show preference for one or the other, <u>provided that human dignity is properly respected and promoted, and provided she herself is allowed the room she needs to exercise her ministry in the world.</u>" (*Sollilicitudo Rei Socialis*, 1987, par.41)

"The condemnation of evils and injustices is also part of that ministry of evangelization in the social field which is an aspect of the Church's prophetic role. But it should be made clear that proclamation is always more important than condemnation, and the latter cannot ignore the former, which gives it true solidity and the force of higher motivation." (*Sollilicitudo Rei Socialis*, 1987, par.41)

"In keeping with Christian piety through the ages, we present to the Blessed Virgin difficult individual situations, so that she may place them before her Son, asking that he alleviate and change them.
… Mary most holy, our Mother and Queen, is the one who turns to her Son and says: "They have no more wine" (Jn 2:3). She is also the one who praises God the Father, because "he has put down the mighty from their thrones and exalted those of low degree; he has filled the hungry with good things, and the rich he has sent empty away" (Lk 1:52-53). Her maternal concern extends to the personal and social aspects of people's life on earth." (*Sollilicitudo Rei Socialis*, 1987, par.49)

"Through Christ's sacrifice on the Cross, the victory of the Kingdom of God has been achieved once and for all. Nevertheless, the Christian life involves a struggle against temptation and the forces of evil. Only at the end of history will the Lord return in glory for the final judgment (cf. Mt 25:31) with the establishment of a new heaven and a new earth (cf. 2 Pt 3:13; Rev 21:1); but as long as time lasts the struggle between good and evil continues even in the human heart itself.

… The Kingdom of God, being in the world without being of the world, throws light on the order of human society, while the power of grace penetrates that order and gives it life.
… <u>To those who are searching today for a new and authentic theory and praxis of liberation, the Church offers not only her social doctrine and, in general, her teaching about the human person redeemed in Christ, but also her concrete commitment and material assistance in the struggle against marginalization and suffering</u>." (*Centesimus annus*, 1991, par. 25-26)

"The Church has no models to present; models that are real and truly effective can only arise within the framework of different historical situations, through the efforts of all those who responsibly confront concrete problems in all their social, economic, political and cultural aspects, as these interact with one another. For such a task the Church offers her social teaching as an indispensable and ideal orientation, a teaching which, as already mentioned, recognizes the positive value of the market and of enterprise, but which at the same time points out that these need to be oriented towards the common good." (*Centesimus annus*, 1991, par. 43)

"<u>The Church respects the legitimate autonomy of the democratic order and is not entitled to express preferences for this or that institutional or constitutional solution. Her contribution to the political order is precisely her vision of the dignity of the person revealed in all its fullness in the mystery of the Incarnate Word</u>.
<u>These general observations also apply to</u> *the role of the State in the economic sector*." (*Centesimus annus*, 1991, par. 47)

"Thus the first and most important task is accomplished within man's heart. The way in which he is involved in building his own future depends on the understanding he has of himself and of his own destiny. It is on this level that the Church's specific and decisive contribution to true culture is to be found… The Church renders this service to human society by preaching the truth about the creation of the world, which God has placed in human hands so that people may make it fruitful and more perfect through their work; and by preaching the truth about the Redemption, whereby the Son of God has saved mankind and at the same time has united all people, making them responsible for one another." (*Centesimus annus*, 1991, par. 51)

"The human sciences and philosophy are helpful for interpreting man's central place within society and for enabling him to understand himself better as a "social being". However, man's true identity is only fully revealed to him through faith, and it is precisely from faith that the Church's social teaching begins. While drawing upon all the contributions made by the sciences and philosophy, her social teaching is aimed at helping man on the path of salvation." (*Centesimus annus*, 1991, par. 54)

"As far as the Church is concerned, the social message of the Gospel must not be considered a theory, but above all else a basis and a motivation for action." (*Centesimus annus*, 1991, par. 57)

-certainly not to say that action is somehow better than or even separate from contemplative communion with God (Luke 10.41) but rather, this inner relationship of prayer with God <u>will</u> express itself in actions. (James 2:14)

"It is true that history has known cases where crimes have been committed in the name of "truth". But equally grave crimes and radical denials of freedom have also been committed and are still being committed in the name of "ethical relativism". When a parliamentary or social majority decrees that it is legal, at least under certain conditions, to kill unborn human life, is it not really making a "tyrannical" decision with regard to the weakest and most defenseless of human beings?" (*Evangelium Vitae*, 1995, par.70)

- "But if Mr. Blatchford really thinks that the gory past of an institution damns it, and if he really wants an institution to damn, an institution which is much older, and much larger, and much gorier than Christianity…[then I give him the] State or Government, the mother of all whips and thumbscrews…" -G.K. Chesterton. *The Church always recognizes that Judas will betray Jesus; but we can never leave Peter because of Judas.*

"<u>Jesus himself has shown us by his own example that prayer and fasting are the first and most effective weapons against the forces of evil</u> (cf. Mt 4:1-11)." (*Evangelium Vitae*, 1995, par.100)

"Building a just social and civil order, wherein each person receives what is his or her due, is an essential task which every generation must take up anew. As a political task, this cannot be the Church's immediate responsibility.

"... The Church cannot and must not take upon herself the political battle to bring about the most just society possible. She cannot and must not replace the State. Yet at the same time she cannot and must not remain on the sidelines in the fight for justice. She has to play her part through rational argument and she has to reawaken the spiritual energy without which justice, which always demands sacrifice, cannot prevail and prosper.' (*Deus Caritas Est*, 2005, par.28)

"The Church can never be exempted from practising charity as an organized activity of believers..."(*Deus Caritas Est*, 2005, par.29)

"Again and again, the Church has acted as a mediator in finding solutions to problems affecting peace, social harmony, the land, the defense of life, human and civil rights, and so forth. And how much good has been done by Catholic schools and universities around the world! This is a good thing. Yet, we find it difficult to make people see that when we raise other questions less palatable to public opinion, we are doing so out of fidelity to precisely the same convictions about human dignity and the common good." (*Evangelii Gaudium*, 2013, par.65)

-Role of Catholics in Public Activity-

"<u>Let no man therefore imagine that a life of activity in the world is incompatible with spiritual perfection. The two can very well be harmonized</u>. It is a gross error to suppose that a man cannot perfect himself except by putting aside all temporal activity, on the plea that such activity will inevitably lead him to compromise his personal dignity as a human being and as a Christian." (*Mater et Magistra*, 1961, par.255)

"We especially urge Catholic men living in developed nations to offer their skills and earnest assistance to public and private organizations, both civil and religious, working to solve the problems of developing nations. They will surely want to be in the first ranks of those who spare no effort to have just and fair laws, based on moral precepts, established among all nations." (*Populorum Progresso*, 1967, par.81)

"The direct duty to work for a just ordering of society, on the other hand, is proper to the lay faithful. As citizens of the State, they are called to take part in public life in a personal capacity." (*Deus Caritas Est*, 2005, par.29)

-Politics & Public Activity -

"Here once more We exhort Our sons to take an active part in public life, and to work together for the benefit of the whole human race, as well as for their own political communities.
…But in a culture and civilization like our own, which is so remarkable for its scientific knowledge and its technical discoveries, clearly no one can insinuate himself into public life unless he be scientifically competent, technically capable, and skilled in the practice of his own profession ." (*Pacem in Terris*, 1963, par.146-148)

"Hence, the will to play one's role in common endeavors should be everywhere encouraged. Praise is due to those national procedures which allow the largest possible number of citizens to participate in public affairs with genuine freedom." (*Gaudium et Spes*, 1965, par. 31)

"The political community exists, consequently, for the sake of the common good, in which it finds its full justification and significance, and the source of its inherent legitimacy.
… Yet the people who come together in the political community are many and diverse, and they have every right to prefer divergent solutions. If the political community is not to be torn apart while everyone follows his own opinion, there must be an authority to direct the energies of all citizens toward the common good, not in a mechanical or despotic fashion, but by acting above all as a moral force which appeals to each one's freedom and sense of responsibility." (*Gaudium et Spes*, 1965, par. 49)

"Various models [of democratic society] are proposed, some are tried out, none of them gives complete satisfaction, and the search goes on between ideological and pragmatic tendencies. The Christian has the duty to take part in this search and in the organization and life of political society… All particular activity must be placed within that wider society, and thereby it takes on the dimension of the common good… This indicates the importance of education for life in society, in which there are called to mind, not only information on each one's rights, but also their necessary correlative: the recognition of the duties of each one in regard to others.
Political activity - need one remark that we are dealing primarily with an activity, not an ideology? - should be the projection of a plan of society which is

consistent in its concrete means and in its inspiration, and which springs from a complete conception of man's vocation and of its differing social expressions. It is not for the State or even for political parties, which would be closed unto themselves, to try to impose an ideology by means that would lead to a <u>dictatorship over minds, the worst kind of all</u>. It is for cultural and religious groupings, in the freedom of acceptance which they presume, to develop in the social body, disinterestedly and in their own ways, those ultimate convictions on the nature, origin and end of man and society." (*Octogesima Adveniens*, 1971, par.25)

-An "ideology" (See above) is any framework of thought that one places <u>before</u> truth, so that all Truth must conform to that framework, rather than the opposite. This happens when one single truth becomes over-emphasized: individuality, sexuality, even freedom, etc. For example, "Partisan Politics" is an ideology, since the determining factor is not Truth, but the party line first, and Truth second.

"The just ordering of society and the State is a central responsibility of politics.
... <u>Politics is more than a mere mechanism for defining the rules of public life</u>: its origin and its goal are found in justice, which by its very nature has to do with ethics. The State must inevitably face the question of how justice can be achieved here and now.
... <u>Here politics and faith meet. Faith by its specific nature is an encounter with the living God—an encounter opening up new horizons extending beyond the sphere of reason. But it is also a purifying force for reason itself. From God's standpoint, faith liberates reason from its blind spots and therefore helps it to be ever more fully itself. Faith enables reason to do its work more effectively and to see its proper object more clearly. This is where Catholic social doctrine has its place: it has no intention of giving the Church power over the State. Even less is it an attempt to impose on those who do not share the faith ways of thinking and modes of conduct proper to faith. Its aim is simply to help purify reason and to contribute, here and now, to the acknowledgment and attainment of what is just.</u>" (*Deus Caritas Est*, 2005, par.28)

"I beg the Lord to grant us more politicians who are genuinely disturbed by the state of society, the people, the lives of the poor!" (*Evangelii Gaudium*, 2013, par.205)

"Not everyone is called to engage directly in political life. Society is also enriched by a countless array of organizations which work to promote the common good and to defend the environment, whether natural or urban... Around these community actions, relationships develop or are recovered and a new social fabric emerges." (*Laudato Si*, 2015, par 232)

-Catholic Social Teaching-

"<u>Charity is at the heart of the Church's social doctrine.</u>
... Through this close link with truth, charity can be recognized as an authentic expression of humanity ...Without truth, charity degenerates into sentimentality. Love becomes an empty shell, to be filled in an arbitrary way. In a culture without truth, this is the fatal risk facing love. It falls prey to contingent subjective emotions and opinions, the word "love" is abused and distorted, to the point where it comes to mean the opposite." (*Caritas in Veritatae*, 2009, par.2-3)

-Separation of Church and State or Church and Public Life-

"Doubtless, this most serious question demands the attention and the efforts of others besides ourselves - to wit, of the rulers of States, of employers of labor, of the wealthy, aye, of the working classes themselves, for whom We are pleading. But We affirm without hesitation that all the striving of men will be vain if they leave out the Church." (*Rerum Novarum*, 1891, par.16)

"Of these facts there cannot be any shadow of doubt: ...civil society was renovated in every part by Christian institutions." (*Rerum Novarum*, 1891, par.27)

"The Church... is not identified in any way with the political community nor bound to any political system. She is at once a sign and a safeguard of the transcendent character of the human person.
The Church and the political community in their own fields are autonomous and independent from each other. Yet both, under different titles, are devoted to the personal and social vocation of the same men. The more that both foster sounder cooperation between themselves with due consideration for the circumstances of time and place, the more effective will their service be exercised for the good of all.

… By preaching the truths of the Gospel, and bringing to bear on all fields of human endeavor the light of her doctrine and of a Christian witness, she respects and fosters the political freedom and responsibility of citizens.

… There are, indeed, close links between earthly things and those elements of man's condition which transcend the world. The Church herself makes use of temporal things insofar as her own mission requires it. She, for her part, does not place her trust in the privileges offered by civil authority. She will even give up the exercise of certain rights which have been legitimately acquired, if it becomes clear that their use will cast doubt on the sincerity of her witness or that new ways of life demand new methods. It is only right, however, that at all times and in all places, the Church should have true freedom to preach the faith, to teach her social doctrine, to exercise her role freely among men, and also to pass moral judgment in those matters which regard public order when the fundamental rights of a person or the salvation of souls require it." (*Gaudium et Spes*, 1965, par.76)

"They are mistaken who, knowing that we have here no abiding city but seek one which is to come,(think that they may therefore shirk their earthly responsibilities. For they are forgetting that by the faith itself they are more obliged than ever to measure up to these duties, each according to his proper vocation. Nor, on the contrary, are they any less wide of the mark who think that religion consists in acts of worship alone and in the discharge of certain moral obligations, and who imagine they can plunge themselves into earthly affairs in such a way as to imply that these are altogether divorced from the religious life. This split between the faith which many profess and their daily lives deserves to be counted among the more serious errors of our age.

… Therefore, let there be no false opposition between professional and social activities on the one part, and religious life on the other.

… Secular duties and activities belong properly although not exclusively to laymen… Laymen should also know that it is generally the function of their well-formed Christian conscience to see that the divine law is inscribed in the life of the earthly city; from priests they may look for spiritual light and nourishment. Let the layman not imagine that his pastors are always such experts, that to every problem which arises, however complicated, they can readily give him a concrete solution, or even that such is their mission. Rather, enlightened by Christian wisdom and giving close attention to the teaching authority of the Church, let the layman take on his own distinctive role." (*Gaudium et Spes*, 1965, par.43)

"The Church, which has long experience in human affairs and has no desire to be involved in the political activities of any nation …Founded to build the kingdom of heaven on earth rather than to acquire temporal power, the Church openly avows that the two powers—Church and State—are distinct from one another; that each is supreme in its own sphere of competency…. So she offers man her distinctive contribution: a global perspective on man and human realities." (*Populorum Progresso*, 1967, par.13)

-Separate not in the sense of divide, apart, and opposed, but in the sense of distinction; similar to the form and matter of a subject. Each works in their respective role within their spheres, but with different goals: the Church's work is eternal; Political work is temporal. Again, temporal is not <u>unrelated</u> to eternal, rather, each <u>compliments</u> each other. Truth is Truth, whether that be religious, scientific, or political. Like all truth, it is not an all-or-nothing, but rather a mutual relationship.

"The State may not impose religion, yet it must guarantee religious freedom and harmony between the followers of different religions. For her part, the Church, as the social expression of Christian faith, has a proper independence and is structured on the basis of her faith as a community which the State must recognize. <u>The two spheres are distinct, yet always interrelated</u>." (*Deus Caritas Est*, 2005, par.28)

"<u>The process of secularization tends to reduce the faith and the Church to the sphere of the private and personal. Furthermore, by completely rejecting the transcendent, it has produced a growing deterioration of ethics, a weakening of the sense of personal and collective sin, and a steady increase in relativism. These have led to a general sense of disorientation, especially in the periods of adolescence and young adulthood which are so vulnerable to change. As the bishops of the United States of America have rightly pointed out, while the Church insists on the existence of objective moral norms which are valid for everyone, "there are those in our culture who portray this teaching as unjust, that is, as opposed to basic human rights. Such claims usually follow from a form of moral relativism that is joined, not without inconsistency, to a belief in the absolute rights of individuals.</u>" (*Evangelii Gaudium*, 2013, par.64)

-Progress & Reform-

"The instruments which [the Church] employs are given to her by Jesus Christ Himself for the very purpose of reaching the hearts of men, and drive their efficiency from God. They alone can reach the innermost heart and conscience, and bring men to act from a motive of duty, to control their passions and appetites, to love God and their fellow men with a love that is outstanding and of the highest degree and to break down courageously every barrier which blocks the way to virtue." (*Rerum Novarum*, 1891, par.26)

"Economic progress must be accompanied by a corresponding social progress, so that all classes of citizens can participate in the increased productivity... From this it follows that the economic prosperity of a nation is not so much its total assets in terms of wealth and property, as the equitable division and distribution of this wealth. " (*Mater et Magistra*, 1961, par.73)

-*See* Private Property *and* Proportional Ownership for All *for related references*. *Also,* Equality & Inequality

"However, it is no less necessary—and justice itself demands—that the riches produced be distributed fairly among all members of the political community...everything must be done to ensure that social progress keeps pace with economic progress.
...Scientific and technical progress, economic development and the betterment of living conditions are certainly valuable elements in a civilization. But we must realize that they are essentially instrumental in character. They are not supreme values in themselves.
It pains Us, therefore, to observe the complete indifference to the true hierarchy of values shown by so many people in the economically developed countries. Spiritual values are ignored, forgotten or denied, while the progress of science, technology and economics is pursued for its own sake, as though material well-being were the be-all and end-all of life." (*Mater et Magistra*, 1961, par.168-177)

"For this reason, love for God and neighbor is the first and greatest commandment. Sacred Scripture, however, teaches us that the love of God cannot be separated from love of neighbor... Man's social nature makes it evident that the progress of the human person and the advance of society itself hinge on one another." (*Gaudium et Spes*, 1965, par. 24-25)

"Sacred Scripture teaches the human family what the experience of the ages confirms: that while human progress is a great advantage to man, it brings with it a strong temptation.
… Hence if anyone wants to know how this unhappy situation can be overcome, Christians will tell him that all human activity, constantly imperiled by man's pride and deranged self-love, must be purified and perfected by the power of Christ's cross and resurrection." (*Gaudium et Spes*, 1965, par. 37)

"…the expectation of a new earth must not weaken but rather stimulate our concern for cultivating this one.
… Hence, while earthly progress must be carefully distinguished from the growth of Christ's kingdom, to the extent that the former can contribute to the better ordering of human society, it is of vital concern to the Kingdom of God." (*Gaudium et Spes*, 1965, par. 31)

"Human society is sorely ill. The cause is not so much the depletion of natural resources, nor their monopolistic control by a privileged few; it is rather the weakening of brotherly ties between individuals and nations." (*Populorum Progresso*, 1967, par.66)

"The ultimate goal is a full-bodied humanism. And does this not mean the fulfillment of the whole man and of every man? A narrow humanism, closed in on itself and not open to the values of the spirit and to God who is their source, could achieve apparent success, for man can set about organizing terrestrial realities without God. But "closed off from God, they will end up being directed against man. A humanism closed off from other realities becomes inhuman."
… Man is not the ultimate measure of man. Man becomes truly man only by passing beyond himself." (*Populorum Progresso*, 1967, par.42)

"Since the nineteenth century, western societies and, as a result, many others have put their hopes in ceaselessly renewed and indefinite progress…Yet a doubt arises today regarding both its value and its result. What is the meaning of this never-ending, breathless pursuit of a progress [if one cannot] enjoy it in peace?
…Overcoming the temptation to wish to measure everything in terms of efficiency and of trade, and in terms of the interplay of forces and interests, man

today wishes to replace these quantitative criteria with the intensity of communication, the spread of knowledge and culture, mutual service and a combining of efforts for a common task. <u>Is not genuine progress to be found in the development of moral consciousness, which will lead man to exercise a wider solidarity and to open himself freely to others and to God?</u>" (*Octogesima Adveniens*, 1971, par.41)

"Let each one examine himself, to see what he has done up to now, and what he ought to do. It is not enough to recall principles, state intentions, point to crying injustice and utter prophetic denunciations; these words will lack real weight unless they are accompanied for each individual by a livelier awareness of personal responsibility and by effective action. It is too easy to throw back on others responsibility for injustice, if at the same time one does not realize how each one shares in it personally…" (*Octogesima Adveniens*, 1971, par.48)

"In this direction it is possible to actuate a plan for universal and proportionate progress by all… The progress in question must be made through man and for man and it must produce its fruit in man." (*Laborem Exercens*, 1981, par. 18)

"The technical forces in play, the global interrelations, the damaging effects on the real economy of badly managed and largely speculative financial dealing, large-scale migration of peoples, often provoked by some particular circumstance and then given insufficient attention, the unregulated exploitation of the earth's resources: all this leads us today to reflect on the measures that would be necessary to provide a solution to problems that are not only new in comparison to those addressed by Pope Paul VI, but also, and above all, of decisive impact upon the present and future good of humanity. The different aspects of the crisis, its solutions, and any new development that the future may bring, are increasingly interconnected, they imply one another, they require new efforts of holistic understanding and a new *humanistic synthesis*." (*Caritas in Veritatae*, 2009, par.21)

"<u>On the part of rich countries there is excessive zeal for protecting knowledge through an unduly rigid assertion of the right to intellectual property, especially in the field of health care.</u>
… Yet it should be stressed that <u>*progress of a merely economic and technological kind is insufficient.*</u>" (*Caritas in Veritatae*, 2009, par.22-23)

"One of the most striking aspects of development in the present day is the important question of *respect for life*, which cannot in any way be detached from questions concerning the development of peoples.

... Not only does the situation of poverty still provoke high rates of infant mortality in many regions, but some parts of the world still experience practices of demographic control, on the part of governments that often promote contraception and even go so far as to impose abortion. In economically developed countries, legislation contrary to life is very widespread, and it has already shaped moral attitudes and praxis, contributing to the spread of an anti-birth mentality; frequent attempts are made to export this mentality to other States as if it were a form of cultural progress.

Some non-governmental Organizations work actively to spread abortion, at times promoting the practice of sterilization in poor countries, in some cases not even informing the women concerned... Further grounds for concern are laws permitting euthanasia as well as pressure from lobby groups, nationally and internationally, in favor of its juridical recognition.

Openness to life is at the center of true development. When a society moves towards the denial or suppression of life, it ends up no longer finding the necessary motivation and energy to strive for man's true good... By cultivating openness to life, wealthy peoples can better understand the needs of poor ones, they can avoid employing huge economic and intellectual resources to satisfy the selfish desires of their own citizens, and instead, they can promote virtuous action within the perspective of production that is morally sound and marked by solidarity, respecting the fundamental right to life of every people and every individual." (*Caritas in Veritatae*, 2009, par.28)

"The demands of love do not contradict those of reason. Human knowledge is insufficient and the conclusions of science cannot indicate by themselves the path towards integral human development. There is always a need to push further ahead: this is what is required by charity in truth. Going beyond, however, never means prescinding from the conclusions of reason, nor contradicting its results. Intelligence and love are not in separate compartments: *love is rich in intelligence and intelligence is full of love.*" (*Caritas in Veritatae*, 2009, par.30)

"Yet we desire even more than this; our dream soars higher. We are not simply talking about ensuring nourishment or a "dignified sustenance" for all people, but also their "general temporal welfare and prosperity". This means education, access to health care, and above all employment, for it is through free, creative, participatory and mutually supportive labor that human beings express and enhance the dignity of their lives. A just wage enables them to have adequate access to all the other goods which are destined for our common use." (*Evangelii Gaudium*, 2013, par.192)

"Progress in building a people in peace, justice and fraternity depends on four principles related to constant tensions present in every social reality. These derive from the pillars of the Church's social doctrine, which serve as "primary and fundamental parameters of reference for interpreting and evaluating social phenomena". In their light I would now like to set forth these four specific principles which can guide the development of life in society and the building of a people where differences are harmonized within a shared pursuit. I do so out of the conviction that their application can be a genuine path to peace within each nation and in the entire world.

Time is greater than Space

This principle enables us to work slowly but surely, without being obsessed with immediate results…

…Unity prevails over conflict

In the midst of conflict, we lose our sense of the profound unity of reality…

…Realities are more important than ideas

It is dangerous to dwell in the realm of words alone, of images and rhetoric… This calls for rejecting the various means of masking reality: angelic forms of purity, dictatorships of relativism, empty rhetoric, objectives more ideal than real, brands of ahistorical fundamentalism, ethical systems bereft of kindness, intellectual discourse bereft of wisdom… cosmetics take the place of real care for our bodies…

…The whole is greater than the part

We need to pay attention to the global so as to avoid narrowness and banality. Yet we also need to look to the local, which keeps our feet on the ground.

Together, the two prevent us from falling into one of two extremes. In the first, people get caught up in an abstract, globalized universe, falling into step behind everyone else, admiring the glitter of other people's world, gaping and applauding at all the right times. At the other extreme, they turn into a museum of local folklore, a world apart, doomed to doing the same things over and over, and incapable of being challenged by novelty or appreciating the beauty which God bestows beyond their borders.
The whole is greater than the part, but it is also greater than the sum of its parts. <u>There is no need, then, to be overly obsessed with limited and particular questions.</u>" (*Evangelii Gaudium*, 2013, par.221-235)

"It is remarkable how weak international political responses have been. The failure of global summits on the environment make it plain that our politics are subject to technology and finance. There are too many special interests, and economic interests easily end up trumping the common good and manipulating information so that their own plans will not be affected… Consequently the most one can expect is superficial rhetoric, sporadic acts of philanthropy and perfunctory expressions of concern for the environment, whereas any genuine attempt by groups within society to introduce change is viewed as a nuisance based on romantic illusions or an obstacle to be circumvented." (*Laudato Si*, 2015, par 54)

"It is not enough to balance, in the medium term, the protection of nature with financial gain, or the preservation of the environment with progress. Halfway measures simply delay the inevitable disaster. Put simply, it is a matter of redefining our notion of progress. A technological and economic development which does not leave in its wake a better world and an integrally higher quality of life cannot be considered progress." (*Laudato Si*, 2015, par 194)

-Legislation & Practical Application of Social Principles-

"The transition from theory to practice is of its very nature difficult; and it is especially so when one tries to reduce to concrete terms a social doctrine such as that of the Church. There are several reasons why this is so; among them We can mention man's deep-rooted selfishness, the materialism in which modern society is steeped, and the difficulty of determining sometimes what precisely the demands of justice are in a given instance.
Consequently, a purely theoretical instruction in man's social and economic obligations is inadequate. People must also be shown ways in which they can properly fulfill these obligations.

In Our view, therefore, formal instruction, to be successful, must be supplemented by the students' active co-operation in their own training. They must gain an experimental knowledge of the subject, and that by their own positive action.

… There are three stages which should normally be followed in the reduction of social principles into practice. <u>First, one reviews the concrete situation; secondly, one forms a judgment on it in the light of these same principles; thirdly, one decides what in the circumstances can and should be done to implement these principles.</u> These are the three stages that are usually expressed in the three terms: look, judge, act.

It is important for our young people to grasp this method and to practice it. Knowledge acquired in this way does not remain merely abstract, but is seen as something that must be translated into action." (*Mater et Magistra*, 1961, par.229-237)

-*See* Role of the State *for general related references*

"If these policies are really to become operative, men must first of all take the utmost care to conduct their various temporal activities in accordance with the laws which govern each and every such activity, observing the principles which correspond to their respective natures. Secondly, men's actions must be made to conform with the precepts of the moral order." (*Pacem in Terris*, 1963, par.150)

-*In context: a unity of faith and action must be restored to fully strengthen society.*

"<u>[Putting] these principles into effect frequently involves extensive co-operation between Catholics and those Christians who are separated from this Apostolic See. It even involves the cooperation of Catholics with men who may not be Christians but who nevertheless are reasonable men, and men of natural moral integrity.</u> "In such circumstances they must, of course, bear themselves as Catholics, and do nothing to compromise religion and morality. Yet at the same time they should show themselves animated by a spirit of understanding and unselfishness, ready to co-operate…" (*Pacem in Terris*, 1963, par.157)

"There are indeed some people who, in their generosity of spirit, burn with a desire to institute wholesale reforms whenever they come across situations which show scant regard for justice or are wholly out of keeping with its claims.

They tackle the problem with such impetuosity that one would think they were embarking on some political revolution.

<u>We would remind such people that it is the law of nature that all things must be of gradual growth.</u> If there is to be any improvement in human institutions, the work must be done slowly and deliberately from within. Pope Pius XII expressed it in these terms: "Salvation and justice consist not in the uprooting of an outdated system, but in a well-designed policy of development. Hotheadedness was never constructive…" (*Pacem in Terris*, 1963, par.161-162)

<u>"An effort must be made, however, to avoid regarding certain customs as altogether unchangeable, if they no longer answer the new needs of this age. On the other hand, imprudent action should not be taken against respectable customs which, provided they are suitably adapted to present-day circumstances, do not cease to be very useful."</u> (*Gaudium et Spes*, 1965, par. 87)

"In many cases legislation does not keep up with real situations. Legislation is necessary, but it is not sufficient for setting up true relationships of justice and equity. In teaching us charity, the Gospel instructs us in the preferential respect due to the poor and the special situation they have in society: the more fortunate should renounce some of their rights so as to place their goods more generously at the service of others. If, beyond legal rules, there is really no deeper feeling of respect for and service to others, then even equality before the law can serve as an alibi for flagrant discrimination, continued exploitation and actual contempt. Without a renewed education in solidarity, an overemphasis of equality can give rise to an individualism in which each one claims his own rights without wishing to be answerable for the common good." (*Octogesima Adveniens*, 1971, par.23)

<u>"No circumstance, no purpose, no law whatsoever can ever make licit an act which is intrinsically illicit, since it is contrary to the Law of God which is written in every human heart, knowable by reason itself, and proclaimed by the Church."</u> (*Evangelium Vitae*, 1995, par.62)

"Laws which authorize and promote abortion and euthanasia are therefore radically opposed not only to the good of the individual but also to the common good; as such they are completely lacking in authentic juridical validity. Disregard for the right to life, precisely because it leads to the killing of the person whom society exists to serve, is what most directly conflicts with the

possibility of achieving the common good. <u>Consequently, a civil law authorizing abortion or euthanasia ceases by that very fact to be a true, morally binding civil law.</u>
<u>Abortion and euthanasia are thus crimes which no human law can claim to legitimize.</u> There is no obligation in conscience to obey such laws; instead there is a grave and clear obligation to oppose them by conscientious objection.
… In the case of an intrinsically unjust law, such as a law permitting abortion or euthanasia, it is therefore never licit to obey it, or to "take part in a propaganda campaign in favor of such a law, or vote for it".
… In a case like the one just mentioned, when it is not possible to overturn or completely abrogate a pro-abortion law, an elected official, whose absolute personal opposition to procured abortion was well known, could licitly support proposals aimed at limiting the harm done by such a law and at lessening its negative consequences at the level of general opinion and public morality. This does not in fact represent an illicit cooperation with an unjust law, but rather a legitimate and proper attempt to limit its evil aspects.
… Sometimes the choices which have to be made are difficult; they may require the sacrifice of prestigious professional positions or the relinquishing of reasonable hopes of career advancement.
…. Indeed, from the moral standpoint, it is never licit to cooperate formally in evil. Such cooperation occurs when an action, either by its very nature or by the form it takes in a concrete situation, can be defined as a direct participation in an act against innocent human life or a sharing in the immoral intention of the person committing it. This cooperation can never be justified either by invoking respect for the freedom of others or by appealing to the fact that civil law permits it or requires it. Each individual in fact has moral responsibility for the acts which he personally performs…
… To refuse to take part in committing an injustice is not only a moral duty; it is also a basic human right… In this sense, the opportunity to refuse to take part in the phases of consultation, preparation and execution of these acts against life should be guaranteed to physicians, health-care personnel, and directors of hospitals, clinics and convalescent facilities. <u>Those who have recourse to conscientious objection must be protected not only from legal penalties but also from any negative effects on the legal, disciplinary, financial and professional plane.</u>" (*Evangelium Vitae*, 1995, par.74)

"Although laws are not the only means of protecting human life, nevertheless they do play a very important and sometimes decisive role in influencing patterns of thought and behaviour. I repeat once more that a law which violates an innocent person's natural right to life is unjust and, as such, is not valid as a law. For this reason I urgently appeal once more to all political leaders not to pass laws which, by disregarding the dignity of the person, undermine the very fabric of society." (*Evangelium Vitae*, 1995, par.90)

"We should not think that political efforts or the force of law will be sufficient to prevent actions which affect the environment because, when the culture itself is corrupt and objective truth and universally valid principles are no longer upheld, then laws can only be seen as arbitrary impositions or obstacles to be avoided." (*Laudato Si*, 2015, par 123)

"It sometimes happens that complete information is not put on the table; a selection is made on the basis of particular interests, be they politico-economic or ideological. This makes it difficult to reach a balanced and prudent judgement on different questions, one which takes into account all the pertinent variables." (*Laudato Si*, 2015, par 135)

"A politics concerned with immediate results, supported by consumerist sectors of the population, is driven to produce short-term growth. In response to electoral interests, governments are reluctant to upset the public with measures which could affect the level of consumption or create risks for foreign investment." (*Laudato Si*, 2015, par 178)

-Regulation-

"Strict and watchful moral restraint enforced vigorously by governmental authority could have banished these enormous evils [see *Reform*] and even forestalled them; this restraint, however, has too often been sadly lacking." (*Quadragesimo Anno*, 1931, par 133)

"The *mobility of labour*, associated with a climate of deregulation, is an important phenomenon with certain positive aspects, because it can stimulate wealth production and cultural exchange. Nevertheless, uncertainty over working conditions caused by mobility and deregulation, when it becomes endemic, tends to create new forms of psychological instability, giving rise to difficulty in forging coherent life-plans, including that of marriage. This leads to situations of human decline, to say nothing of the waste of social resources." (*Caritas in Veritatae*, 2009, par.25)

"A number of countries have a relatively low level of institutional effectiveness, which results in greater problems for their people while benefiting those who profit from this situation... Laws may be well framed yet remain a dead letter. Can we hope, then, that in such cases, legislation and regulations dealing with the environment will really prove effective? We know, for example, that countries which have clear legislation about the protection of forests continue to keep silent as they watch laws repeatedly being broken." (*Laudato Si*, 2015, par 142)

"The existence of laws and regulations is insufficient in the long run to curb bad conduct, even when effective means of enforcement are present. If the laws are to bring about significant, long-lasting effects, the majority of the members of society must be adequately motivated to accept them, and personally transformed to respond." (*Laudato Si*, 2015, par 211)

-Welfare & State Subsidies-

"At the present day many there are who, like the heathen of old, seek to blame and condemn the Church for such eminent charity. They would substitute in its stead a system of relief organized by the State. But no human expedients will ever make up for the devotedness and self-sacrifice of Christian charity." (*Rerum Novarum*, 1891, par.30)

-In context: The State does have a role in providing for the poor, but it must always defer, whenever possible, to specific, local institutions – see Principle of Subsidiarity

"Experience has shown that where personal initiative is lacking, political tyranny ensues and, in addition, economic stagnation in the production of a wide range of consumer goods and of services of the material and spiritual order—those, namely, which are in a great measure dependent upon the exercise and stimulus of individual creative talent." (*Mater et Magistra*, 1961, par.57)

-This reference is not necessarily directed towards welfare, but may help elucidate later reasons why the Popes state that welfare must only be a temporary measure.

"With demographic growth… the number of those failing to find work and driven to misery or parasitism will grow in the coming years unless the conscience of man rouses itself and gives rise to a general movement of solidarity through an effective policy of investment and of organization of production and trade, as well as of education.

…It is disquieting in this regard to note a kind of fatalism which is gaining a hold even on people in positions of responsibility. This feeling sometimes leads to Malthusian solutions inculcated by active propaganda for contraception and abortion. In this critical situation, it must on the contrary be affirmed that the family, without which no society can stand, has a right to the assistance which will assure it of the conditions for a healthy development.

… In no other age has the appeal to the imagination of society been so explicit. To this should be devoted enterprises of invention and capital as important as those invested for armaments or technological achievements. If man lets himself rush ahead without foreseeing in good time the emergence of new social problems, they will become too grave for a peaceful solution to be hoped for." (*Octogesima Adveniens*, 1971, par.18-19)

"In addition to the tasks of harmonizing and guiding development, in exceptional circumstances the State can also exercise a *substitute function*, when social sectors or business systems are too weak or are just getting under way, and are not equal to the task at hand. Such supplementary interventions, which are justified by urgent reasons touching the common good, must be as brief as possible, so as to avoid removing permanently from society and business systems the functions which are properly theirs, and so as to avoid enlarging excessively the sphere of State intervention to the detriment of both economic and civil freedom.

In recent years the range of such intervention has vastly expanded, to the point of creating a new type of State, the so-called "Welfare State"…However, excesses and abuses, especially in recent years, have provoked very harsh criticisms of the Welfare State, dubbed the "Social Assistance State". Malfunctions and defects in the Social Assistance State are the result of an inadequate understanding of the tasks proper to the State. Here again the *principle of subsidiarity* must be respected: a community of a higher order should not interfere in the internal life of a community of a lower order, depriving the latter of its functions, but rather should support it in case of need and help to coordinate its activity with the activities of the rest of society, always with a view to the common good.

By intervening directly and depriving society of its responsibility, the Social Assistance State leads to a loss of human energies and an inordinate increase of public agencies, which are dominated more by bureaucratic ways of thinking than by concern for serving their clients, and which are accompanied by an enormous increase in spending. In fact, it would appear that needs are best understood and satisfied by people who are closest to them and who act as neighbors to those in need. It should be added that certain kinds of demands often call for a response which is not simply material but which is capable of perceiving the deeper human need. One thinks of the condition of refugees, immigrants, the elderly, the sick, and all those in circumstances which call for assistance, such as drug abusers: all these people can be helped effectively only by those who offer them genuine fraternal support, in addition to the necessary care." (*Centesimus annus*, 1991, par. 48)

-*See* Principle of Subsidiarity *for related references*.

"At times it happens that those who receive aid become subordinate to the aid-givers, and the poor serve to perpetuate expensive bureaucracies which consume an excessively high percentage of funds intended for development." (*Caritas in Veritatae*, 2009, par.47)

"Such aid, whatever the donors' intentions, can sometimes lock people into a state of dependence and even foster situations of localized oppression and exploitation in the receiving country. Economic aid, in order to be true to its purpose, must not pursue secondary objectives. It must be distributed with the involvement not only of the governments of receiving countries, but also local economic agents and the bearers of culture within civil society, including local Churches. Aid programmes must increasingly acquire the characteristics of participation and completion from the grass roots… Too often in the past, aid has served to create only fringe markets for the products of these donor countries." (*Caritas in Veritatae*, 2009, par.58)

"In the search for solutions to the current economic crisis, *development aid for poor countries must be considered a valid means of creating wealth for all*… From this perspective, more economically developed nations should do all they can to allocate larger portions of their gross domestic product to development aid, thus respecting the obligations that the international community has undertaken in this regard. One way of doing so is by reviewing their internal social assistance and welfare policies, applying the principle of subsidiarity and creating better integrated welfare systems, with the active participation of private individuals and civil society. In this way, it is actually possible to improve social services and welfare programmes, and at the same time to save resources

— by eliminating waste and rejecting fraudulent claims — which could then be allocated to international solidarity." *(Caritas in Veritatae*, 2009, par.60)

"Welfare projects, which meet certain urgent needs, should be considered merely temporary responses." *(Evangelii Gaudium*, 2013, par.202)

"We can no longer trust in the unseen forces and the invisible hand of the market. Growth in justice requires more than economic growth, while presupposing such growth: it requires decisions, programmes, mechanisms and processes specifically geared to a better distribution of income, the creation of sources of employment and an integral promotion of the poor which goes beyond a simple welfare mentality." *(Evangelii Gaudium*, 2013, par.204)

-There is a subtle correlation between the mindset of profit, of the liberal "Laissez-Faire" market, and the welfare state. Liberalism's core principle that society's objective is to solely supply material goods. The underlying assumption therefore – namely, that exchange and mere access to money will take care of people on its own – is the same.

"Helping the poor financially must always be a provisional solution in the face of pressing needs. The broader objective should always be to allow them a dignified life through work." *(Laudato Si*, 2015, par 128)

-Healthcare-

"A unique responsibility belongs to health-care personnel [Doctors, Nurses, Volunteers, etc.]… Its deepest inspiration and strongest support lie in the intrinsic and undeniable ethical dimension of the health-care profession, something already recognized by the ancient and still relevant Hippocratic Oath, which requires every doctor to commit himself to absolute respect for human life and its sacredness." *(Evangelium Vitae*, 1995, par.89)

"On the part of rich countries there is excessive zeal for protecting knowledge through an unduly rigid assertion of the right to intellectual property, especially in the field of health care." *(Caritas in Veritatae*, 2009, par.22)

-Taxes & Tax Evasion-

"These [benefits of equitable ownership] benefits, however, can be reckoned on only provided that a man's means be not drained and exhausted by excessive taxation. <u>The right to possess private property is derived from nature, not from man; and the State has the right to control its use in the interests of the public good alone, but by no means to absorb it altogether.</u> The State would therefore be unjust and cruel if under the name of taxation it were to deprive the private owner of more than is fair." (*Rerum Novarum*, 1891, par.47)

"Wherefore the wise Pontiff declared that it is grossly unjust for a State to exhaust private wealth through the weight of imposts and taxes." (*Quadragesimo Anno*, 1931, par 49)

"<u>Consequently, it is not permissible for citizens who have garnered sizeable income from the resources and activities of their own nation to deposit a large portion of their income in foreign countries for the sake of their own private gain alone, taking no account of their country's interests; in doing this, they clearly wrong their country.</u>" (*Populorum Progresso*, 1967, par.24)

-It is worth noting: the Popes, in this case Pope Paul VI, are not concerned with the legal hair-splitting of tax evasion vs. tax reduction. This is not a legal exhortation, rather, an ethical, moral, and human one. It may be perfectly legal to find a loophole to avoid taxes – but is it just? That is the question. Perhaps it is, given what the government might use it for! But perhaps there is a better alternative? Note, too, the Pope specifies "for the sake of private gain alone."

"Government leaders, your task is to draw your communities into closer ties of solidarity with all men, and to convince them that they must accept the necessary taxes on their luxuries and their wasteful expenditures in order to promote the development of nations and the preservation of peace." (*Populorum Progresso*, 1967, par.84)

"One possible approach to development aid would be to apply effectively what is known as fiscal subsidiarity, allowing citizens to decide how to allocate a portion of the taxes they pay to the State. Provided it does not degenerate into the promotion of special interests, this can help to stimulate forms of welfare solidarity from below, with obvious benefits in the area of solidarity for development as well." (*Caritas in Veritatae*, 2009, par.60)

"To all this we can add widespread corruption and self-serving tax evasion, which have taken on worldwide dimensions. The thirst for power and possessions knows no limits. In this system, which tends to devour everything which stands in the way of increased profits, whatever is fragile, like the environment, is defenseless before the interests of a deified market, which become the only rule." (*Evangelii Gaudium*, 2013, par.56)

-Class Warfare-

"The great mistake made in regard to the matter now under consideration is to take up with the notion that class is naturally hostile to class, and that the wealthy and the working men are intended by nature to live in mutual conflict... Each needs the other: capital cannot do without labor, nor labor without capital... there is no intermediary more powerful than religion (whereof the Church is the interpreter and guardian) in drawing the rich and the working class together..." (*Rerum Novarum*, 1891, par.19)

-Freedom of Press & Freedom of Speech-

-*See* Freedom *for a more complete and necessary understanding of these terms.*

"Moreover, man has a natural right to be respected. He has a right to his good name. He has a right to freedom in investigating the truth, and—within the limits of the moral order and the common good—to freedom of speech and publication... He has the right, also, to be accurately informed about public events." (*Pacem in Terris*, 1963, par.12)

"All this supposes that, within the limits of morality and the common utility, man can freely search for the truth, express his opinion and publish it; that he can practice any art he chooses; that finally, he can avail himself of true information concerning events of a public nature.
As for public authority, it is not its function to determine the character of the civilization, but rather to establish the conditions and to use the means which are capable of fostering the life of culture among all..." (*Gaudium et Spes*, 1965, par.59)

-Media, Social Media, & the News-

"Among the major changes of our times, we do not wish to forget to emphasize the growing role being assumed by the media of social communication and their influence on the transformation of mentalities of knowledge, of organizations and of society itself. Certainly they have many positive aspects… Nevertheless, by their very action the media of social communication are reaching the point of representing as it were a new power. One cannot but ask about those who really hold this power, the aims that they pursue and the means they use, and finally, about the effect of their activity on the exercise of individual liberty, both in the political and ideological spheres and in social, economic and cultural life. The men who hold this power have a grave moral responsibility with respect to the truth of the information that they spread, the needs and the reactions that they generate and the values which they put forward.

… Naturally, the public authorities cannot ignore the growing power and influence of the media of social communication and the advantages and risks which their use involves for the civic community and for its development and real perfecting.

Consequently they are called upon to perform their own positive function for the common good by encouraging every constructive expression, by supporting individual citizens and groups in defending the fundamental values of the person and of human society, and also by taking suitable steps to prevent the spread of what would harm the common heritage of values on which orderly civil progress is based." (*Octogesima Adveniens*, 1971, par.20)

"It is here that the *phenomenon of consumerism* arises. In singling out new needs and new means to meet them, one must be guided by a comprehensive picture of man which respects all the dimensions of his being and which subordinates his material and instinctive dimensions to his interior and spiritual ones. If, on the contrary, a direct appeal is made to his instincts — while ignoring in various ways the reality of the person as intelligent and free — then *consumer attitudes* and *life-styles* can be created which are objectively improper and often damaging to his physical and spiritual health. Of itself, an economic system does not possess criteria for correctly distinguishing new and higher forms of satisfying human needs from artificial new needs which hinder the formation of a mature personality. *Thus a great deal of educational and cultural work* is urgently needed, including the education of consumers in the responsible use of their power of

choice, the formation of a strong sense of responsibility among producers and among people in the mass media in particular, as well as the necessary intervention by public authorities.
…[an example of this artificial consumption contrary to health and human dignity is drugs…]
…<u>It is not wrong to want to live better; what is wrong is a style of life which is presumed to be better when it is directed towards "having" rather than "being"</u>, and which wants to have more, not in order to be more but in order to spend life in enjoyment as an end in itself. It is therefore necessary to create life-styles in which the quest for truth, beauty, goodness and communion with others for the sake of common growth are the factors which determine consumer choices, savings and investments." (*Centesimus annus*, 1991, par. 36)

"This growth [of Freedom and Truth] can be hindered as a result of manipulation by the means of mass communication, which impose fashions and trends of opinion through carefully orchestrated repetition, without it being possible to subject to critical scrutiny the premises on which these fashions and trends are based." (*Centesimus annus*, 1991, par. 41)

"An important and serious responsibility belongs to those involved in the mass media… They need to present noble models of life and make room for instances of people's positive and sometimes heroic love for others. With great respect they should also present the positive values of sexuality and human love, and not insist on what defiles and cheapens human dignity. In their interpretation of things, they should refrain from emphasizing anything that suggests or fosters feelings or attitudes of indifference, contempt or rejection in relation to life. With scrupulous concern for factual truth, they are called to combine freedom of information with respect for every person and a profound sense of humanity." (*Evangelium Vitae*, 1995, par.98)

"Today the means of mass communication have made our planet smaller, rapidly narrowing the distance between different peoples and cultures…. Despite the great advances made in science and technology, each day we see how much suffering there is in the world on account of different kinds of poverty, both material and spiritual. Our times call for a new readiness to assist our neighbors in need." (*Deus Caritas Est*, 2005, par.30)

"Linked to technological development is the increasingly pervasive presence of the means of *social communications*. It is almost impossible today to imagine the life of the human family without them. For better or for worse, they are so integral a part of life today that it seems quite absurd to maintain that they are neutral — and hence unaffected by any moral considerations concerning people… Given the media's fundamental importance in engineering changes in attitude towards reality and the human person, we must reflect carefully on their influence, especially in regard to the ethical-cultural dimension of globalization and the development of peoples in solidarity… This means that they can have a civilizing effect not only when, thanks to technological development, they increase the possibilities of communicating information, but above all when they are geared towards a vision of the person and the common good that reflects truly universal values. Just because social communications increase the possibilities of interconnection and the dissemination of ideas, it does not follow that they promote freedom or internationalize development and democracy for all…. The media can make an important contribution towards the growth in communion of the human family and the *ethos* of society when they are used to promote universal participation in the common search for what is just." (*Caritas in Veritatae*, 2009, par.73)

"What is astonishing is the arbitrary and selective determination of what to put forward today as worthy of respect. <u>Insignificant matters are considered shocking, yet unprecedented injustices seem to be widely tolerated. While the poor of the world continue knocking on the doors of the rich, the world of affluence runs the risk of no longer hearing those knocks, on account of a conscience that can no longer distinguish what is human.</u>" (*Caritas in Veritatae*, 2009, par.75)

"We are living in an information-driven society which bombards us indiscriminately with data – <u>all treated as being of equal importance</u> – and which leads to remarkable <u>superficiality</u> in the area of moral discernment. In response, we need to provide an education which teaches critical thinking and encourages the development of mature moral values." (*Evangelii Gaudium*, 2013, par.64)

"True wisdom, as the fruit of self-examination, dialogue and generous encounter between persons, is not acquired by a mere accumulation of data which eventually leads to overload and confusion, a sort of mental pollution." (*Laudato Si*, 2015, par 47)

Popular media controls thought, not by telling people what to think, but — almost as important — telling people what to think about. The key distinction is that <u>information is not wisdom</u>.

-Propaganda-

"Truth further demands an attitude of unruffled impartiality in the use of the many aids to the promotion and spread of mutual understanding between nations which modern scientific progress has made available. This does not mean that people should be prevented from drawing particular attention to the virtues of their own way of life, but it does mean <u>the utter rejection</u> of ways of disseminating information which violate the principles of truth and justice, <u>and injure the reputation of another nation.</u>" (*Pacem in Terris*, 1963, par.90)

-Advertising & Consumerism-

See Media, Communication, & the News *for related references.*

"We must not omit to mention those crafty men who, wholly unconcerned about any honest usefulness of their work, do not scruple to stimulate the baser human desires and, when they are aroused, use them for their own profit." (*Quadragesimo Anno*, 1931, par 132)

-Note: the above reference is not specifically in regard to advertising, but does have important relevance therein.

"Everything therefore in the modern means of social communication which arouses men's baser passions and encourages low moral standards, as well as every obscenity in the written word and every form of indecency on the stage and screen, <u>should be condemned publicly and unanimously</u> by all those who have at heart the advance of civilization and the safeguarding of the outstanding values of the human spirit. It is quite absurd to defend this kind of depravity in the name of art or culture or by pleading the liberty which may be allowed in this field by the public authorities." (*Humanae Vitae*,1968, par.22)

"<u>Unlimited competition utilizing the modern means of publicity incessantly launches new products and tries to attract the consumer</u> …<u>While very large areas of the population are unable to satisfy their primary needs, superfluous needs are ingeniously created</u>. It can thus rightly be asked if, in spite of all his conquests, man is not turning back against himself the results of his activity. Having rationally endeavored to control nature, is he not now becoming the slave of the objects which he makes?" (*Octogesima Adveniens*, 1971, par.9)

"All of us experience firsthand the sad effects of this blind submission to pure consumerism: in the first place a crass materialism, and at the same time a radical dissatisfaction, because one quickly learns - unless one is shielded from the flood of publicity and the ceaseless and tempting offers of products - that the more one possesses the more one wants, while deeper aspirations remain unsatisfied and perhaps even stifled.
… To "have" objects and goods does not in itself perfect the human subject, unless it contributes to the maturing and enrichment of that subject's "being," that is to say unless it contributes to the realization of the human vocation as such." (*Sollilicitudo Rei Socialis*, 1987, par.28)

"The pace of consumption, waste and environmental change has so stretched the planet's capacity that our contemporary lifestyle, unsustainable as it is, can only precipitate catastrophes, such as those which even now periodically occur in different areas of the world... We need to reflect on our accountability before those who will have to endure the dire consequences. Our difficulty in taking up this challenge seriously has much to do with an ethical and cultural decline which has accompanied the deterioration of the environment. (*Laudato Si*, 2015, par 161, 162)

"Since the market tends to promote extreme consumerism in an effort to sell its products, people can easily get caught up in a whirlwind of needless buying and spending… This paradigm leads people to believe that they are free as long as they have the supposed freedom to consume. But those really free are the minority who wield economic and financial power… We have too many means and only a few insubstantial ends." (*Laudato Si*, 2015, par 203)

-Consumers-

"It is good for people to realize that purchasing is always a moral — and not simply economic — act. Hence the *consumer has a specific social responsibility*, which goes hand-in- hand with the social responsibility of the enterprise." (*Caritas in Veritatae*, 2009, par.66)

"Consumers should be continually educated regarding their daily role, which can be exercised with respect for moral principles without diminishing the intrinsic economic rationality…particularly at times like the present when purchasing power has diminished and people must live more frugally, it is necessary to explore other paths: for example, forms of cooperative purchasing like the consumer cooperatives… In addition, it can be helpful to promote new ways of marketing products from deprived areas of the world, so as to guarantee their producers a decent return. However, certain conditions need to be met: the market should be genuinely transparent; the producers, as well as increasing their profit margins, should also receive improved formation in professional skills and technology; and finally, trade of this kind must not become hostage to partisan ideologies. A more incisive role for consumers, as long as they themselves are not manipulated by associations that do not truly represent them, is a desirable element for building economic democracy." (*Caritas in Veritatae*, 2009, par.66)

"The emptier a person's heart is, the more he or she needs things to buy, own and consume. It becomes almost impossible to accept the limits imposed by reality." (*Laudato Si*, 2015, par 204)

"[Quoting Benedict XVI's *Caritas in Veritatae*] 'Purchasing is always a moral – and not simply economic – act'." (*Laudato Si*, 2015, par 206)

"We need to take up an ancient lesson, found in different religious traditions and also in the Bible. It is the conviction that 'less is more'." (*Laudato Si*, 2015, par 222)

-Public versus Private-

"…in the economic order first place must be given to the personal initiative of private citizens working either as individuals or in association…
But—for reasons explained by Our predecessors—the civil power must also have a hand in the economy. It has to promote production in a way best calculated to achieve social progress and the well-being of all citizens." (*Mater et Magistra*, 1961, par.51-52)

"It is well-known that in recent years in the larger industrial concerns distinction has been growing between the ownership of productive goods and the responsibility of company managers. ... Experience shows that these problems arise whether the capital which makes possible these vast undertakings belongs to private citizens or to public corporations." (*Mater et Magistra*, 1961, par.104)

"[The Right of Private Property], of course, is not to deny the lawfulness of State and public ownership of productive goods, especially those which "carry with them a power too great to be left to private individuals without injury to the community at large."" (*Mater et Magistra*, 1961, par.116)

"In recent years the State and other agencies of public law have extended, and are continuing to extend, the sphere of their activity and initiative. But this does not mean that the doctrine of the social function of private ownership is out of date, as some would maintain. It is inherent in the very right of private ownership.
Then, too, a further consideration arises. Tragic situations and urgent problems of an intimate and personal nature are continually arising which the State with all its machinery is unable to remedy or assist. There will always remain, therefore, a vast field for the exercise of human sympathy and the Christian charity of individuals. We would observe, finally, that the efforts of individuals, or of groups of private citizens, are definitely more effective in promoting spiritual values than is the activity of public authority." (*Mater et Magistra*, 1961, par.120)

-*See* Principle of Subsidiarity *for related references.*

"The continuing hegemony of the binary model of market-plus-State has accustomed us to think only in terms of the private business leader of a capitalistic bent on the one hand, and the State director on the other. In reality, business has to be understood in an articulated way. There are a number of reasons, of a meta-economic kind, for saying this. Business activity has a human significance, prior to its professional one… It is in response to the needs and the dignity of the worker, as well as the needs of society, that there exist various types of business enterprise, over and above the simple distinction between "private" and "public". Each of them requires and expresses a specific business capacity. In order to construct an economy that will soon be in a position to serve the national and global common good, it is appropriate to take account of this broader significance of business activity." (*Caritas in Veritatae*, 2009, par.41)

-Education-

"It is of the utmost importance that parents exercise their right and obligation toward the younger generation by securing for their children a sound cultural and religious formation." (*Mater et Magistra*, 1961, par.195)

"It is therefore Our urgent desire that [Catholic Social Teaching] be studied more and more. First of all it should be taught as part of the daily curriculum in Catholic schools of every kind…" (*Mater et Magistra*, 1961, par.223)

"[Man] has the natural right to share in the benefits of culture, and hence to receive a good general education, and a technical or professional training consistent with the degree of educational development in his own country. Furthermore, a system must be devised for affording gifted members of society the opportunity of engaging in more advanced studies, with a view to their occupying, as far as possible, positions of responsibility in society in keeping with their natural talent and acquired skill." (*Pacem in Terris*, 1963, par.13)

"Of course, the support and education of children is a right which belongs primarily to the parents." (*Pacem in Terris*, 1963, par.17)

"We consider too that a further reason for this very frequent divorce between faith and practice in Christians is an inadequate education in Christian teaching and Christian morality." (*Pacem in Terris*, 1963, par.153)

"Above all the education of youth from every social background has to be undertaken, so that there can be produced not only men and women of refined talents, but those great-souled persons who are so desperately required by our times." (*Gaudium et Spes*, 1965, par. 31)

"Graced with the dignity and office of fatherhood and motherhood, parents will energetically acquit themselves of a duty which devolves primarily on them, namely education and especially religious education." (*Gaudium et Spes*, 1965, par. 49)

"With the more or less generalized reduction of working hours, the leisure time of most men has increased. May this leisure be used properly to relax, to fortify the health of soul and body through spontaneous study and activity, through

tourism which refines man's character and enriches him with understanding of others, through sports activity which helps to preserve equilibrium of spirit even in the community, and to establish fraternal relations among men of all conditions, nations and races
…<u>All these leisure activities however are not able to bring man to a full cultural development unless there is at the same time a profound inquiry into the meaning of culture and science for the human person.</u>" (*Gaudium et Spes*, 1965, par. 49)

"<u>Lack of education is as serious as lack of food; the illiterate is a starved spirit.</u>
…We also rejoice at the good work accomplished in this field by private initiative, by the public authorities, and by international organizations. These are the primary agents of development, because they enable man to act for himself." (*Populorum Progresso*, 1967, par.35)

"Technical expertise is necessary, but it must be accompanied by concrete signs of genuine love… They must realize that their expert knowledge does not give them superiority in every sphere of life… If [their technical expertise] is introduced into foreign lands, it must undergo adaptation.
… those who undertake such work must realize they are guests in a foreign land; they must see to it that they studiously observe its historical traditions, its rich culture, and its peculiar genius. A rapprochement between cultures will thus take place, bringing benefits to both sides." (*Populorum Progresso*, 1967, par.72)

"This *unemployment of intellectuals* occurs or increases when the education available is not oriented towards the types of employment or service required by the true needs of society, or when there is less demand for work which requires education, at least professional education, than for manual labour, or when it is less well paid." (*Laborem Exercens*, 1981, par. 8)

"In particular, I wish [Catholic Social Teaching, especially *Rerum* Novarum] to be made known and applied in the countries which, following the collapse of "Real Socialism", are experiencing a serious lack of direction in the work of rebuilding. The Western countries, in turn, run the risk of seeing this collapse as a one-sided victory of their own economic system, and thereby failing to make necessary corrections in that system. Meanwhile, the countries of the Third World are experiencing more than ever the tragedy of underdevelopment, which is becoming more serious with each passing day." (*Centesimus annus*, 1991, par. 56)

"Closely connected with the formation of conscience is the work of education, which helps individuals to be ever more human, leads them ever more fully to the truth, instils in them growing respect for life, and trains them in right interpersonal relationships.
In particular, there is a need for education about the value of life from its very origins. It is an illusion to think that we can build a true culture of human life if we do not help the young to accept and experience sexuality and love and the whole of life according to their true meaning and in their close interconnection.
… The trivialization of sexuality is among the principal factors which have led to contempt for new life. Only a true love is able to protect life.
… The work of educating in the service of life involves the training of married couples in responsible procreation. In its true meaning, responsible procreation requires couples to be obedient to the Lord's call and to act as faithful interpreters of his plan. This happens when the family is generously open to new lives, and when couples maintain an attitude of openness and service to life, even if, for serious reasons and in respect for the moral law, they choose to avoid a new birth for the time being or indefinitely. The moral law obliges them in every case to control the impulse of instinct and passion, and to respect the biological laws inscribed in their person. It is precisely this respect which makes legitimate, at the service of responsible procreation, the use of <u>natural methods</u> of regulating fertility." (*Evangelium Vitae*, 1995, par.97)

-The Pope is referring, in part, to Natural Family Planning (NFP), which is, in brief, a scientifically demonstrated method (~99% reliable given thousands of test subjects) which uses knowledge of the Woman's fertility cycle to either abstain or have sex. While it can be wrongly employed with a "contraceptive mentality," NFP is not contraceptive as the couple is a) not obstructing life and b) still completely open to life as a gift from God.

"The work of education cannot avoid a consideration of suffering and death. These are a part of human existence, and it is futile, not to say misleading, to try to hide them or ignore them. On the contrary, people must be helped to understand their profound mystery in all its harsh reality." (*Evangelium Vitae*, 1995, par.97)

"Intellectuals can also do much to build a new culture of human life. A special task falls to Catholic intellectuals, who are called to be present and active in the leading centres where culture is formed, in schools and universities, in places of scientific and technological research, of artistic creativity and of the study of man. Allowing their talents and activity to be nourished by the living force of the Gospel, they ought to place themselves at the service of a new culture of life by offering serious and well documented contributions, capable of commanding general respect and interest by reason of their merit." (*Evangelium Vitae*, 1995, par.98)

"The Church, in her concern for man's authentic development, urges him to have full respect for human values in the exercise of his sexuality. It cannot be reduced merely to pleasure or entertainment, nor can sex education be reduced to technical instruction aimed solely at protecting the interested parties from possible disease or the "risk" of procreation. This would be to impoverish and disregard the deeper meaning of sexuality, a meaning which needs to be acknowledged and responsibly appropriated not only by individuals but also by the community. It is irresponsible to view sexuality merely as a source of pleasure, and likewise to regulate it through strategies of mandatory birth control. In either case materialistic ideas and policies are at work, and individuals are ultimately subjected to various forms of violence." (*Caritas in Veritatae*, 2009, par.44)

"Pope Paul VI noted that 'the world is in trouble because of lack of thinking.'" (*Caritas in Veritatae*, 2009, par.53)

"The term 'education' refers not only to classroom teaching and vocational [i.e. job] training… but to the complete formation of the person." (*Caritas in Veritatae*, 2009, par.61)

". It is imperative to evangelize cultures in order to inculturate the Gospel. In countries of Catholic tradition, this means encouraging, fostering and reinforcing a richness which already exists. In countries of other religious traditions, or profoundly secularized countries, it will mean sparking new processes for evangelizing culture…
… Nor can we overlook the fact that in recent decades there has been a breakdown in the way Catholics pass down the Christian faith to the young." (*Evangelii Gaudium*, 2013, par.69-70)

"If someone has not learned to stop and admire something beautiful, we should not be surprised if he or she treats everything as an object to be used and abused without scruple." (*Laudato Si*, 2015, par 215)

-Youth-

"<u>We cannot insist too much on the duty of giving foreigners a hospitable reception.</u>
… <u>Young people, in particular,</u> must be given a warm reception; more and more families and hostels must open their doors to them. This must be done, first of all, that they may be shielded from feelings of loneliness, distress and despair that would sap their strength… And finally, it must be done so that they may be protected from subversive notions and temptations to violence, which gain headway in their minds when they ponder their "wretched plight."
… We are deeply distressed by what happens to many of these young people. They come to wealthier nations to acquire scientific knowledge, professional training, and a high-quality education that will enable them to serve their own land with greater effectiveness. They do get a fine education,<u> but very often they lose their respect for the priceless cultural heritage of their native land.</u>"
(*Populorum Progresso*, 1967, par.67-68)

"We are fully aware of the fact that many young people have already responded wholeheartedly to the invitation… to take part in missionary work…. We commend such undertakings and the men of good will who take part in them."
(Populorum Progresso, 1967, par.74)

"It is in fact the weakest who are the victims of dehumanizing living conditions, degrading for conscience and harmful for the family institution. The promiscuity of working people's housing makes a minimum of intimacy impossible; young couples waiting in vain for a decent dwelling at a price they can afford are demoralized and their union can thereby even be endangered; youth escape from a home which is too confined and seek in the streets compensations and companionships which cannot be supervised. It is the grave duty of those responsible to strive to control this process and to give it direction." (*Octogesima Adveniens*, 1971, par.11)

"Urban life and industrial change bring strongly to light questions which until now were poorly grasped. What place, for example, in this world being brought to birth, should be given to youth? Everywhere dialogue is proving to be difficult between youth, with its aspirations, renewal and also insecurity for the future, and the adult generations. It is obvious to all that here we have a source of serious conflicts, division and opting out, even within the family, and a questioning of modes of authority, education for freedom and the handing on of values and beliefs, which strikes at the deep roots of society." (*Octogesima Adveniens*, 1971, par.13)

"Once we start to think about the kind of world we are leaving to future generations, we look at things differently… we can no longer view reality in a purely utilitarian way, in which efficiency and productivity are entirely geared to our individual benefit." (*Laudato Si*, 2015, par 159)

-Utopias & Ideologies-

"The attempt to find a solution to this problem [of how to build a new social order of balanced human relationships] has given birth to a number of theories. Some of these were little more than ephemeral; others have undergone, and are still undergoing, substantial change; others again are proving themselves less and less attractive to modern man.
Why is this? It is because these ideologies do not take account of the whole man, nor even of his most important part. In particular, they take little account of certain inevitable human weaknesses such as sickness and suffering, weaknesses which even the most advanced economic and social systems cannot completely eliminate. Finally, they fail to take account of that deep-rooted sense of religion which exists in all men everywhere, and which nothing, neither violence nor cunning, can eradicate.
The most fundamental modern error is that of imagining that man's natural sense of religion is nothing more than the outcome of feeling or fantasy, to be eradicated from his soul as an anachronism and an obstacle to human progress." (*Mater et Magistra*, 1961, par.213-214)

-Only a brief perusal of online futuristic utopian films or literature is needed to understand what sort of ephemeral and ideological thinking the Pope is referring to, even in 1961…

"There is, alas, a spirit of hedonism abroad today which beguiles men into thinking that life is nothing more than the quest for pleasure and the satisfaction of human passions. This attitude is disastrous. Its evil effects on soul and body are undeniable. Even on the natural level temperance and simplicity of life are the dictates of sound policy." (*Mater et Magistra*, 1961, par.235)

"The Christian faith is above and is sometimes opposed to the ideologies, in that it recognizes God, who is transcendent and the Creator, and who, through all the levels of creation, calls on man as endowed with responsibility and freedom." (*Octogesima Adveniens*, 1971, par.27)

-In context: specifically Marxism and Liberalism are mentioned.

"The appeal to a utopia is often a convenient excuse for those who wish to escape from concrete tasks in order to take refuge in an imaginary world. To live in a hypothetical future is a facile alibi for rejecting immediate responsibilities. But it must clearly be recognized that this kind of criticism of existing society often provokes the forward-looking imagination both to perceive in the present the disregarded possibility hidden within it, and to direct itself towards a fresh future…[But sometimes, forward-looking criticism] can also meet the Christian appeal. The Spirit of the Lord, who animates man renewed in Christ, continually breaks down the horizons within which his understanding likes to find security and the limits to which his activity would willingly restrict itself…" (*Octogesima Adveniens*, 1971, par.37)

"Moreover, man, who was created for freedom, bears within himself the wound of original sin, which constantly draws him towards evil and puts him in need of redemption. Not only is this doctrine an integral part of Christian revelation; it also has great hermeneutical value insofar as it helps one to understand human reality. Man tends towards good, but he is also capable of evil. He can transcend his immediate interest and still remain bound to it. The social order will be all the more stable, the more it takes this fact into account and does not place in opposition personal interest and the interests of society as a whole, but rather seeks ways to bring them into fruitful harmony. In fact, where self-interest is violently suppressed, it is replaced by a burdensome system of bureaucratic control which dries up the wellsprings of initiative and creativity. When people think they possess the secret of a perfect social organization which makes evil impossible, they also think that they can use any means, including violence and deceit, in order to bring that organization into being. Politics then becomes a "secular religion" which operates under the illusion of creating paradise in this world. But no political society — which possesses its own autonomy and laws

— can ever be confused with the Kingdom of God. The Gospel parable of the weeds among the wheat (cf. Mt 13:24-30; 36-43) teaches that it is for God alone to separate the subjects of the Kingdom from the subjects of the Evil One, and that this judgment will take place at the end of time. By presuming to anticipate judgment here and now, man puts himself in the place of God and sets himself against the patience of God." (*Centesimus annus*, 1991, par. 25)

"<u>The conviction that man is self-sufficient and can successfully eliminate the evil present in history by his own action alone has led him to confuse happiness and salvation with immanent forms of material prosperity and social action.</u>" (*Caritas in Veritatae*, 2009, par.34)

-In context: this particular passage is not referring to Utopias per se, *but rather Liberalism, which argues for a "hidden hand," unregulated economy – i.e. the philosophy of Adam Smith.*

-Evangelization-

"In this context [of the preservation and development of culture], it is appropriate to *recall that evangelization too plays a role in the culture of the various nations*, sustaining culture in its progress towards the truth, and assisting in the work of its purification and enrichment." (*Centesimus annus*, 1991, par. 50)

-Dialogue & Differences in Opinion -

"Differences of opinion in the application of principles can sometimes arise even among sincere Catholics. <u>When this happens, they should be careful not to lose their respect and esteem for each other. Instead, they should strive to find points of agreement for effective and suitable action, and not wear themselves out in interminable arguments, and, under pretext of the better or the best, omit to do the good that is possible and therefore obligatory.</u>
In their economic and social activities, Catholics often come into contact with others who do not share their view of life. In such circumstances, they must, of course, bear themselves as Catholics and do nothing to compromise religion and morality. Yet at the same time they should show themselves animated by a spirit of understanding and unselfishness, ready to <u>cooperate</u> loyally in achieving objects which are good in themselves, or can be turned to good. <u>Needless to say, when the [Catholic] Hierarchy has made a decision on any point Catholics are bound to obey their directives.</u> The Church has the right and obligation not

merely to guard ethical and religious principles, but also to declare its authoritative judgment in the matter of putting these principles into practice." (*Mater et Magistra*, 1961, par.238-239)

-In regards to Papal Infallibility: The Catholic Church regards the Pope and the Bishops in union with him, as infallible, <u>when teaching on matters of Faith and Morals – where "teaching" is specifically designated with the full teaching authority of the Church.</u> A distinction between infallibility and obedience: Catholics are bound by specific teaching statements (i.e. encyclicals) even though not each and every sentence within those encyclicals is necessarily infallible. This is what makes a Catholic a Catholic – if he believes, internally and externally, the teachings of Jesus Christ and His Apostolic Church. Much confusion and misunderstandings can be made of the above (i.e. a "free pass" to sin if you believe, etc.) and a knowledgeable source should be consulted if one desires to truly know the specifics of the above teachings of the Church.

"<u>It is always perfectly justifiable to distinguish between error as such and the person who falls into error—even in the case of men who err regarding the truth or are led astray as a result of their inadequate knowledge, in matters either of religion or of the highest ethical standards. A man who has fallen into error does not cease to be a man.</u>
… <u>Catholics who, in order to achieve some external good, collaborate with unbelievers or with those who through error lack the fullness of faith in Christ, may possibly provide the occasion or even the incentive for their conversion to the truth.</u>" (*Pacem in Terris*, 1963, par.158)

"Respect and love ought to be extended also to those who think or act differently than we do in social, political and even religious matters.
… This love and good will, to be sure, must in no way render us indifferent to truth and goodness. Indeed love itself impels the disciples of Christ to speak the saving truth to all men. But it is necessary to distinguish between error, which always merits repudiation, and the person in error, who never loses the dignity of being a person even when he is flawed by false or inadequate religious notions." (*Gaudium et Spes*, 1965, par. 28)

"In addition, the Catholic Church gladly holds in high esteem the things which other Christian Churches and ecclesial communities have done or are doing cooperatively by way of achieving the same goal." (*Gaudium et Spes*, 1965, par. 40)

"Often enough the Christian view of things will itself suggest some specific solution in certain circumstances. Yet it happens rather frequently, and legitimately so, that with equal sincerity some of the faithful will disagree with others on a given matter. Even against the intentions of their proponents, however, solutions proposed on one side or another may be easily confused by many people with the Gospel message. Hence it is necessary for people to remember that no one is allowed in the aforementioned situations to appropriate the Church's authority for his opinion. They should always try to enlighten one another through honest discussion, preserving mutual charity and caring above all for the common good." (*Gaudium et Spes*, 1965, par. 43)

"Of the many subjects arousing universal concern today, it may be helpful to concentrate on these: marriage and the family, human progress, life in its economic, social and political dimensions, the bonds between the family of nations, and peace." (*Gaudium et Spes*, 1965, par. 46)

"In order that they may fulfill their function, let it be recognized that all the faithful, whether clerics or laity, possess a lawful freedom of inquiry, freedom of thought and of expressing their mind with humility and fortitude in those matters on which they enjoy competence." (*Gaudium et Spes*, 1965, par. 62)

-This comes with responsibilities: first, to be competent in areas which one speaks about by study, especially of the Church's official teachings found in encyclicals and the Catechism; second, to speak with humility and fortitude; and third, to speak respectfully, in regards for both the intellectual stance of the other, and their position of authority. There are always many wrong ways of being right. Any married person can attest to this…

"In this way [Christians] are to demonstrate concretely how authority can be compatible with freedom, personal initiative with the solidarity of the whole social organism, and the advantages of unity with fruitful diversity." (*Gaudium et Spes*, 1965, par. 75)

"One would hope that also men and women without an explicit faith would be convinced that the obstacles to integral development are not only economic but rest on more profound attitudes which human beings can make into absolute values.

... For Christians, as for all who recognize the precise theological meaning of the word "sin," a change of behavior or mentality or mode of existence is called "conversion," to use the language of the Bible (cf. Mk 13:3, 5, Is 30:15)" (*Sollilicitudo Rei Socialis*, 1987, par.38)

"Commitment to ecumenism responds to the prayer of the Lord Jesus that "they may all be one" (Jn 17:21).... <u>We must never forget that we are pilgrims journeying alongside one another.</u>
... Given the seriousness of the counter-witness of division among Christians, particularly in Asia and Africa, the search for paths to unity becomes all the more urgent. Missionaries on those continents often mention the criticisms, complaints and ridicule to which the scandal of divided Christians gives rise. If we concentrate on the convictions we share, and if we keep in mind the principle of the hierarchy of truths, we will be able to progress decidedly towards common expressions of proclamation, service and witness... How many important things unite us! If we really believe in the abundantly free working of the Holy Spirit, we can learn so much from one another!" (*Evangelii Gaudium*, 2013, par.244-246)

"<u>We hold the Jewish people in special regard because their covenant with God has never been revoked...</u> With them, we believe in the one God who acts in history, and with them we accept his revealed word.
Dialogue and friendship with the children of Israel are part of the life of Jesus' disciples. The friendship which has grown between us makes us bitterly and sincerely regret the terrible persecutions which they have endured, and continue to endure, especially those that have involved Christians.
... While it is true that certain Christian beliefs are unacceptable to Judaism, and that the Church cannot refrain from proclaiming Jesus as Lord and Messiah, there exists as well a <u>rich complementarity</u> which allows us to read the texts of the Hebrew Scriptures together and to help one another to mine the riches of God's word. We can also share many ethical convictions and a common concern for justice and the development of peoples.
An attitude of openness in truth and in love must characterize the dialogue with the followers of non-Christian religions, in spite of various obstacles and difficulties, especially forms of fundamentalism on both sides. Interreligious dialogue is a necessary condition for peace in the world... Efforts made in dealing with a specific theme can become a process in which, by mutual listening, both parts can be purified and enriched.

… A facile syncretism [i.e. all religions are equally good] would ultimately be a totalitarian gesture on the part of those who would ignore greater values of which they are not the masters. True openness involves remaining steadfast in one's deepest convictions, clear and joyful in one's own identity, while at the same time being "open to understanding those of the other party" and "knowing that dialogue can enrich each side". What is not helpful is a diplomatic openness which says "yes" to everything in order to avoid problems, for this would be a way of deceiving others and denying them the good which we have been given to share generously with others. Evangelization and interreligious dialogue, far from being opposed, mutually support and nourish one another.

Our relationship with the followers of Islam has taken on great importance, since they are now significantly present in many traditionally Christian countries, where they can freely worship and become fully a part of society. We must never forget that they "profess to hold the faith of Abraham, and together with us they adore the one, merciful God, who will judge humanity on the last day". … In order to sustain dialogue with Islam, suitable training is essential for all involved, not only so that they can be solidly and joyfully grounded in their own identity, but so that they can also acknowledge the values of others, appreciate the concerns underlying their demands and shed light on shared beliefs. We Christians should embrace with affection and respect Muslim immigrants to our countries in the same way that we hope and ask to be received and respected in countries of Islamic tradition…. Faced with disconcerting episodes of violent fundamentalism, our respect for true followers of Islam should lead us to avoid hateful generalizations, for authentic Islam and the proper reading of the Koran are opposed to every form of violence.

… Non-Christians, by God's gracious initiative, when they are faithful to their own consciences, can live "justified by the grace of God", and thus be "associated to the paschal mystery of Jesus Christ"… While these lack the meaning and efficacy of the sacraments instituted by Christ, they can be channels which the Holy Spirit raises up in order to liberate non-Christians from atheistic immanentism [i.e. "God is merely everything taken together"] or from purely individual religious experiences." (*Evangelii Gaudium*, 2013, par.247-254)

-Women & Women in the Workplace-

"…Women are now playing in political life is everywhere evident. This is a development that is perhaps of swifter growth among Christian nations ... Women are gaining an increasing awareness of their natural dignity." (*Pacem in Terris*, 1963, par. 41)

"Women must be accorded such conditions of work as are consistent with their needs and responsibilities as wives and mothers." (*Pacem in Terris*, 1963, par. 19)

"Similarly, in many countries a charter for women which would put an end to an actual discrimination and would establish relationships of equality in rights and of respect for their dignity is the object of study and at times of lively demands. We do not have in mind that false equality which would deny the distinction with woman's proper role, which is of such capital importance, at the heart of the family as well as within society. Developments in legislation should on the contrary be directed to protecting her proper vocation and at the same time recognizing her independence as a person, and her equal rights to participate in cultural, economic, social and political life." (*Octogesima Adveniens*, 1971, par.13)

"Experience confirms that there must be a social re-evaluation of the mother's role, of the toil connected with it, and of the need that children have for care, love and affection in order that they may develop into responsible, morally and religiously mature and psychologically stable persons. It will redound to the credit of society to make it possible for a mother - without inhibiting her freedom, without psychological or practical discrimination, and without penalizing her as compared with other women - to devote herself to taking care of her children and educating them in accordance with their needs, which vary with age. Having to abandon these tasks in order to take up paid work outside the home is wrong from the point of view of the good of society and of the family when it contradicts or hinders these primary goals of the mission of a mother.
It is a fact that in many societies women work in nearly every sector of life. But it is fitting that they should be able to fulfil their tasks in accordance with their own nature, without being discriminated against and without being excluded from jobs for which they are capable, but also without lack of respect for their family aspirations and for their specific role in contributing, together with men,

to the good of society. The true advancement of women requires that labour should be structured in such a way that women do not have to pay for their advancement by abandoning what is specific to them and at the expense of the family, in which women as mothers have an irreplaceable role." (*Laborem Exercens*, 1981, par. 19)

"The one who accepted "Life" in the name of all and for the sake of all was Mary, the Virgin Mother; she is thus most closely and personally associated with the Gospel of life. Mary's consent at the Annunciation and her motherhood stand at the very beginning of the mystery of life which Christ came to bestow on humanity (cf. Jn 10:10). Through her acceptance and loving care for the life of the Incarnate Word, human life has been rescued from condemnation to final and eternal death.
For this reason, Mary, "like the Church of which she is the type, is a mother of all who are reborn to life."" (*Evangelium Vitae*, 1995, par.102)

-Racism-

"Truth calls for the elimination of every trace of racial discrimination..." (*Pacem in Terris*, 1963, par. 86)

-Minorities-

"It is quite clear that any attempt to check the vitality and growth of these ethnic minorities is a flagrant violation of justice; the more so if such perverse efforts are aimed at their very extinction.
… It is worth noting, however, that these minority groups, in reaction, perhaps…frequently tend to magnify unduly characteristics proper to their own people.
… [to cooperate and contribute] minority groups must enter into some kind of association with the people in whose midst they are living, and learn to share their customs and way of life." (*Pacem in Terris*, 1963, par.95-97)

-Discrimination-

"True, all men are not alike from the point of view of varying physical power and the diversity of intellectual and moral resources. Nevertheless, with respect to the fundamental rights of the person, every type of discrimination, whether social or cultural, whether based on sex, race, color, social condition, language or religion, is to be overcome and eradicated as contrary to God's intent." (*Gaudium et Spes*, 1965, par. 29)

"Among the victims of situations of injustice - unfortunately no new phenomenon - must be placed those who are discriminated against, in law or in fact, on account of their race, origin, color, culture, sex or religion.... Men rightly consider unjustifiable and reject as inadmissible the tendency to maintain or introduce legislation or behavior systematically inspired by racialist prejudice. The members of mankind share the same basic rights and duties, as well as the same supernatural destiny." (*Octogesima Adveniens*, 1971, par.16)

-Form of Government-

"... it is not possible to give a general ruling on the most suitable form of government..."(*Pacem in Terris*, 1963, par.67)

"However, those political systems, prevailing in some parts of the world are to be reproved which hamper civic or religious freedom, victimize large numbers through avarice and political crimes, and divert the exercise of authority from the service of the common good to the interests of one or another faction or of the rulers themselves." (*Gaudium et Spes*, 1965, par.73)

-Democracy-

"The Church values the democratic system inasmuch as it ensures the participation of citizens in making political choices, guarantees to the governed the possibility both of electing and holding accountable those who govern them, and of replacing them through peaceful means when appropriate. Thus she cannot encourage the formation of narrow ruling groups which usurp the power of the State for individual interests or for ideological ends.
...Authentic democracy is possible only in a State ruled by law, and on the basis of a correct conception of the human person... As history demonstrates, a democracy without values easily turns into open or thinly disguised totalitarianism." (*Centesimus annus*, 1991, par. 46)

"This [distortion of what Freedom is] is what is happening also at the level of politics and government: the original and inalienable right to life is questioned or denied on the basis of a parliamentary vote or the will of one part of the people-even if it is the majority... In this way democracy, contradicting its own principles effectively moves towards a form of totalitarianism. The State is no longer the "common home" where all can live together on the basis of principles of fundamental equality, but is transformed into a tyrant State, which arrogates to itself the right to dispose of the life of the weakest and most defenseless members, from the unborn child to the elderly, in the name of a public interest which is really nothing but the interest of one part." (*Evangelium Vitae*, 1995, par.20)

"Democracy cannot be idolized to the point of making it a substitute for morality or a panacea for immorality. Fundamentally, democracy is a "system" and as such is a means and not an end. Its "moral" value is not automatic, but depends on conformity to the moral law to which it, like every other form of human behaviour, must be subject: in other words, its morality depends on the morality of the ends which it pursues and of the means which it employs." (*Evangelium Vitae*, 1995, par.71)

"When the Church declares that unconditional respect for the right to life of every innocent person-from conception to natural death-is one of the pillars on which every civil society stands, she "wants simply to promote a human State. A State which recognizes the defense of the fundamental rights of the human person, especially of the weakest, as its primary duty".
... There can be no true democracy without a recognition of every person's dignity and without respect for his or her rights." (*Evangelium Vitae*, 1995, par.101)

-Public Authority-

"Profound and rapid changes make it more necessary that no one ignoring the trend of events or drugged by laziness, content himself with a merely individualistic morality.
... Yet there are those who, while possessing grand and rather noble sentiments, nevertheless in reality live always as if they cared nothing for the needs of society. Many in various places even make light of social laws and precepts, and do not hesitate to resort to various frauds and deceptions in avoiding just taxes or other debts due to society. Others think little of certain norms of social life, for example those designed for the protection of health, or laws establishing

speed limits; they do not even avert to the fact that by such indifference they imperil their own life and that of others.

Let everyone consider it his sacred obligation to esteem and observe social necessities as belonging to the primary duties of modern man." (*Gaudium et Spes*, 1965, par. 30)

"The political community exists, consequently, for the sake of the common good, in which it finds its full justification and significance, and the source of its inherent legitimacy.

… Yet the people who come together in the political community are many and diverse, and they have every right to prefer divergent solutions. If the political community is not to be torn apart while everyone follows his own opinion, there must be an authority to direct the energies of all citizens toward the common good, not in a mechanical or despotic fashion, but by acting above all as a moral force which appeals to each one's freedom and sense of responsibility.

… It follows also that political authority, both in the community as such and in the representative bodies of the state, must always be exercised within the limits of the moral order and directed toward the common good—with a dynamic concept of that good—according to the juridical order legitimately established or due to be established. When authority is so exercised, citizens are bound in conscience to obey.

… But where citizens are oppressed by a public authority overstepping its competence, they should not protest against those things which are objectively required for the common good; but it is legitimate for them to defend their own rights and the rights of their fellow citizens against the abuse of this authority, while keeping within those limits drawn by the natural law and the Gospels." (*Gaudium et Spes*, 1965, par. 74)

-Peace-

"Yet peace is but an empty word, if it does not rest upon that order which Our hope prevailed upon Us to set forth in outline in this encyclical. It is an order that is founded on truth, built up on justice, nurtured and animated by charity, and brought into effect under the auspices of freedom." (*Pacem in Terris*, 1963, par.167)

"Peace is not merely the absence of war; nor can it be reduced solely to the maintenance of a balance of power between enemies; nor is it brought about by dictatorship. Instead, it is rightly and appropriately called an enterprise of justice. Peace results from that order structured into human society by its divine Founder, and actualized by men as they thirst after ever greater justice.
...But this is not enough. This peace on earth cannot be obtained unless personal well-being is safeguarded and men freely and trustingly share with one another the riches of their inner spirits and their talents... Hence peace is likewise the fruit of love, which goes beyond what justice can provide."
(*Gaudium et Spes*, 1965, par. 78)

"Motivated by this same spirit, we cannot fail to praise those who renounce the use of violence in the vindication of their rights ... provided this can be done without injury to the rights and duties of others or of the community itself."
(*Gaudium et Spes*, 1965, par. 78)

"For peace is not simply the absence of warfare, based on a precarious balance of power; it is fashioned by efforts directed day after day toward the establishment of the ordered universe willed by God, with a more perfect form of justice among men.
... Regional mutual aid agreements among the poorer nations, broader based programs of support for these nations, major alliances between nations to coordinate these activities—these are the road signs that point the way to national development and world peace." (*Populorum Progresso*, 1967, par.76-77)

"Also to be mentioned here, as a sign of respect for life - despite all the temptations to destroy it by abortion and euthanasia - is a concomitant concern for peace, together with an awareness that peace is indivisible. It is either for all or for none." (*Sollilicitudo Rei Socialis*, 1987, par.26)

", it must be remembered that true peace is never simply the result of military victory, but rather implies both the removal of the causes of war and genuine reconciliation between peoples. For many years there has been in Europe and the world a situation of non-war rather than genuine peace." (*Centesimus annus*, 1991, par. 18)

"For this reason, another name for peace is development. Just as there is a collective responsibility for avoiding war, so too there is a collective responsibility for promoting development." (*Centesimus annus*, 1991, par. 52)

"<u>Even peace can run the risk of being considered a technical product, merely the outcome of agreements between governments or of initiatives aimed at ensuring effective economic aid.</u> It is true that *peace-building* requires the constant interplay of diplomatic contacts, economic, technological and cultural exchanges, agreements on common projects, as well as joint strategies to curb the threat of military conflict and to root out the underlying causes of terrorism. Nevertheless, if such efforts are to have lasting effects, they must be based on values rooted in the truth of human life." (*Caritas in Veritatae*, 2009, par.72)

"Peace in society cannot be understood as <u>pacification</u> or the mere <u>absence of violence</u> resulting from the domination of one part of society over others." (*Evangelii Gaudium*, 2013, par.218)

-War-

"On the subject of war, quite a large number of nations have subscribed to international agreements aimed at making military activity and its consequences less inhuman. Their stipulations deal with such matters as the treatment of wounded soldiers and prisoners. <u>Agreements of this sort must be honored.</u>
… As long as the danger of war remains and there is no competent and sufficiently powerful authority at the international level, governments cannot be denied the right to <u>legitimate defense</u> once every means of peaceful settlement has been exhausted.
… <u>Any act of war aimed indiscriminately at the destruction of entire cities of extensive areas along with their population is a crime against God and man himself. It merits unequivocal and unhesitating condemnation.</u>" (*Gaudium et Spes*, 1965, par. 79-80)

"It is our clear duty, therefore, to strain every muscle in working for the time when all war can be completely outlawed by international consent." (*Gaudium et Spes*, 1965, par. 81)

"…all the causes of discord among men, especially injustice, which foment wars must be rooted out. Not a few of these causes come from excessive economic inequalities and from putting off the steps needed to remedy them. Other causes of discord, however, have their source in the desire to dominate and in a contempt for persons. And, if we look for deeper causes, we find them in human envy, distrust, pride, and other egotistical passions. Man cannot bear so many ruptures in the harmony of things. Consequently, the world is constantly beset by strife and violence between men, even when no war is being waged." (*Gaudium et Spes*, 1965, par. 83)

"It is foreseeable that, once certain resources have been depleted, the scene will be set for new wars, albeit under the guise of noble claims." (*Laudato Si*, 2015, par 57)

-Global and Foreign Relationships-

"With respect to States themselves… nations are the subjects of reciprocal rights and duties.
… <u>They are still bound by the natural law, which is the rule that governs all moral conduct, and they have no authority to depart from its slightest precepts.</u>
… even when it regulates the relations between States, authority must be exercised for the promotion of the common good." (*Pacem in Terris*, 1963, par.80-84)

"…<u>all States are by nature equal in dignity.</u>
… men frequently differ widely in knowledge, virtue, intelligence and wealth, but that is no valid argument in favor of a system whereby those who are in a position of superiority impose their will arbitrarily on others.
… <u>States have the right to existence, to self development, and to the means necessary to achieve this. They have the right to play the leading part in the process of their own development, and the right to their good name and due honors.</u>
… States must further [inter-State] relationships by taking positive steps to pool their material and spiritual resources." (*Pacem in Terris*, 1963, par.86-98)

"Furthermore, relations between States must be regulated by the principle of freedom. This means that no country has the right to take any action that would constitute an <u>unjust oppression</u> of other countries, or an <u>unwarranted interference in their affairs.</u>
… They must also repudiate any policy of domination." (*Pacem in Terris*, 1963, par.120)

-Foreign Policy-

"Yet although individuals and nations are becoming more and more convinced of this twofold necessity [of co-operation and understanding], it would seem that men in general, and particularly those with high responsibility in public life, are showing themselves quite incapable of achieving it. The root of such inability is not to be sought in scientific, technical or economic reasons, but in the absence of mutual trust.

…The result is a vast expenditure of human energy and natural resources on projects which are disruptive of human society rather than beneficial to it [including armament]; while a growing uneasiness gnaws at men's hearts and makes them less responsive to the call of nobler enterprises.

The root cause of so much mistrust is the presence of ideological differences between nations, and more especially between their rulers. There are some indeed who go so far as to deny the existence of a moral order which is transcendent, absolute, universal and equally binding upon all. And where the same law of justice is not adhered to by all, men cannot hope to come to open and full agreement on vital issues." (*Mater et Magistra*, 1961, par.202-205)

"This duty concerns first and foremost the wealthier nations. Their obligations stem from the human and supernatural brotherhood of man, and present a three-fold obligation: 1) mutual solidarity—the aid that the richer nations must give to developing nations; 2) social justice—the rectification of trade relations between strong and weak nations; 3) universal charity—the effort to build a more humane world community, where all can give and receive, and where the progress of some is not bought at the expense of others. The matter is urgent, for on it depends the future of world civilization." (Populorum Progresso, 1967, par.44)

"Up to now relations between nations have too often been governed by force; indeed, that is the hallmark of past history.

May the day come when international relationships will be characterized by respect and friendship, when mutual cooperation will be the hallmark of collaborative efforts, and when concerted effort for the betterment of all nations will be regarded as a duty by every nation. The developing nations now emerging are asking that they be allowed to take part in the construction of a better world, a world which would provide better protection for every man's rights and duties. It is certainly a legitimate demand, so everyone must heed and fulfill it." (Populorum Progresso, 1967, par.65)

""But, as we have often stated, the most important duty in the realm of justice is to allow each country to promote its own development, within the framework of a cooperation free from any spirit of domination, whether economic or political…Thus it is necessary to have the courage to undertake a revision of the relationships between nations, whether it is a question of the international division of production, the structure of exchanges, the control of profits, the monetary system- without forgetting the actions of human solidarity - to question the models of growth of the rich nations and change people's outlooks, so that they may realize the prior call of international duty, and to renew international organizations so that they may increase in effectiveness." (*Octogesima Adveniens*, 1971, par.43)

-Culture -

"Just as it is in the world's interest to acknowledge the Church as an historical reality, and to recognize her good influence, so the Church herself knows how richly she has profited by the history and development of humanity." (*Gaudium et Spes*, 1965, par.44)

"Culture… has constant need of a just liberty in order to develop; it needs also the legitimate possibility of exercising its autonomy according to its own principles. It therefore rightly demands respect and enjoys a certain inviolability within the limits of the common good, as long, of course, as it preserves the rights of the individual and the community, whether particular or universal. … this Sacred Synod affirms the legitimate autonomy of human culture and especially of the sciences." (*Gaudium et Spes*, 1965, par. 58-59)

"Although the Church has contributed much to the development of culture, experience shows that, for circumstantial reasons, it is sometimes difficult to harmonize culture with Christian teaching." (*Gaudium et Spes*, 1965, par. 62)

"Other people are not rivals from whom we must defend ourselves, but brothers and sisters to be supported. They are to be loved for their own sakes, and they enrich us by their very presence." (*Evangelium Vitae*, 1995, par.98)

"Let it not be forgotten that the increased commercialization of cultural exchange today leads to a twofold danger. First, one may observe a cultural eclecticism that is often assumed uncritically: cultures are simply placed alongside one another and viewed as substantially equivalent and interchangeable. This easily yields to a relativism that does not serve true intercultural dialogue; on the social plane, cultural relativism has the effect that cultural groups coexist side by side, but remain separate, with no authentic dialogue and therefore with no true integration. Secondly, the opposite danger exists, that of cultural levelling and indiscriminate acceptance of types of conduct and life-styles. In this way one loses sight of the profound significance of the culture of different nations, of the traditions of the various peoples, by which the individual defines himself in relation to life's fundamental questions. What eclecticism and cultural levelling have in common is the separation of culture from human nature. Thus, cultures can no longer define themselves within a nature that transcends them, and man ends up being reduced to a mere cultural statistic. When this happens, humanity runs new risks of enslavement and manipulation." (*Caritas in Veritatae*, 2009, par.26)

"In all cultures there are examples of ethical convergence, some isolated, some interrelated, as an expression of the one human nature, willed by the Creator; the tradition of ethical wisdom knows this as the natural law." (*Caritas in Veritatae*, 2009, par.59)

"In many countries globalization has meant a hastened deterioration of their own cultural roots and the invasion of ways of thinking and acting proper to other cultures which are economically advanced but ethically debilitated. This fact has been brought up by bishops from various continents in different Synods." (*Evangelii Gaudium*, 2013, par.62)

"The disappearance of a culture can be just as serious, or even more serious, than the disappearance of a species of plant or animal." (*Laudato Si*, 2015, par 145)

-Urbanization-

"A major phenomenon draws our attention, as much in the industrialized countries as in those which are developing: urbanization.
After long centuries, agrarian civilization is weakening. Is sufficient attention being devoted to the arrangement and improvement of the life of the country

people, whose inferior and at times miserable economic situation provokes the flight to the unhappy crowded conditions of the city outskirts, where neither employment nor housing awaits them?

… Man is experiencing a new loneliness; it is not in the face of a hostile nature which it has taken him centuries to subdue, but in an anonymous crowd which surrounds him and in which he feels himself a stranger. Urbanization, undoubtedly an irreversible stage in the development of human societies, confronts man with difficult problems. How is he to master its growth, regulate its organization, and successfully accomplish its animation for the good of all? In this disordered growth, new proletariats are born. They install themselves in the heart of the cities sometimes abandoned by the rich; they dwell on the outskirts - which become a belt of misery besieging in a still silent protest the luxury which blatantly cries out from centers of consumption and waste.

… There is an urgent need to remake at the level of the street, of the neighborhood or of the great agglomerative dwellings the social fabric whereby man may be able to develop the needs of his personality. Centers of special interest and of culture must be created or developed at the community and parish levels with different forms of associations, recreational centers, and spiritual and community gatherings where the individual can escape from isolation and form anew fraternal relationships." (*Octogesima Adveniens*, 1971, par.8-11)

"The lack of housing is being experienced universally and is due in large measure to the growing phenomenon of urbanization.

… The lack of housing, an extremely serious problem in itself, should be seen as a sign and summing-up of a whole series of shortcomings: economic, social, cultural or simply human in nature. Given the extent of the problem, we should need little convincing of how far we are from an authentic development of peoples.

… Another indicator common to the vast majority of nations is the phenomenon of unemployment and underemployment." (*Sollilicitudo Rei Socialis*, 1987, par.17)

"The feeling of asphyxiation brought on by densely populated residential areas is countered if close and warm relationships develop, if communities are created, if the limitations of the environment are compensated for in the interior of each person who feels held within a network of solidarity and belonging." (*Laudato Si*, 2015, par 148)

"The quality of life in cities has much to do with systems of transport, which are often a source of much suffering for those who use them…Many specialists agree on the need to give priority to public transportation. Yet some measures needed will not prove easily acceptable to society unless substantial improvements are made in the systems themselves…" (*Laudato Si*, 2015, par 153)

-Atheism-

"The word atheism is applied to phenomena which are quite distinct from one another. For while God is expressly denied by some, others believe that man can assert absolutely nothing about Him. Still others use such a method to scrutinize the question of God as to make it seem devoid of meaning. Many, unduly transgressing the limits of the positive sciences, contend that everything can be explained by this kind of scientific reasoning alone, or by contrast, they altogether disallow that there is any absolute truth. Some laud man so extravagantly that their faith in God lapses into a kind of anemia, though they seem more inclined to affirm man than to deny God. Again some form for themselves such a fallacious idea of God that when they repudiate this figment they are by no means rejecting the God of the Gospel. Some never get to the point of raising questions about God, since they seem to experience no religious stirrings nor do they see why they should trouble themselves about religion. Moreover, atheism results not rarely from a violent protest against the evil in this world, or from the absolute character with which certain human values are unduly invested, and which thereby already accords them the stature of God. Modern civilization itself often complicates the approach to God not for any essential reason but because it is so heavily engrossed in earthly affairs.
… taken as a whole, atheism is not a spontaneous development but stems from a variety of causes, including a critical reaction against religious beliefs …Hence believers can have more than a little to do with the birth of atheism." (*Gaudium et Spes*, 1965, par. 19)

"If we then inquire as to the source of this mistaken concept of the nature of the person and the "subjectivity" of society, we must reply that its first cause is atheism… <u>The denial of God deprives the person of his foundation, and consequently leads to a reorganization of the social order without reference to the person's dignity and responsibility.</u>
The atheism of which we are speaking is also closely connected with the rationalism of the Enlightenment, which views human and social reality in a

mechanistic way. Thus there is a denial of the supreme insight concerning man's true greatness, his transcendence in respect to earthly realities, the contradiction in his heart between the desire for the fullness of what is good and his own inability to attain it and, above all, the need for salvation which results from this situation." (*Centesimus annus*, 1991, par. 13)

"Marxism had promised to uproot the need for God from the human heart, but the results have shown that it is not possible to succeed in this without throwing the heart into turmoil." (*Centesimus annus*, 1991, par. 24)

"[When Man lives as if God does not exist, he is] Enclosed in the narrow horizon of his physical nature, he is somehow reduced to being "a thing", and no longer grasps the "transcendent" character of his "existence as man". <u>He no longer considers life as a splendid gift of God, something "sacred" entrusted to his responsibility and thus also to his loving care and "veneration". Life itself becomes a mere "thing"</u>, which man claims as his exclusive property, completely subject to his control and manipulation.
Thus, in relation to life at birth or at death, man is no longer capable of posing the question of the truest meaning of his own existence, nor can he assimilate with genuine freedom these crucial moments of his own history. He is concerned only with "doing", and, using all kinds of technology, he busies himself with programming, controlling and dominating birth and death. <u>Birth and death, instead of being primary experiences demanding to be "lived", become things to be merely "possessed" or "rejected".</u>
… Something similar happens when concern about the consequences of such a "freedom without law" leads some people to the opposite position of a "law without freedom", as for example in ideologies which consider it unlawful to interfere in any way with nature, practically "divinizing" it." (*Evangelium Vitae*, 1995, par.22)

"The eclipse of the sense of God and of man inevitably leads to a practical materialism, which breeds individualism, utilitarianism and hedonism.
…Within this same cultural climate, the body is no longer perceived as a properly personal reality, a sign and place of relations with others, with God and with the world. It is reduced to pure materiality: it is simply a complex of organs, functions and energies to be used according to the sole criteria of pleasure and efficiency. Consequently, sexuality too is depersonalized and exploited…

... In the materialistic perspective described so far, interpersonal relations are seriously impoverished. The first to be harmed are women, children, the sick or suffering, and the elderly. The criterion of personal dignity-which demands respect, generosity and service-is replaced by the criterion of efficiency, functionality and usefulness: others are considered not for what they "are", but for what they "have, do and produce". <u>This is the supremacy of the strong over the weak.</u>" (*Evangelium Vitae*, 1995, par.23)

-Terrorism-

"Nor may we close our eyes to another painful wound in today's world: the phenomenon of terrorism, understood as the intention to kill people and destroy property indiscriminately, and to create a climate of terror and insecurity, often including the taking of hostages. Even when some ideology or the desire to create a better society is adduced as the motivation for this inhuman behavior, acts of terrorism are never justifiable." (*Sollilicitudo Rei Socialis*, 1987, par.24)

"Violence puts the brakes on authentic development and impedes the evolution of peoples towards greater socio-economic and spiritual well-being. This applies especially to terrorism motivated by fundamentalism, which generates grief, destruction and death, obstructs dialogue between nations and diverts extensive resources from their peaceful and civil uses." (*Caritas in Veritatae*, 2009, par.29)

-Patriotism-

"<u>Citizens must cultivate a generous and loyal spirit of patriotism, but without being narrow-minded.</u> This means that they will always direct their attention to the good of the <u>whole human family</u>, united by the different ties which bind together races, people and nations." (*Gaudium et Spes*, 1965, par. 75)

-Voting-

"<u>All citizens, therefore, should be mindful of the right and also the duty to use their free vote to further the common good.</u>" (*Gaudium et Spes*, 1965, par. 75)

-Tourism-

"An illustration of the significance of [the problem of taking advantage of needy populations] is offered by the phenomenon of international tourism, which can be a major factor in economic development and cultural growth, but can also become an occasion for exploitation and moral degradation… In many cases this is what happens, but in other cases international tourism has a negative educational impact both for the tourist and the local populace. The latter are often exposed to immoral or even perverted forms of conduct, as in the case of so-called sex tourism, to which many human beings are sacrificed even at a tender age. It is sad to note that this activity often takes place with the support of local governments, with silence from those in the tourists' countries of origin, and with the complicity of many of the tour operators. Even in less extreme cases, international tourism often follows a consumerist and hedonistic pattern, as a form of escapism planned in a manner typical of the countries of origin, and therefore not conducive to authentic encounter between persons and cultures. We need, therefore, to develop a different type of tourism that has the ability to promote genuine mutual understanding, without taking away from the element of rest and healthy recreation." (*Caritas in Veritatae*, 2009, par.61)

3. Rights & Responsibilities

-Charity (Caritas)-

"Following the example given in the parable of the Good Samaritan, Christian charity is first of all the simple response to immediate needs and specific situations: feeding the hungry, clothing the naked, caring for and healing the sick, visiting those in prison, etc.
… Yet, while professional competence is a primary, fundamental requirement, it is not of itself sufficient. We are dealing with human beings, and human beings always need something more than technically proper care. They need humanity. They need heartfelt concern. Those who work for the Church's charitable organizations must be distinguished by the fact that they do not merely meet the needs of the moment, but they dedicate themselves to others with heartfelt concern, enabling them to experience the richness of their humanity. Consequently, in addition to their necessary professional training, these charity workers need a "formation of the heart": they need to be led to that encounter with God in Christ which awakens their love and opens their spirits to others.
… Christian charitable activity must be independent of parties and ideologies." (*Deus Caritas Est*, 2005, par.31)

"Charity, furthermore, cannot be used as a means of engaging in what is nowadays considered proselytism. Love is free; it is not practiced as a way of achieving other ends. But this does not mean that charitable activity must somehow leave God and Christ aside… Those who practice charity in the Church's name will never seek to impose the Church's faith upon others. They realize that a pure and generous love is the best witness to the God in whom we believe and by whom we are driven to love. A Christian knows when it is time to speak of God and when it is better to say nothing and to let love alone speak… Consequently, the best defense of God and man consists precisely in love." (*Deus Caritas Est*, 2005, par.31)

"This proper way of serving others also leads to humility. The one who serves does not consider himself superior to the one served, however miserable his situation at the moment may be." (*Deus Caritas Est*, 2005, par.35)

-Rights-

"...<u>man's personal dignity involves his right to take an active part in public life</u>...
...As a human person he is entitled to the legal protection of his rights, and such protection must be effective, unbiased, and strictly just."(*Pacem in Terris*, 1963, par.26-27)

"[Natural rights] are inextricably bound up with as many duties, all applying to one and the same person. These rights and duties derive their origin, their sustenance, and their indestructibility from the natural law, which in conferring the one imposes the other.
Thus, for example, the right to live involves the duty to preserve one's life; the right to a decent standard of living, the duty to live in a becoming fashion; the right to be free to seek out the truth, the duty to devote oneself to an ever deeper and wider search for it." (*Pacem in Terris*, 1963, par.28-29)

"It is generally accepted today that the common good is best safeguarded when personal rights and duties are guaranteed." (*Pacem in Terris*, 1963, par.60)

"While rejecting atheism, root and branch, the Church sincerely professes that all men, believers and unbelievers alike, ought to work for the rightful betterment of this world in which all alike live; such an ideal cannot be realized, however, apart from sincere and prudent dialogue. Hence the Church protests against the distinction which some state authorities make between believers and unbelievers, with prejudice to the fundamental rights of the human person." (*Gaudium et Spes*, 1965, par. 21)

"Every social group must take account of the needs and legitimate aspirations of other groups, and even of the general welfare of the entire human family.
... Therefore, there must be made available to all men everything necessary for leading a life truly human, such as food, clothing, and shelter; the right to choose a state of life freely and to found a family, the right to education, to employment, to a good reputation, to respect, to appropriate information, to activity in accord with the upright norm of one's own conscience, to protection of privacy and rightful freedom even in matters religious.'" (*Gaudium et Spes*, 1965, par. 26)

"For we are tempted to think that our personal rights are fully ensured only when we are exempt from every requirement of divine law. But this way lies not the maintenance of the dignity of the human person, but its annihilation."
(*Gaudium et Spes*, 1965, par. 41)

"The protection of the rights of a person is indeed a necessary condition so that citizens, individually or collectively, can take an active part in the life and government of the state.
(*Gaudium et Spes*, 1965, par. 73)

"On the internal level of every nation, respect for all rights takes on great importance, especially: the right to life at every stage of its existence; the rights of the family, as the basic social community, or "cell of society"; justice in employment relationships; the rights inherent in the life of the political community as such; the rights based on the transcendent vocation of the human being, beginning with the right of freedom to profess and practice one's own religious belief.
On the international level, that is, the level of relations between States or, in present-day usage, between the different "worlds," there must be complete respect for the identity of each people, with its own historical and cultural characteristics." (*Sollilicitudo Rei Socialis*, 1987, par.33)

"But for this very reason it is necessary for peoples in the process of reforming their systems to give democracy an authentic and solid foundation through the explicit recognition of those rights. Among the most important of these rights, mention must be made of the right to life, an integral part of which is the right of the child to develop in the mother's womb from the moment of conception; the right to live in a united family and in a moral environment conducive to the growth of the child's personality; the right to develop one's intelligence and freedom in seeking and knowing the truth; the right to share in the work which makes wise use of the earth's material resources, and to derive from that work the means to support oneself and one's dependents; and the right freely to establish a family, to have and to rear children through the responsible exercise of one's sexuality. In a certain sense, the source and synthesis of these rights is religious freedom, understood as the right to live in the truth of one's faith and in conformity with one's transcendent dignity as a person.
Even in countries with democratic forms of government, these rights are not always fully respected." (*Centesimus annus*, 1991, par. 47)

"The theory of human rights is based precisely on the affirmation that the human person, unlike animals and things, cannot be subjected to domination by others. We must also mention the mentality which tends to equate personal dignity with the capacity for verbal and explicit, or at least perceptible, communication... In this case it is force which becomes the criterion for choice and action in interpersonal relations and in social life." (*Evangelium Vitae*, 1995, par.19)

"First and fundamental among these is the inviolable right to life of every innocent human being." (*Evangelium Vitae*, 1995, par.71)

"Many people today would claim that they owe nothing to anyone, except to themselves. They are concerned only with their rights, and they often have great difficulty in taking responsibility for their own and other people's integral development. Hence it is important to call for a renewed reflection on how *rights presuppose duties, if they are not to become mere licence.* Nowadays we are witnessing a grave inconsistency. On the one hand, appeals are made to alleged rights, arbitrary and non-essential in nature, accompanied by the demand that they be recognized and promoted by public structures, while, on the other hand, elementary and basic rights remain unacknowledged and are violated in much of the world. A link has often been noted between claims to a "right to excess", and even to transgression and vice, within affluent societies, and the lack of food, drinkable water, basic instruction and elementary health care in areas of the underdeveloped world and on the outskirts of large metropolitan centres. The link consists in this: individual rights, when detached from a framework of duties which grants them their full meaning, can run wild, leading to an escalation of demands which is effectively unlimited and indiscriminate. An overemphasis on rights leads to a disregard for duties. Duties set a limit on rights because they point to the anthropological and ethical framework of which rights are a part, in this way ensuring that they do not become licence. Duties thereby reinforce rights and call for their defence and promotion as a task to be undertaken in the service of the common good. Otherwise, if the only basis of human rights is to be found in the deliberations of an assembly of citizens, those rights can be changed at any time, and so the duty to respect and pursue them fades from the common consciousness. Governments and international bodies can then lose sight of the objectivity and "inviolability" of rights. When this happens, the authentic development of peoples is endangered... *The sharing of reciprocal duties is a more powerful incentive to action than the mere assertion of rights." (Caritas in Veritatae, 2009, par.43)*

-Right to Life-

"<u>Morally responsible openness to life represents a rich social and economic resource.</u> Populous nations have been able to emerge from poverty thanks not least to the size of their population and the talents of their people. On the other hand, formerly prosperous nations are presently passing through a phase of uncertainty and in some cases decline, precisely because of their falling birth rates; this has become a crucial problem for highly affluent societies. The decline in births, falling at times beneath the so-called "replacement level", also puts a strain on social welfare systems, increases their cost, eats into savings and hence the financial resources needed for investment, reduces the availability of qualified laborers, and narrows the "brain pool" upon which nations can draw for their needs. Furthermore, smaller and at times miniscule families run the risk of impoverishing social relations, and failing to ensure effective forms of solidarity." (*Caritas in Veritatae*, 2009, par.44)

-When discussing "Rights," especially the right to life, it is important to proceed from the weaker party to the stronger, always. In the case of "Right to Life," it is vital to first speak of children's rights (the weaker party), and the corresponding right to Life of the Mother (the stronger party) – they originate from the same source.

-Freedom-

"Man's personal dignity requires besides that he enjoy freedom and be able to make up his own mind when he acts... Each man should act on his own initiative, conviction, and sense of responsibility, not under the constant pressure of external coercion or enticement. There is nothing human about a society that is welded together by force... And so, dearest sons and brothers, we must think of human society as being primarily a spiritual reality." (*Pacem in Terris*, 1963, par. 34-36)

"<u>Only in freedom can man direct himself toward goodness. Our contemporaries make much of this freedom and pursue it eagerly; and rightly to be sure. Often however they foster it perversely as a license for doing whatever pleases them, even if it is evil.</u>" (*Gaudium et Spes*, 1965, par. 62)

"Now a man can scarcely arrive at the needed sense of responsibility, unless his living conditions allow him to become conscious of his dignity, and to rise to his destiny by spending himself for God and for others. But human freedom is often crippled when a man encounters extreme poverty just as it withers when he indulges in too many of life's comforts and imprisons himself in a kind of splendid isolation. Freedom acquires new strength, by contrast, when a man consents to the unavoidable requirements of social life, takes on the manifold demands of human partnership, and commits himself to the service of the human community." (*Gaudium et Spes*, 1965, par. 31)

"<u>As has been mentioned, this error consists in an understanding of human freedom which detaches it from obedience to the truth, and consequently from the duty to respect the rights of others.</u> The essence of freedom then becomes self-love carried to the point of contempt for God and neighbour, a self-love which leads to an unbridled affirmation of self-interest and which refuses to be limited by any demand of justice." (*Centesimus annus*, 1991, par. 17)

"Nevertheless, it cannot be forgotten that the manner in which the individual exercises his freedom is conditioned in innumerable ways… Where society is so organized as to reduce arbitrarily or even suppress the sphere in which freedom is legitimately exercised, the result is that the life of society becomes progressively disorganized and goes into decline." (*Centesimus annus*, 1991, par. 25)

"<u>All of this can be summed up by repeating once more that economic freedom is only one element of human freedom.</u> When it becomes autonomous, when man is seen more as a producer or consumer of goods than as a subject who produces and consumes in order to live, then economic freedom loses its necessary relationship to the human person and ends up by alienating and oppressing him." (*Centesimus annus*, 1991, par. 39)

"A person who is concerned solely or primarily with possessing and enjoying, who is no longer able to control his instincts and passions, or to subordinate them by obedience to the truth, cannot be free: obedience to the truth about God and man is the first condition of freedom, making it possible for a person to order his needs and desires and to choose the means of satisfying them according to a correct scale of values, so that the ownership of things may become an occasion of growth for him." (*Centesimus annus*, 1991, par. 41)

"But freedom attains its full development only by accepting the truth. In a world without truth, freedom loses its foundation and man is exposed to the violence of passion and to manipulation, both open and hidden… While paying heed to every fragment of truth which he encounters in the life experience and in the culture of individuals and of nations, he will not fail to affirm in dialogue with others all that his faith and the correct use of reason have enabled him to understand." (*Centesimus annus*, 1991, par. 46)

"At another level, the roots of the contradiction between the solemn affirmation of human rights and their tragic denial in practice lies in a notion of freedom which exalts the isolated individual in an absolute way, and gives no place to solidarity, to openness to others and service of them.
… freedom negates and destroys itself, and becomes a factor leading to the destruction of others, when it no longer recognizes and respects its essential link with the truth. When freedom, out of a desire to emancipate itself from all forms of tradition and authority, shuts out even the most obvious evidence of an objective and universal truth, which is the foundation of personal and social life, then the person ends up by no longer taking as the sole and indisputable point of reference for his own choices the truth about good and evil, but only his subjective and changeable opinion or, indeed, his selfish interest and whim." (*Evangelium Vitae*, 1995, par.19)

-Freedom of Religion and Conscience-

"And here we are reminded of the confraternities, societies, and religious orders which have arisen… The annals of every nation down to our own days bear witness to what they have accomplished for the human race… In their religious aspect they claim rightly to be responsible to the Church alone. The rulers of the State accordingly have no rights over them, nor can they claim any share in their control; on the contrary, it is the duty of the State to respect and cherish them, and, if need be, to defend them from attack." (*Rerum Novarum*, 1891, par.53)

"Also among man's rights is that of being able to worship God in accordance with the right dictates of his own conscience, and to profess his religion both in private and in public." (*Pacem in Terris*, 1963, par.14)

-In context: this is the most important form of "Freedom of Speech." See Freedom of Press & Freedom of Speech *for contextual references.*

"But it must not be imagined that authority knows no bounds.
…Hence, representatives of the State have no power to bind men in conscience, unless their own authority is tied to God's authority, and is a participation in it." (*Pacem in Terris*, 1963, par.47-49)

"Finally, development must not be understood solely in economic terms, but in a way that is fully human. It is not only a question of raising all peoples to the level currently enjoyed by the richest countries, but rather of building up a more decent life through united labor, of concretely enhancing every individual's dignity and creativity, as well as his capacity to respond to his personal vocation, and thus to God's call. The apex of development is the exercise of the right and duty to seek God, to know him and to live in accordance with that knowledge. In the totalitarian and authoritarian regimes, the principle that force predominates over reason was carried to the extreme. Man was compelled to submit to a conception of reality imposed on him by coercion, and not reached by virtue of his own reason and the exercise of his own freedom. This principle must be overturned and total recognition must be given to the rights of the human conscience, which is bound only to the truth, both natural and revealed. The recognition of these rights represents the primary foundation of every authentically free political order." (*Centesimus annus*, 1991, par. 29)

"Nor does the Church close her eyes to the danger of fanaticism or fundamentalism among those who, in the name of an ideology which purports to be scientific or religious, claim the right to impose on others their own concept of what is true and good. Christian truth is not of this kind. Since it is not an ideology, the Christian faith does not presume to imprison changing socio-political realities in a rigid schema, and it recognizes that human life is realized in history in conditions that are diverse and imperfect. Furthermore, in constantly reaffirming the transcendent dignity of the person, the Church's method is always that of respect for freedom." (*Centesimus annus*, 1991, par. 46)

"There is another aspect of modern life that is very closely connected to development: the denial of the *right to religious freedom.*

… Yet it should be added that, as well as religious fanaticism that in some contexts impedes the exercise of the right to religious freedom, so too the deliberate promotion of religious indifference or practical atheism on the part of many countries obstructs the requirements for the development of peoples, depriving them of spiritual and human resources. *God is the guarantor of man's true development…*When the State promotes, teaches, or actually imposes forms of practical atheism, it deprives its citizens of the moral and spiritual strength that is indispensable for attaining integral human development and it impedes them from moving forward with renewed dynamism as they strive to offer a more generous human response to divine love." (*Caritas in Veritatae*, 2009, par.29)

"Religious freedom does not mean religious indifferentism, nor does it imply that all religions are equal. Discernment is needed regarding the contribution of cultures and religions, especially on the part of those who wield political power, if the social community is to be built up in a spirit of respect for the common good. Such discernment has to be based on the criterion of charity and truth." (*Caritas in Veritatae*, 2009, par.55)

"The Synod Fathers spoke of the importance of respect for religious freedom, viewed as a fundamental human right… A healthy pluralism, one which genuinely respects differences and values them as such, does not entail privatizing religions in an attempt to reduce them to the quiet obscurity of the individual's conscience or to relegate them to the enclosed precincts of churches, synagogues or mosques. This would represent, in effect, a new form of discrimination and authoritarianism…. Intellectuals and serious journalists frequently descend to crude and superficial generalizations in speaking of the shortcomings of religion, and often prove incapable of realizing that not all believers – or religious leaders – are the same. Some politicians take advantage of this confusion to justify acts of discrimination." (*Evangelii Gaudium*, 2013, par.255-256)

4. Poor and Vulnerable

-Poor-

"Today more than in the past, the Church's social doctrine must be open to an international outlook...
... Here I would like to indicate one [emphasis of Catholic Social principles]: the option or love of preference for the poor.
... Today, furthermore, given the worldwide dimension which the social question has assumed, this love of preference for the poor, and the decisions which it inspires in us, cannot but embrace the immense multitudes of the hungry, the needy, the homeless, those without medical care and, above all, those without hope of a better future." (*Sollicitudo Rei Socialis*, 1987, par.42)

"Faithful to the mission received from Christ her Founder, the Church has always been present and active among the needy, offering them material assistance in ways that neither humiliate nor reduce them to mere objects of assistance, but which help them to escape their precarious situation by promoting their dignity as persons...In this regard, special mention must be made of *volunteer work*, which the Church favors and promotes by urging everyone to cooperate in supporting and encouraging its undertakings." (*Centesimus annus*, 1991, par. 49)

"One of the deepest forms of poverty a person can experience is isolation... Poverty is often produced by a rejection of God's love... All of humanity is alienated when too much trust is placed in merely human projects, ideologies and false utopias..." (*Caritas in Veritatae*, 2009, par.53)

"Our commitment does not consist exclusively in activities or programs of promotion and assistance... True love is always contemplative, and permits us to serve the other not out of necessity or vanity, but rather because he or she is beautiful above and beyond mere appearances... Only on the basis of this real and sincere closeness can we properly accompany the poor on their path of liberation.
... Since this Exhortation is addressed to members of the Catholic Church, I want to say, with regret, that the worst discrimination which the poor suffer is the lack of spiritual care.

… No one must say that they cannot be close to the poor because their own lifestyle demands more attention to other areas. This is an excuse commonly heard in academic, business or professional, and even ecclesial circles." (*Evangelii Gaudium*, 2013, par.199-201)

"At times this attitude [of ignoring of the poor] exists side by side with a "green" rhetoric. Today, however, we have to realize that a true ecological approach always becomes a social approach; it must integrate questions of justice in debates on the environment, so as to hear both the cry of the earth and the cry of the poor." (*Laudato Si*, 2015, par 49)

"For poor countries, the priorities must be to eliminate extreme poverty and to promote the social development of their people. At the same time, they need to acknowledge the scandalous level of consumption in some privileged sectors of their population and to combat corruption more effectively." (*Laudato Si*, 2015, par 172)

-Foreign Aid-

"[As an obligation of wealthy nations] The solidarity which binds all men together as members of a common family makes it impossible for wealthy nations to look with indifference upon the hunger, misery and poverty of other nations whose citizens are unable to enjoy even elementary human rights… We are all equally responsible for the undernourished peoples.
… It is therefore a great source of joy to Us to see those nations which enjoy a high degree of economic wealth helping the nations not so well provided…
Justice and humanity demand that those countries which produce consumer goods, especially farm products, in excess of their own needs should come to the assistance of those other countries where large sections of the population are suffering from want and hunger. It is nothing less than an outrage to justice and humanity to destroy or to squander goods that other people need for their very lives.
We are, of course, well aware that overproduction, especially in agriculture, can cause economic harm to a certain section of the population. But it does not follow that one is thereby exonerated from extending emergency aid to those who need it. On the contrary, everything must be done to minimize the ill effects of overproduction, and to spread the burden equitably over the entire population.
Of itself, however, emergency aid will not go far in relieving want and famine when these are caused—as they so often are—by the primitive state of a

nation's economy. The only permanent remedy for this is to make use of every possible means of providing these citizens with the scientific, technical and professional training they need, and to put at their disposal the necessary capital for speeding up their economic development with the help of modern methods." (*Mater et Magistra*, 1961, par.157-163)

- see Progress *for related references. All progress must be balanced, or else, like all good things, it will become disproportionate to the point of harming, instead of helping.*

"There is also a further temptation which the economically developed nations must resist: that of giving technical and financial aid with a view to gaining control over the political situation in the poorer countries, and furthering their own plans for world domination." (*Mater et Magistra*, 1961, par.171)

Scientific and technical progress... are certainly valuable elements in a civilization. But we must realize that they are essentially instrumental in character. They are not supreme values in themselves.
It pains Us, therefore, to observe the complete indifference to the true hierarchy of values shown by so many people in the economically developed countries. Spiritual values are ignored, forgotten or denied, while the progress of science, technology and economics is pursued for its own sake, as though material well-being were the be-all and end-all of life... To attempt to undermine this national integrity is clearly immoral." (*Mater et Magistra*, 1961, par.175-177)

"Again and again We must insist on the need for helping these peoples in a way which guarantees to them the preservation of their own freedom. They must be conscious that they are themselves playing the major role in their economic and social development; that they are themselves to shoulder the main burden of it." (*Pacem in Terris*, 1963, par.123)

"The development of a nation depends on human and financial aids... Such help should be accorded with generosity and without greed on the one side, and received with complete honesty on the other side." (*Gaudium et Spes*, 1965, par. 85)

"In many cases there is an urgent need to revamp economic and social structures. But one must guard against proposals of technical solutions that are untimely. This is particularly true of those solutions providing man with material conveniences, but nevertheless contrary to man's spiritual nature and advancement." (*Gaudium et Spes*, 1965, par. 86)

"Those Christians are to be praised and supported, therefore, who volunteer their services to help other men and nations… They should do this too, as was the ancient custom in the Church, out of the substance of their goods, and not only out of what is superfluous." (*Gaudium et Spes*, 1965, par. 88)

-It is essential to remember that "Foreign Aid" does not necessarily mean Governmental Aid. See Principle of Subsidiarity. *This of course does not mean that the government has no role in Foreign Aid, but its role may be, for instance, indirect, rather than one-dimensionally pouring money or resources into another country. In fact, the latter would be more often detrimental, than helpful, by creating a slavery of dependence.*

"The poorer nations can never be too much on guard against the temptation posed by the wealthier nations.
…The developing nations must choose wisely from among the things that are offered to them. They must test and reject false values that would tarnish a truly human way of life, while accepting noble and useful values in order to develop them in their own distinctive way, along with their own indigenous heritage." (*Populorum Progresso*, 1967, par.41)

""If a brother or a sister be naked and in want of daily food," says St. James, "and one of you say to them, 'Go in peace, be warm and filled,' yet you do not give them what is necessary for the body, what does it profit?" Today no one can be unaware of the fact that on some continents countless men and women are ravished by hunger and countless children are undernourished.
… But these efforts, as well as public and private allocations of gifts, loans and investments, are not enough. It is not just a question of eliminating hunger and reducing poverty. It is not just a question of fighting wretched conditions, though this is an urgent and necessary task. It involves building a human community… On the part of the rich man, it calls for great generosity, willing sacrifice and diligent effort. Each man must examine his conscience, which sounds a new call in our present times. Is he prepared to support, at his own expense, projects and undertakings designed to help the needy? Is he prepared to pay higher taxes so that public authorities may expand their efforts in the work of development? Is he prepared to pay more for imported goods, so that the foreign producer may make a fairer profit? Is he prepared to emigrate from

his homeland if necessary and if he is young, in order to help the emerging nations?" (*Populorum Progresso*, 1967, par.45-48)

-*See* Private Property *for related references. Being rich is not an evil; on the contrary, it is an opportunity that God gives some. It does, however, come with heavy responsibilities mentioned above, depending on context and personal situation.*

"Efforts are being made to help the developing nations financially and technologically. Some of these efforts are considerable. Yet all these efforts will prove to be vain and useless, if their results are nullified to a large extent by the unstable trade relations between rich and poor nations. The latter will have no grounds for hope or trust if they fear that what is being given them with one hand is being taken away with the other." (*Populorum Progresso*, 1967, par.56)

"We certainly rejoice over the fact that an ever increasing number of experts are being sent on development missions by private groups, bilateral associations and international organizations." (*Populorum Progresso*, 1967, par.71)

"Concern for our neighbor transcends the confines of national communities and has increasingly broadened its horizon to the whole world." (*Deus Caritas Est*, 2005, par.30)

"Today's economic mechanisms promote inordinate consumption, yet it is evident that unbridled consumerism combined with inequality proves doubly damaging to the social fabric. Inequality eventually engenders a violence which recourse to arms cannot and never will be able to resolve… Some simply content themselves with blaming the poor and the poorer countries themselves for their troubles; indulging in unwarranted generalizations, they claim that the solution is an "education" that would tranquilize them, making them tame and harmless." (*Evangelii Gaudium*, 2013, par.60)

"The foreign debt of poor countries has become a way of controlling them… The land of the southern poor is rich and mostly unpolluted, yet access to ownership of goods and resources for meeting vital needs is inhibited by a system of commercial relations and ownership which is structurally perverse. The developed countries ought to help pay this debt by significantly limiting their consumption of non-renewable energy and by assisting poorer countries to support policies and programmes of sustainable development." (*Laudato Si*, 2015, par 52)

-Volunteer Aid-

"Significantly, our time has also seen the growth and spread of different kinds of volunteer work, which assume responsibility for providing a variety of services. I wish here to offer a special word of gratitude and appreciation to all those who take part in these activities in whatever way… The anti-culture of death, which finds expression for example in drug use, is thus countered by an unselfish love which shows itself to be a culture of life by the very willingness to "lose itself" (cf. Lk 17:33 *et passim*) for others." (*Deus Caritas Est*, 2005, par.30)

-Development-

"True development cannot consist in the simple accumulation of wealth and in the greater availability of goods and services, if this is gained at the expense of the development of the masses, and without due consideration for the social, cultural and spiritual dimensions of the human being." (*Sollilicitudo Rei Socialis*, 1987, par.9)

"Hence at this point we have to ask ourselves if the sad reality of today might not be, at least in part, the result of a too narrow idea of development, that is, a mainly economic one." (*Sollilicitudo Rei Socialis*, 1987, par.15)

"On the other hand, it is very alarming to see governments in many countries launching systematic campaigns against birth, contrary not only to the cultural and religious identity of the countries themselves but also contrary to the nature of true development. It often happens that these campaigns are the result of pressure and financing coming from abroad, and in some cases they are made a condition for the granting of financial and economic aid and assistance. In any event, there is an absolute lack of respect for the freedom of choice of the parties involved, men and women often subjected to intolerable pressures, including economic ones, in order to force them to submit to this new form of oppression. It is the poorest populations which suffer such mistreatment, and this sometimes leads to a tendency towards a form of racism, or the promotion of certain equally racist forms of eugenics.

This fact too, which deserves the most forceful condemnation, is a sign of an erroneous and perverse idea of true human development." (*Sollilicitudo Rei Socialis*, 1987, par.25)

"...development is not a straightforward process, as it were, automatic and in itself limitless, as though, given certain conditions, the human race was able to progress rapidly towards an undefined perfection of some kind.
Such an idea - linked to a notion of "progress" with philosophical connotations deriving from the Enlightenment... now seems to be seriously called into doubt... A naive mechanistic optimism has been replaced by a well-founded anxiety for the fate of humanity.
... In fact there is a better understanding today that the mere accumulation of goods and services, even for the benefit of the majority, is not enough for the realization of human happiness. Nor, in consequence, does the availability of the many real benefits provided in recent times by science and technology, including the computer sciences, bring freedom from every form of slavery. On the contrary, the experience of recent years shows that unless all the considerable body of resources and potential at man's disposal is guided by a moral understanding and by an orientation towards the true good of the human race, it easily turns against man to oppress him.
A disconcerting conclusion about the most recent period should serve to enlighten us: side-by-side with the miseries of underdevelopment, themselves unacceptable, we find ourselves up against a form of superdevelopment, equally inadmissible. because like the former it is contrary to what is good and to true happiness. This super-development, which consists in an excessive availability of every kind of material goods for the benefit of certain social groups, easily makes people slaves of "possession" and of immediate gratification, with no other horizon than the multiplication or continual replacement of the things already owned with others still better. This is the so-called civilization of "consumption" or " consumerism ," which involves so much "throwing-away" and "waste." An object already owned but now superseded by something better is discarded, with no thought of its possible lasting value in itself, nor of some other human being who is poorer." (*Sollilicitudo Rei Socialis*, 1987, par.27-28)

"In order to be genuine, development must be achieved within the framework of solidarity and freedom, without ever sacrificing either of them under whatever pretext." (*Sollilicitudo Rei Socialis*, 1987, par.33)

"…among the actions and attitudes opposed to the will of God, the good of neighbor and the "structures" created by them, two are very typical: on the one hand, the all-consuming desire for profit, and on the other, the thirst for power, with the intention of imposing one's will upon others. In order to characterize better each of these attitudes, one can add the expression: "at any price." In other words, we are faced with the absolutizing of human attitudes with all its possible consequences.
Since these attitudes can exist independently of each other, they can be separated; however in today's world both are indissolubly united, with one or the other predominating." (*Sollilicitudo Rei Socialis*, 1987, par.37)

"<u>Peoples or nations too have a right to their own full development</u>, which while including - as already said - the economic and social aspects, should also include individual cultural identity and openness to the transcendent. <u>Not even the need for development can be used as an excuse for imposing on others one's own way of life or own religious belief.</u>" (*Sollilicitudo Rei Socialis*, 1987, par.32)

"Development demands above all a spirit of initiative on the part of the countries which need it.81Each of them must act in accordance with its own responsibilities, not expecting everything from the more favored countries, and acting in collaboration with others in the same situation.
… Some nations will have to increase food production…
… Other nations need to reform certain unjust structures, and in particular their political institutions…
…None of what has been said can be achieved without the collaboration of all - especially the international community - in the framework of a solidarity which includes everyone, beginning with the most neglected. But the developing nations themselves have the duty to practice solidarity among themselves and with the neediest countries of the world.
It is desirable, for example, that nations of the some geographical area should establish forms of cooperation which will make them less dependent on more powerful producers…
… An essential condition for global solidarity is autonomy and free self-determination, also within associations such as those indicated. But at the same time solidarity demands a readiness to accept the sacrifices necessary for the good of the whole world community." (*Sollilicitudo Rei Socialis*, 1987, par.44-45)

"Now, as then, we need to repeat that there can be *no genuine solution of the "social question" apart from the Gospel...*" (*Centesimus annus*, 1991, par. 5)

"Finally, development must not be understood solely in economic terms, but in a way that is fully human. It is not only a question of raising all peoples to the level currently enjoyed by the richest countries, but rather of building up a more decent life through united labor, of concretely enhancing every individual's dignity and creativity, as well as his capacity to respond to his personal vocation, and thus to God's call. The apex of development is the exercise of the right and duty to seek God, to know him and to live in accordance with that knowledge." (*Centesimus annus*, 1991, par. 29)

"If there is no transcendent truth… Their self-interest as a class, group or nation would inevitably set them in opposition to one another… People are then respected only to the extent that they can be exploited for selfish ends. Thus, the root of modern totalitarianism is to be found in the denial of the transcendent dignity of the human person who, as the visible image of the invisible God, is therefore by his very nature the subject of rights which no one may violate — no individual, group, class, nation or State. Not even the majority of a social body may violate these rights, by going against the minority, by isolating, oppressing, or exploiting it, or by attempting to annihilate it." (*Centesimus annus*, 1991, par. 44)

"In the course of history, it was often maintained that the creation of institutions was sufficient to guarantee the fulfilment of humanity's right to development. Unfortunately, too much confidence was placed in those institutions, as if they were able to deliver the desired objective automatically. In reality, institutions by themselves are not enough, because integral human development is primarily a vocation, and therefore it involves a free assumption of responsibility in solidarity on the part of everyone. Moreover, such development requires a transcendent vision of the person, it needs God: without him, development is either denied, or entrusted exclusively to man, who falls into the trap of thinking he can bring about his own salvation, and ends up promoting a dehumanized form of development." (*Caritas in Veritatae*, 2009, par.11)

"*The development of peoples depends, above all, on a recognition that the human race is a single family* working together in true communion, not simply a group of subjects who happen to live side by side." (*Caritas in Veritatae*, 2009, par.53)

"The development of peoples is intimately linked to the development of individuals... *A person's development is compromised, if he claims to be solely responsible for producing what he becomes.* By analogy, the development of peoples goes awry if humanity thinks it can re-create itself through the "wonders" of technology, just as economic development is exposed as a destructive sham if it relies on the "wonders" of finance in order to sustain unnatural and consumerist growth." (*Caritas in Veritatae*, 2009, par.68)

"This deviation from solid humanistic principles that a technical mindset can produce is seen today in certain technological applications in the fields of development and peace. Often the development of peoples is considered a matter of financial engineering, the freeing up of markets, the removal of tariffs, investment in production, and institutional reforms — in other words, a purely technical matter. All these factors are of great importance, but we have to ask why technical choices made thus far have yielded rather mixed results. We need to think hard about the cause. Development will never be fully guaranteed through automatic or impersonal forces, whether they derive from the market or from international politics. *Development is impossible without upright men and women, without financiers and politicians whose consciences are finely attuned to the requirements of the common good.* Both professional competence and moral consistency are necessary." (*Caritas in Veritatae*, 2009, par.71)

"One aspect of the contemporary technological mindset is the tendency to consider the problems and emotions of the interior life from a purely psychological point of view, even to the point of neurological reductionism... *The question of development is closely bound up with our understanding of the human soul,* insofar as we often reduce the self to the psyche and confuse the soul's health with emotional well-being. These over-simplifications stem from a profound failure to understand the spiritual life... Development must include not just material growth but also spiritual growth, since the human person is a "unity of body and soul", born of God's creative love and destined for eternal life." (*Caritas in Veritatae*, 2009, par.76)

"*A humanism which excludes God is an inhuman humanism.*

... *Development needs Christians with their arms raised towards God* in prayer" (*Caritas in Veritatae*, 2009, par.78-79)

"Even as the quality of available water is constantly diminishing, in some places there is a growing tendency, despite its scarcity, to privatize this resource, turning it into a commodity subject to the laws of the market. Yet access to safe drinkable water is a basic and universal human right, since it is essential to human survival and, as such, is a condition for the exercise of other human rights." (*Laudato Si*, 2015, par 30)

"A consumerist vision of human beings, encouraged by the mechanisms of today's globalized economy, has a levelling effect on cultures, diminishing the immense variety which is the heritage of all humanity. Attempts to resolve all problems through uniform regulations or technical interventions can lead to overlooking the complexities of local problems which demand the active participation of all members of the community. New processes taking shape cannot always fit into frameworks imported from outside; they need to be based in the local culture itself." (*Laudato Si*, 2015, par 144)

-Liberation Theology-

"Recently, in the period following the publication of the encyclical Populorum Progressio, a new way of confronting the problems of poverty and underdevelopment has spread in some areas of the world, especially in Latin America. This approach makes liberation the fundamental category and the first principle of action. <u>The positive values, as well as the deviations and risks of deviation, which are damaging to the faith and are connected with this form of theological reflection and method, have been appropriately pointed out by the Church's Magisterium.</u>
It is fitting to add that the aspiration to freedom from all forms of slavery affecting the individual and society is something noble and legitimate.
...<u>Development which is merely economic is incapable of setting man free, on the contrary, it will end by enslaving him further.</u> Development that does not include the cultural, transcendent and religious dimensions of man and society, to the extent that it does not recognize the existence of such dimensions and does not endeavor to direct its goals and priorities toward the same, is even less conducive to authentic liberation. Human beings are totally free only when they are completely themselves, in the fullness of their rights and duties. The same can be said about society as a whole.

The principal obstacle to be overcome on the way to authentic liberation is sin and the structures produced by sin as it multiplies and spreads." (*Sollilicitudo Rei Socialis*, 1987, par.46)

-Non-Violent Resistance-

"It seemed that the European order resulting from the Second World War and sanctioned by the Yalta Agreements could only be overturned by another war. Instead, it has been overcome by the non-violent commitment of people who, while always refusing to yield to the force of power, succeeded time after time in finding effective ways of bearing witness to the truth. <u>This disarmed the adversary, since violence always needs to justify itself through deceit, and to appear, however falsely, to be defending a right or responding to a threat posed by others.</u> Once again I thank God for having sustained people's hearts amid difficult trials, and I pray that this example will prevail in other places and other circumstances." (*Centesimus annus*, 1991, par. 23)

-In the eyes of the Church, non-violent recourses must be sought before violent ones. This does not negate simple prudence, nor legitimate self-defense. Cf. Catechism of the Catholic Church, 2263-2265.

5. Work & the Economy

-Economics-

"Even though economics and moral science employs each its own principles in its own sphere, it is, nevertheless, <u>an error to say that the economic and moral orders are so distinct from and alien to each other that the former depends in no way on the latter</u>... If we faithfully observe [moral] law, then it will follow that the particular purposes, both individual and social, that are sought in the economic field will fall in their proper place in the universal order of purposes..." (*Quadragesimo Anno*, 1931, par.42)

"Wherefore it is wholly false to ascribe to property alone or to labor alone whatever has been obtained through the combined effort of both, and it is wholly unjust for either, denying the efficacy of the other, to arrogate to itself whatever has been produced." (*Quadragesimo Anno*, 1931, par.53)

"<u>Labor… is not a mere commodity.</u>" (*Quadragesimo Anno*, 1931, par.83)

"What We have taught about the reconstruction and perfection of social order can surely in no wise be brought to realization without reform of morality, the very record of history clearly shows." (*Quadragesimo Anno*, 1931, par 97)

"Therefore, technical progress, an inventive spirit, an eagerness to create…in a word, all the elements making for such development—must be promoted. The fundamental finality of this production is not the mere increase of products nor profit or control but rather the service of man…
<u>Growth is not to be left solely to a kind of mechanical course of the economic activity of individuals, nor to the authority of government.</u> For this reason, doctrines which obstruct the necessary reforms under the guise of a false liberty, and those which subordinate the basic rights of individual persons and groups to the collective organization of production must be shown to be erroneous." (*Gaudium et Spes*, 1965, par.64-65)

"It happens too often, however, even in our days that workers are reduced to the level of being slaves to their own work. <u>This is by no means justified by the so-called economic laws.</u> The entire process of productive work, therefore, must be adapted to the needs of the person and to his way of life, above all to his domestic life, especially in respect to <u>mothers of families</u>, always with due regard for sex and age." (*Gaudium et Spes*, 1965, par.67)

"<u>Is it not here that there appears a radical limitation to economics? Economic activity is necessary and, if it is at the service of man, it can be "a source of brotherhood and a sign of Providence"...Yet it runs the risk of taking up too much strength and freedom. This is why the need is felt to pass from economics to politics.</u> It is true that in the term "politics" many confusions are possible and must be clarified...

...Political power, which is the natural and necessary link for ensuring the cohesion of the social body, must have as its aim the achievement of the common good. While respecting the legitimate liberties of individuals, families and subsidiary groups, it acts in such a way as to create, effectively and for the well-being of all, the conditions required for attaining man's true and complete good, including his spiritual end...It does not, for all [its interventions, while it acts within its limits], deprive individuals and intermediary bodies of the field of activity and responsibility which are proper to them and which lead them to collaborate in the attainment of this common good. In fact, "the true aim of all social activity should be to help individual members of the social body, but never to destroy or absorb them."... Without of course solving every problem, it endeavors to apply solutions to the relationships men have with one another." (*Octogesima Adveniens*, 1971, par.46)

"The break occurred in such a way that labour was separated from capital and set in opposition to it, and capital was set in opposition to labour, as though they were two impersonal forces, two production factors juxtaposed in the same "economistic" perspective. This way of stating the issue contained a fundamental error, what we can call the *error of economism*, that of considering human labour solely according to its economic purpose. This fundamental error of thought can and must be called an *error of materialism*, in that economism directly or indirectly includes a conviction of the primacy and superiority of the material, and directly or indirectly places the spiritual and the personal (man's activity, moral values and such matters) in a position of subordination to material reality. This is still not *theoretical materialism* in the full sense of the term, but it is certainly *practical materialism*..." (*Laborem Exercens*, 1981, par. 13)

"Rational planning and the proper organization of human labour in keeping with individual societies and States should also facilitate the discovery of the right proportions between the different kinds of employment: work on the land, in industry, in the various services, white-collar work and scientific or artistic work, in accordance with the capacities of individuals and for the common good of each society and of the whole of mankind.

… As we view the whole human family throughout the world, we cannot fail to be struck by a disconcerting fact of immense proportions: the fact that, while conspicuous natural resources remain unused, there are huge numbers of people who are unemployed or under-employed and countless multitudes of people suffering from hunger. This is a fact that without any doubt demonstrates that both within the individual political communities and in their relationships on the continental and world level there is something wrong with the organization of work and employment, precisely at the most critical and socially most important points." (*Laborem Exercens*, 1981, par. 18)

"Following the example of my predecessors, I must repeat that whatever affects the dignity of individuals and peoples, such as authentic development, cannot be reduced to a "technical" problem." (*Sollilicitudo Rei Socialis*, 1987, par.41)

"To this must be added the cultural and national dimension: it is not possible to understand man on the basis of economics alone, nor to define him simply on the basis of class membership… Different cultures are basically different ways of facing the question of the meaning of personal existence. When this question is eliminated, the culture and moral life of nations are corrupted." (*Centesimus annus*, 1991, par. 24)

"The economy in fact is only one aspect and one dimension of the whole of human activity. If economic life is absolutized, if the production and consumption of goods become the center of social life and society's only value, not subject to any other value, the reason is to be found not so much in the economic system itself as in the fact that the entire socio-cultural system, by ignoring the ethical and religious dimension, has been weakened, and ends by limiting itself to the production of goods and services alone." (*Centesimus annus*, 1991, par. 39)

"…the primary capital to be safeguarded and valued is man, the human person in his or her integrity…" (*Caritas in Veritatae*, 2009, par.25)

"Economic science tells us that structural insecurity generates anti-productive attitudes wasteful of human resources, inasmuch as workers tend to adapt passively to automatic mechanisms, rather than to release creativity. On this point too, there is a convergence between economic science and moral evaluation. <u>Human costs always include economic costs</u>, and economic dysfunctions always involve human costs." (*Caritas in Veritatae*, 2009, par.32)

"Economic activity cannot solve all social problems through the simple application of *commercial logic*. This needs to be *directed towards the pursuit of the common good*, for which the political community in particular must also take responsibility. Therefore, it must be borne in mind that grave imbalances are produced when economic action, conceived merely as an engine for wealth creation, is detached from political action, conceived as a means for pursuing justice through redistribution.
The Church has always held that economic action is not to be regarded as something opposed to society. In and of itself, the market is not, and must not become, the place where the strong subdue the weak… Admittedly, the market can be a negative force, not because it is so by nature, but because a certain ideology can make it so. <u>It must be remembered that the market does not exist in the pure state.</u> It is shaped by the cultural configurations which define it and give it direction. Economy and finance, as instruments, can be used badly when those at the helm are motivated by purely selfish ends. Instruments that are good in themselves can thereby be transformed into harmful ones. But it is man's darkened reason that produces these consequences, not the instrument *per se*. Therefore it is not the instrument that must be called to account, but individuals, their moral conscience and their personal and social responsibility.
…<u>The economic sphere is neither ethically neutral, nor inherently inhuman and opposed to society. It is part and parcel of human activity and precisely because it is human, it must be structured and governed in an ethical manner.</u>
The great challenge before us, accentuated by the problems of development in this global era and made even more urgent by the economic and financial crisis, is to demonstrate, in thinking and behavior, not only that traditional principles of social ethics like transparency, honesty and responsibility cannot be ignored or attenuated, but also that in *commercial relationships the principle of gratuitousness* and the logic of gift as an expression of fraternity can and must *find their place within normal economic activity*. This is a human demand at the present time, but it is also demanded by economic logic. It is a demand both of charity and of truth.

The Church's social doctrine has always maintained that *justice must be applied to every phase of economic activity*, because this is always concerned with man and his needs. Locating resources, financing, production, consumption and all the other phases in the economic cycle inevitably have moral implications. <u>Thus every economic decision has a moral consequence.</u>" (*Caritas in Veritatae*, 2009, par.36-37)

"Politics and the economy tend to blame each other when it comes to poverty and environmental degradation. It is to be hoped that they can acknowledge their own mistakes... While some are concerned only with financial gain, and others with holding on to or increasing their power, what we are left with are conflicts or spurious agreements where the last thing either party is concerned about is caring for the environment and protecting those who are most vulnerable." (*Laudato Si*, 2015, par 198)

-Labor-

"But [St. Paul's admonition: "If any man will not work neither let him eat."] is in <u>no wise teaches</u> that labor is the sole title to a living or an income." (*Quadragesimo Anno*, 1931, par. 57)

"Every man has, of his very nature, a need to express himself in his work and thereby to perfect his own being." (*Mater et Magistra*, 1961, par.82)

"Just as [Human Activity] proceeds from man, so it is ordered toward man. For when a man works he not only alters things and society, he develops himself as well. He learns much, he cultivates his resources, he goes outside of himself and beyond himself. Rightly understood this kind of growth is of greater value than any external riches which can be garnered. A man is more precious for what he is than for what he has.
... Hence, the norm of human activity is this: that in accord with the divine plan and will, it harmonize with the genuine good of the human race, and that it allow men as individuals and as members of society to pursue their total vocation and fulfill it." (*Gaudium et Spes*, 1965, par. 35)

"Sometimes there exist conditions of life and of work which impede the cultural striving of men and destroy in them the eagerness for culture. This is especially true of farmers and workers. It is necessary to provide for them those working conditions which will not impede their human culture but rather favor it." (*Gaudium et Spes*, 1965, par. 60)

"The concept of work can turn into an exaggerated mystique. Yet, for all that, it is something willed and approved by God.
… Our predecessor John XXIII stressed the urgent need of restoring dignity to the worker and making him a real partner in the common task." (*Populorum Progresso*, 1967, par.27)

"…even in the age of ever more mechanized "work", <u>the proper subject of work continues to be man.</u>" (*Laborem Exercens*, 1981, par. 6)

"…however true it may be that man is destined for work and called to it, in the first place work is "for man" and not man "for work"." (*Laborem Exercens*, 1981, par. 6)

"In the modern period, from the beginning of the industrial age, the Christian truth about work had to oppose the various trends of materialistic and economistic thought.
For certain supporters of such ideas, work was understood and treated as a sort of "merchandise" that the worker-especially the industrial worker-sells to the employer, who at the same time is the possessor of the capital, that is to say, of all the working tools and means that make production possible… Since then, explicit expressions of this sort have almost disappeared, and have given way to more human ways of thinking about work and evaluating it… <u>Nevertheless, the danger of treating work as a special kind of "merchandise", or as an impersonal "force" needed for production (the expression "workforce" is in fact in common use) always exists, especially when the whole way of looking at the question of economics is marked by the premises of materialistic economism.</u>" (*Laborem Exercens*, 1981, par. 7)

"[in materialistic perspectives] there is a confusion or even a reversal of the order laid down from the beginning by the words of the Book of Genesis: man is treated as an instrument of production, whereas he - he alone, independently of the work he does - ought to be treated as the effective subject of work and its true maker and creator." (*Laborem Exercens*, 1981, par. 7)

"And yet, in spite of all this toil-perhaps, in a sense, because of it - work is a good thing for man… because through work man not only transforms nature,

adapting it to his own needs, but he also achieves fulfilment as a human being and indeed, in a sense, becomes "more a human being".
... This fact in no way alters our justifiable anxiety that in work, whereby matter gains in nobility, man himself should not experience a lowering of his own dignity." (*Laborem Exercens*, 1981, par. 9)

"In view of [modern conflicts] we must first of all recall a principle that has always been taught by the Church: <u>*the principle of the priority of labour over capital*</u>... *Capacity for work* - that is to say, for sharing efficiently in the modern production process - demands greater and greater *preparation* and, before all else, proper *training*.... We must emphasize and give prominence to the primacy of man in the production process, <u>*the primacy of man over things*</u>. Everything contained in the concept of capital in the strict sense is only a collection of things.
... In the light of the above truth we see clearly, first of all, that capital cannot be separated from labour... A labour system can be right, in the sense of being in conformity with the very essence of the issue, and in the sense of being intrinsically true and also morally legitimate, if in its very basis it overcomes the opposition between labour and capital through an effort at being shaped in accordance with the principle put forward above: the principle of the substantial and real priority of labour, of the subjectivity of human labour and its effective participation in the whole production process, independently of the nature of the services provided by the worker." (*Laborem Exercens*, 1981, par. 13)

"Thus, the principle of the priority of labour over capital is a postulate of the order of social morality.... Labour is in a sense inseparable from capital; in no way does it accept the [opposition]... But here it must be emphasized, in general terms, that the person who works desires not only due remuneration for his work; he also wishes that, within the production process, provision be made for him to be able to know that in his work, even on something that is owned in common, he is working "for himself". This awareness is extinguished within him in a system of excessive bureaucratic centralization, which makes the worker feel that he is just a cog in a huge machine moved from above, that he is for more reasons than one a mere production instrument rather than a true subject of work with an initiative of his own. The Church's teaching has always expressed the strong and deep conviction that man's work concerns not only the economy but also, and especially, personal values." (*Laborem Exercens*, 1981, par. 15)

"Indeed, the key to reading the Encyclical is the *dignity of the worker* as such, and, for the same reason, the *dignity of work*… Work thus belongs to the vocation of every person; indeed, man expresses and fulfils himself by working." (*Centesimus annus*, 1991, par. 6)

"More than ever, work is work with others and work for others: it is a matter of doing something for someone else. Work becomes ever more fruitful and productive to the extent that people become more knowledgeable of the productive potentialities of the earth and more profoundly cognisant of the needs of those for whom their work is done." (*Centesimus annus*, 1991, par. 31)

"Alienation is found also in work, when it is organized so as to ensure maximum returns and profits with no concern whether the worker, through his own labour, grows or diminishes as a person, either through increased sharing in a genuinely supportive community or through increased isolation in a maze of relationships marked by destructive competitiveness and estrangement, in which he is considered only a means and not an end." (*Centesimus annus*, 1991, par. 41)

"What is meant by the word "decent" in regard to work? It means work that expresses the essential dignity of every man and woman in the context of their particular society: work that is freely chosen, effectively associating workers, both men and women, with the development of their community; work that enables the worker to be respected and free from any form of discrimination; work that makes it possible for families to meet their needs and provide schooling for their children, without the children themselves being forced into labor; work that permits the workers to organize themselves freely, and to make their voices heard; work that leaves enough room for rediscovering one's roots at a personal, familial and spiritual level; work that guarantees those who have retired a decent standard of living." (*Caritas in Veritatae*, 2009, par.63)

-The Market-

"How can it be that it is not a news item when an elderly homeless person dies of exposure, but it is news when the stock market loses two points? This is a case of exclusion." (*Evangelii Gaudium*, 2013, par.53)

-Free Market-

-or-

-*Laissez Faire* Market-

-*See* Consumers *for a better contextual understanding of the Catholic Position on the Free Market (chapter 2.)*

-*See* Liberalism *and* Capitalism *for related references.*

"<u>Wages, as we are told, are regulated by free consent</u>, and therefore the employer, when he pays what was agreed upon, has done his part and seemingly is not called upon to do anything beyond. The only way, it is said, in which injustice might occur would be if the master refused to pay the whole of the wages, or if the workman should not complete the work undertaken; in such cases the public authority should intervene. <u>To this kind of argument a fair-minded man will not easily or entirely assent; it is not complete</u>, for there are important considerations which it leaves out of account altogether… <u>Let the working man and the employer make free agreements, and in particular let them agree freely as to the wages; nevertheless, there underlies a dictate of natural justice more imperious and ancient than any bargain between man and man, namely, that wages ought not to be insufficient to support a frugal and well-behaved wage-earner.</u> If through necessity or fear of a worse evil the workman accept harder conditions because an employer or contractor will afford him no better, he is made the victim of force and injustice. In these and similar questions, … it is advisable that recourse be had to societies or boards such as We shall mention presently, or to some other mode of safeguarding the interests of the wage-earners; the State being appealed to, should circumstances require, for its sanction and protection. (*Rerum Novarum*, 1891, par.43-44)

"For from [the teaching that the economy can be regulated exclusively by free competition], as from a poisoned spring, have originated and spread all the errors of individualist economic teaching. Destroying through forgetfulness or ignorance the social and moral character of economic life, it held that economic life must be considered and treated as altogether free from and independent of public authority, because in the market, i.e., in the free struggle of competitors, it would have a principle of self-direction which governs it much more perfectly

"Human society can be neither well-ordered nor prosperous without the presence of those who, invested with legal authority, preserve its institutions and do all that is necessary to sponsor actively the interests of all its members." (*Pacem in Terris*, 1963, par. 46)

"Hence, a regime which governs solely or mainly by means of threats and intimidation or promises of reward, provides men with no effective incentive to work for the common good. And even if it did, it would certainly be offensive to the dignity of free and rational human beings. Authority is before all else a moral force. For this reason the appeal of rulers should be to the individual conscience, to the duty which every man has of voluntarily contributing to the common good." (*Pacem in Terris*, 1963, par. 48)

"Now if the earth truly was created to provide man with the necessities of life and the tools for his own progress, it follows that every man has the right to glean what he needs from the earth.

... All other rights, whatever they may be, including the rights of property and free trade, are to be subordinated to this principle." (*Populorum Progresso*, 1967, par.22)

"Individual initiative alone and the interplay of competition will not ensure satisfactory development. We cannot proceed to increase the wealth and power of the rich while we entrench the needy in their poverty and add to the woes of the oppressed. Organized programs are necessary for "directing, stimulating, coordinating, supplying and integrating" the work of individuals and intermediary organizations.

It is for the public authorities to establish and lay down the desired goals, the plans to be followed, and the methods to be used in fulfilling them; and it is also their task to stimulate the efforts of those involved in this common activity. Organized programs designed to increase productivity should have but one aim: to serve human nature. They should reduce inequities, eliminate discrimination, free men from the bonds of servitude... When we speak of development, we should mean social progress as well as economic growth.

It is not enough to increase the general fund of wealth and then distribute it more fairly. It is not enough to develop technology so that the earth may become a more suitable living place for human beings. The mistakes of those who led the way should help those now on the road to development to avoid certain dangers. The reign of technology—technocracy, as it is called—can cause as much harm to the world of tomorrow as liberalism did to the world of yesteryear. Economics and technology are meaningless if they do not benefit man, for it is he they are to serve. Man is truly human only if he is the master of his own actions and the judge of their worth, only if he is the architect of his own progress. He must act according to his God-given nature, freely accepting its potentials and its claims upon him."" (*Populorum Progresso*, 1967, par.33-34)

"It is evident that the principle of free trade, by itself, is no longer adequate for regulating international agreements. It certainly can work when both parties are about equal economically; in such cases it stimulates progress and rewards effort. That is why industrially developed nations see an element of justice in this principle.
But the case is quite different when the nations involved are far from equal. Market prices that are freely agreed upon can turn out to be most unfair. It must be avowed openly that, in this case, the fundamental tenet of liberalism (as it is called), as the norm for market dealings, is open to serious question.
The teaching set forth by Our predecessor Leo XIII in Rerum Novarum is still valid today: when two parties are in very unequal positions, their mutual consent alone does not guarantee a fair contract; the rule of free consent remains subservient to the demands of the natural law. In Rerum Novarum this principle was set down with regard to a just wage for the individual worker; but it should be applied with equal force to contracts made between nations: trade relations can no longer be based solely on the principle of free, unchecked competition, for it very often creates an economic dictatorship. Free trade can be called just only when it conforms to the demands of social justice.
As a matter of fact, the highly developed nations have already come to realize this. At times they take appropriate measures to restore balance to their own economy, a balance which is frequently upset by competition when left to itself.
... Now in this matter one standard should hold true for all. What applies to national economies and to highly developed nations must also apply to trade relations between rich and poor nations. Indeed, competition should not be eliminated from trade transactions; but it must be kept within limits so that it operates justly and fairly, and thus becomes a truly human endeavor... In order that international trade be human and moral, social justice requires that it restore to the participants a certain equality of opportunity." (*Populorum Progresso*, 1967, par.58-61)

"Moreover, one must denounce the existence of economic, financial and social mechanisms which, although they are manipulated by people, often function almost automatically, thus accentuating the situation of wealth for some and poverty for the rest. These mechanisms, which are maneuvered directly or indirectly by the more developed countries, by their very functioning favor the interests of the people manipulating them at in the end they suffocate or condition the economies of the less developed countries." (*Sollilicitudo Rei Socialis*, 1987, par.16)

-In context: though "automatic mechanisms" are not dealt with specifically for the rest of the Encyclical, the implication is that all principles of Catholic Social teaching re-enforce why such mechanisms are detrimental to society.

"It would appear that, on the level of individual nations and of international relations, the *free market* is the most efficient instrument for utilizing resources and effectively responding to needs. But this is true only for those needs which are "solvent", insofar as they are endowed with purchasing power, and for those resources which are "marketable", insofar as they are capable of obtaining a satisfactory price. But there are many human needs which find no place on the market. It is a strict duty of justice and truth not to allow fundamental human needs to remain unsatisfied, and not to allow those burdened by such needs to perish. It is also necessary to help these needy people to acquire expertise, to enter the circle of exchange, and to develop their skills in order to make the best use of their capacities and resources. Even prior to the logic of a fair exchange of goods and the forms of justice appropriate to it, there exists *something which is due to man because he is man*, by reason of his lofty dignity. Inseparable from that required "something" is the possibility to survive and, at the same time, to make an active contribution to the common good of humanity." (*Centesimus annus*, 1991, par. 34)

-It is simplistic to think that the "hidden hand of the market" could give each person their due according to their human dignity. Freedom in the Market is a good and necessary thing, and is proper in specific situations, i.e. when all parties involved are solvent and equal; however, when – and it happens quite often – one or more parties involved are comparatively powerless in terms of negotiating, the "Free Market" market in truth becomes something more like a "Market at Gunpoint."

"In a climate of mutual trust, the market is the economic institution that permits encounter between persons, inasmuch as they are economic subjects who make use of contracts to regulate their relations as they exchange goods and services of equivalent value between them, in order to satisfy their needs and desires. The market is subject to the principles of so-called *commutative justice*... <u>In fact, if the market is governed solely by the principle of the equivalence in value of exchanged goods, it cannot produce the social cohesion that it requires in order to function well.</u> *Without internal forms of solidarity and mutual trust, the market cannot completely fulfil its proper economic function.* And today it is this trust which has ceased to exist, and the loss of trust is a grave loss." (*Caritas in Veritatae*, 2009, par.35)

"Perhaps at one time it was conceivable that first the creation of wealth could be entrusted to the economy, and then the task of distributing it could be assigned to politics. Today that would be more difficult, given that economic activity is no longer circumscribed within territorial limits, while the authority of governments continues to be principally local. Hence the canons of justice must be respected from the outset, as the economic process unfolds, and not just afterwards or incidentally. Space also needs to be created within the market for economic activity carried out by subjects who freely choose to act according to principles other than those of pure profit, without sacrificing the production of economic value in the process. The many economic entities that draw their origin from religious and lay initiatives demonstrate that this is concretely possible.
... *Economic life* undoubtedly requires *contracts*, in order to regulate relations of exchange between goods of equivalent value. But it also needs *just laws* and *forms of redistribution* governed by politics, and what is more, it needs works redolent of the *spirit of gift*." (*Caritas in Veritatae*, 2009, par.37)

"While in the past it was possible to argue that justice had to come first and gratuitousness could follow afterwards, as a complement, today it is clear that without gratuitousness, there can be no justice in the first place. What is needed, therefore, is a market that permits the free operation, in conditions of equal opportunity, of enterprises in pursuit of different institutional ends. Alongside profit-oriented private enterprise and the various types of public enterprise, there must be room for commercial entities based on mutualist principles and pursuing social ends to take root and express themselves. It is from their reciprocal encounter in the marketplace that one may expect hybrid forms of commercial behavior to emerge, and hence an attentiveness to ways of *civilizing the economy.*" (*Caritas in Veritatae*, 2009, par.38)

"In this context, some people continue to defend trickle-down theories which assume that economic growth, encouraged by a free market, will inevitably succeed in bringing about greater justice and inclusiveness in the world. This opinion, which has never been confirmed by the facts, expresses a crude and naïve trust in the goodness of those wielding economic power and in the sacralized workings of the prevailing economic system. Meanwhile, the excluded are still waiting." (*Evangelii Gaudium*, 2013, par.54)

-Note that "trickle-down" here does not refer to the policy of relaxing taxes; rather, it refers to the idea that unbridled wealth-accumulation will automatically benefit those whom are secured to create said wealth – usually undeveloped countries or stagnant economic sectors.

"While the earnings of a minority are growing exponentially, so too is the gap separating the majority from the prosperity enjoyed by those happy few. This imbalance is the result of ideologies which defend the absolute autonomy of the marketplace and financial speculation.... A new tyranny is thus born, invisible and often virtual, which unilaterally and relentlessly imposes its own laws and rules." (*Evangelii Gaudium*, 2013, par.56)

"Some circles maintain that current economics and technology will solve all environmental problems, and argue, in popular and non-technical terms, that the problems of global hunger and poverty will be resolved simply by market growth. They are less concerned with certain economic theories which today scarcely anybody dares defend, than with their actual operation in the functioning of the economy. They may not affirm such theories with words, but nonetheless support them with their deeds by showing no interest in more balanced levels of production, a better distribution of wealth, concern for the environment and the rights of future generations. Their behaviour shows that for them maximizing profits is enough. Yet by itself the market cannot guarantee integral human development and social inclusion." (*Laudato Si*, 2015, par 109)

"The culture of relativism is the same disorder which drives one person to take advantage of another, to treat others as mere objects, imposing forced labour on them or enslaving them to pay their debts. The same kind of thinking leads to the sexual exploitation of children and abandonment of the elderly who no longer serve our interests. It is also the mindset of those who say: Let us allow the invisible forces of the market to regulate the economy, and consider their impact on society and nature as collateral damage." (*Laudato Si*, 2015, par 123)

"Here too, it should always be kept in mind that 'environmental protection cannot be assured solely on the basis of financial calculations of costs and benefits. The environment is one of those goods that cannot be adequately safeguarded or promoted by market forces'. [quoting *Compendium of Catholic Social Teaching*] " (*Laudato Si*, 2015, par 190)

"Once more, we need to reject a magical conception of the market, which would suggest that problems can be solved simply by an increase in the profits of companies or individuals. Is it realistic to hope that those who are obsessed with maximizing profits will stop to reflect on the environmental damage which they will leave behind for future generations? Where profits alone count, there can be no thinking about the rhythms of nature, its phases of decay and regeneration, or the complexity of ecosystems which may be gravely upset by human intervention. Moreover, biodiversity is considered at most a deposit of economic resources available for exploitation, with no serious thought for the real value of things, their significance for persons and cultures, or the concerns and needs of the poor.
Whenever these questions are raised, some react by accusing others of irrationally attempting to stand in the way of progress and human development... If we look at the larger picture, we can see that more diversified and innovative forms of production which impact less on the environment can prove very profitable. It is a matter of openness to different possibilities which do not involve stifling human creativity and its ideals of progress, but rather directing that energy along new channels." (*Laudato Si*, 2015, par 190-191)

-Free Consent-

-See Free Market; *see also Phillipians 2:4 in relation to the concept of "Self Interest."*

"Jesus reminded us that we have God as our common Father and that this makes us brothers and sisters. Fraternal love can only be gratuitous; it can never be a means of repaying others for what they have done or will do for us. That is why it is possible to love our enemies." (*Laudato Si*, 2015, par 228)

-"Self-interest" may often seem to have the same appearance as "love," but it is but a mere shadow of it. Love does not calculate; therefore, we can love our enemies and all humans even when there is truly no calculable benefit to us. Philosophies which teach that self-interest should be the motivating force of society crush human nature into a one-dimensional materialistic animal. Self-interest is important and has its place, but when it becomes the master rather than the servant, it destroys by treating what is infinitely valuable as valuable only to a calculated measure.

-Contracts-

"In all agreements between masters and work people there is always the condition expressed or understood that there should be allowed proper rest for soul and body. <u>To agree in any other sense would be against what is right and just</u>; for it can never be just or right to require on the one side, or to promise on the other, the giving up of those duties which a man owes to his God and to himself." (*Rerum Novarum*, 1891, par.42)

-In context: this includes <u>all</u> duties or claims, including support of family, etc. A man cannot in good conscience enter a contract that will not allow him to provide for himself and his family, for instance — -nor, as an employer, can one pressure another into doing so. <u>There is a law above mere economics</u>.

"First of all, those who declare that a contract of hiring and being hired is unjust of its own nature, and hence a partnership-contract must take its place, are certainly in error and gravely misrepresent [Pope Leo XIII]... We consider it more advisable, however, in the present condition of human society that, so far as is possible, the work-contract be somewhat modified by a partnership-contract, as is already being done in various ways and with no small advantage to workers and owners." (*Quadragesimo Anno*, 1931, par 64)

"It was said [at the time of the Industrial Revolution] that the State does not have the power to intervene in the terms of these contracts, except to ensure the fulfilment of what had been explicitly agreed upon. This concept of relations between employers and employees, purely pragmatic and inspired by a thorough-going individualism, is severely censured in the [*Rerum Novarum*] as contrary to the twofold nature of work as a personal and necessary reality." (*Centesimus annus*, 1991, par. 8)

-Production-

"Justice is to be observed not only in the distribution of wealth, but also in regard to the conditions in which men are engaged in producing this wealth. ...<u>Consequently, if the whole structure and organization of an economic system is such as to compromise human dignity, to lessen a man's sense of responsibility or rob him of opportunity for exercising personal initiative, then</u>

such a system, We maintain, is altogether unjust—no matter how much wealth it produces, or how justly and equitably such wealth is distributed." (*Mater et Magistra*, 1961, par.74)

"Neither individuals nor nations should regard the possession of more and more goods as the ultimate objective. Every kind of progress is a two-edged sword. It is necessary if man is to grow as a human being; yet it can also enslave him, if he comes to regard it as the supreme good and cannot look beyond it. When this happens, men harden their hearts, shut out others from their minds and gather together solely for reasons of self-interest rather than out of friendship…
Thus the exclusive pursuit of material possessions prevents man's growth as a human being and stands in opposition to his true grandeur. Avarice, in individuals and in nations, is the most obvious form of stultified moral development." (*Populorum Progresso*, 1967, par.19)

"Christ's question is directed to nations also: "What does it profit a man, if he gain the whole world but suffer the loss of his own soul?" (*Populorum Progresso*, 1967, par.40)

"We must repeat that the superfluous goods of wealthier nations ought to be placed at the disposal of poorer nations… Continuing avarice on their part will arouse the judgment of God and the wrath of the poor, with consequences no one can foresee." (*Populorum Progresso*, 1967, par.49)

"Environmental impact assessment should not come after the drawing up of a business proposition or the proposal of a particular policy, plan or programme. It should be part of the process from the beginning, and be carried out in a way which is interdisciplinary, transparent and free of all economic or political pressure." (*Laudato Si*, 2015, par 183)

"Production is not always rational, and is usually tied to economic variables which assign to products a value that does not necessarily correspond to their real worth. This frequently leads to an overproduction of some commodities, with unnecessary impact on the environment and with negative results on regional economies." (*Laudato Si*, 2015, par 189)

-Obligations of Workers to Employers-

"Of these duties, the following bind the proletarian and the worker: fully and faithfully to perform the work which has been freely and equitably agreed upon; never to injure the property, nor to outrage the person of an employer; never to resort to violence in defending their own cause, nor to engage in riot or disorder; and to have nothing to do with men of evil principles, who work upon the people with artful promises of great results, and excite foolish hopes which usually end in useless regrets and grievous loss." (*Rerum Novarum*, 1891, par.20)

"All this serves to create an environment in which workers are encouraged to assume greater responsibility in their own sphere of employment." (*Mater et Magistra*, 1961, par.96)

-Strikes-

See Obligations of Workers to Employers *or* Unions & Non-Government Organizations.

-Obligations of Employers to Workers-

"The following duties bind the wealthy owner and the employer: not to look upon their work people as their bondsmen, but to respect in every man his dignity as a person ennobled by Christian character. They are reminded that, according to natural reason and Christian philosophy, working for gain is creditable, not shameful, to a man, since it enables him to earn an honorable livelihood; but to misuse men as though they were things in the pursuit of gain, or to value them solely for their physical powers - that is truly shameful and inhuman. Again justice demands that, in dealing with the working man, religion and the good of his soul must be kept in mind. Hence, the employer is bound to see that the worker has time for his religious duties; that he be not exposed to corrupting influences and dangerous occasions; and that he be not led away to neglect his home and family, or to squander his earnings. Furthermore, the employer must never tax his work people beyond their strength, or employ them in work unsuited to their sex and age. His great and principal duty is to give every one what is just. Doubtless, before deciding whether wages are fair, many things have to be considered; but wealthy owners and all masters of labor should be mindful of this - that to exercise pressure upon the indigent and the destitute for the sake of gain, and to gather one's profit out of the need of another, is condemned by all laws, human and divine. To defraud any one of wages that are his due is a great crime which cries to the avenging anger of Heaven. "Behold, the hire of the laborers... which by fraud has been kept back by you, crieth; and the cry of them hath entered into the ears of the Lord of Sabaoth."(6) Lastly, the rich must religiously refrain from cutting down the workmen's earnings, whether by force, by fraud, or by usurious dealing; and with all the greater reason because the laboring man is, as a rule, weak and unprotected, and because his slender means should in proportion to their scantiness be accounted sacred. Were these precepts carefully obeyed and followed out, would they not be sufficient of themselves to keep under all strife and all its causes?" (*Rerum Novarum*, 1891, par.20)

"[today] a greater technical skill is required of the workers, and more exacting professional qualifications. Which means that they must be given more assistance, and more free time in which to complete their vocational training as well as to carry out more fittingly their cultural, moral and religious education." (*Mater et Magistra*, 1961, par.94)

"The responsibility of the indirect employer [i.e. those who direct the whole orientation of labor policy] differs from that of the direct employer-the term itself indicates that the responsibility is less direct-but it remains a true responsibility: the indirect employer substantially determines one or other facet of the labour relationship, thus conditioning the conduct of the direct employer when the latter determines in concrete terms the actual work contract and labour relations.
… they must also give attention to organizing that work in a correct and rational way. In the final analysis this overall concern weighs on the shoulders of the State, but it cannot mean one-sided centralization by the public authorities. Instead, what is in question is a just and rational coordination, within the framework of which the initiative of individuals, free groups and local work centres and complexes must be safeguarded, keeping in mind what has been said above with regard to the subject character of human labour." (*Laborem Exercens*, 1981, par. 17-18)

"Besides wages, various social benefits intended to ensure the life and health of workers and their families play a part here. The expenses involved in health care, especially in the case of accidents at work, demand that medical assistance should be easily available for workers, and that as far as possible it should be cheap or even free of charge. Another sector regarding benefits is the sector associated with the right to rest. In the first place this involves a regular weekly rest comprising at least Sunday, and also a longer period of rest, namely the holiday or vacation taken once a year or possibly in several shorter periods during the year. A third sector concerns the right to a pension and to insurance for old age and in case of accidents at work. Within the sphere of these principal rights, there develops a whole system of particular rights which, together with remuneration for work, determine the correct relationship between worker and employer. Among these rights there should never be overlooked the right to a working environment and to manufacturing processes which are not harmful to the workers' physical health or to their moral integrity." *(Laborem Exercens,* 1981, par. 19)

-Wages & Profit-

"Now, were we to consider labor merely in so far as it is personal, doubtless it would be within the workman's right to accept any rate of wages whatsoever; for in the same way as he is free to work or not, so is he free to accept a small wage or even none at all. But our conclusion must be very different if, together with the personal element in a man's work, we consider the fact that work is also necessary for him to live: these two aspects of his work are separable in thought, but not in reality. The preservation of life is the bounden duty of one and all, and to be wanting therein is a crime. It necessarily follows that each one has a natural right to procure what is required in order to live, and the poor can procure that in no other way than by what they can earn through their work." (*Rerum Novarum,* 1891, par.44)

-*See Free Market* for related references.

"The just amount of pay, however, must be calculated not on a single basis but on several... By this statement he plainly condemned the shallowness of those who think that this most difficult matter is easily solved by the application of a single rule or measure - and one quite false.
For they are greatly in error who do not hesitate to spread the principle that labor is worth and must be paid as much as its products are worth, and that consequently the one who hires out his labor has the right to demand all that is produced through his labor." (*Quadragesimo Anno,* 1931, par 66-68)

"<u>In the first place, the worker must be paid a wage sufficient to support him and his family.</u> That the rest of the family should also contribute to the common support, according to the capacity of each... can be observed [in family farms or businesses]. But to abuse the years of childhood and the limited strength of women is grossly wrong. <u>Mothers, concentrating on household duties, should work primarily in the home or in its immediate vicinity.</u> It is an intolerable abuse, and to be abolished at all cost, for mothers on account of the father's low wage to be forced to engage in gainful occupations outside the home to the neglect of their proper cares and duties, especially the training of children. Every effort must therefore be made that fathers of families receive a wage large enough to meet ordinary family needs adequately. But if this cannot always be done under existing circumstances, social justice demands that changes be introduced as soon as possible whereby such a wage will be assured to every adult workingman...

In determining the amount of the wage, the condition of a business and of the one carrying it on must also be taken into account; for it would be unjust to demand excessive wages which a business cannot stand without its ruin and consequent calamity to the workers. If, however, a business makes too little money, because of lack of energy or lack of initiative or because of indifference to technical and economic progress, that must not be regarded a just reason for reducing the compensation of the workers. But if the business in question is not making enough money to pay the workers an equitable wage because it is being crushed by unjust burdens or forced to sell its product at less than a just price, those who are thus the cause of the injury are guilty of grave wrong, for they deprive workers of their just wage and force them under the pinch of necessity to accept a wage less than fair... If, however, matters come to an extreme crisis, it must be finally considered whether the business can continue or the workers are to be cared for in some other way. In such a situation, certainly most serious, a feeling of close relationship and a Christian concord of minds ought to prevail and function effectively among employers and workers...

Lastly, the amount of the pay must be adjusted to the public economic good... For everyone knows that an excessive lowering of wages, or their increase beyond due measure, causes unemployment... Hence it is contrary to social justice when, for the sake of personal gain and without regard for the common good, wages and salaries are excessively <u>lowered or raised</u>; and this same social justice demands that wages and salaries be so managed, through agreement of plans and wills, in so far as can be done, as to offer to the greatest possible number the opportunity of getting work and obtaining suitable means of livelihood." (*Quadragesimo Anno*, 1931, par 71-74)

-In context: Pope Pius XI's follows this by noting that these precepts are essential for proper distribution of property. Hence the accurate meaning of "distribution of property." See Proportional Ownership *for related references.*

"In the majority of cases a man's work is his sole means of livelihood. <u>Its remuneration, therefore, cannot be made to depend on the state of the market.</u> It must be determined by the laws of justice and equity. Any other procedure would be a clear violation of justice, even supposing the contract of work to have been freely entered into by both parties.
…It is furthermore the duty of the State to ensure that terms of employment are regulated in accordance with justice and equity, and to safeguard the human dignity of workers by making sure that they are not required to work in an environment which may prove harmful to their material and spiritual interests." (*Mater et Magistra*, 1961, par.18-21)

"In some parts of the world men are being subjected to inhuman privations so that the output of the national economy can be increased at a rate of acceleration beyond what would be possible if regard were had to social justice and equity. And in other countries a notable percentage of income is absorbed in building up an ill-conceived national prestige, and vast sums are spent on armaments.
In economically developed countries, relatively unimportant services, and services of doubtful value, frequently carry a disproportionately high rate of remuneration, while the diligent and profitable work of whole classes of honest, hard-working men gets scant reward.
We therefore consider it Our duty to reaffirm that the remuneration of work is not something that can be left to the laws of the marketplace; nor should it be a decision left to the will of the more powerful. It must be determined in accordance with justice and equity; which means that workers must be paid a wage which allows them to live a truly human life and to fulfill their family obligations in a worthy manner. Other factors too enter into the assessment of a just wage: namely, the effective contribution which each individual makes to the economic effort, the financial state of the company for which he works, the requirements of the general good of the particular country—having regard especially to the repercussions on the overall employment of the working force

in the country as a whole—and finally the requirements of the common good of the universal family of nations of every kind, both large and small.
The above principles are valid always and everywhere. So much is clear. But their degree of applicability to concrete cases cannot be determined without reference to the quantity and quality of available resources; and these can—and in fact do—vary from country to country, and even, from time to time, within the same country." (*Mater et Magistra*, 1961, par.69-72)

"What are these demands [of the Common Good]? On the national level they include: employment of the greatest possible number of workers; care lest privileged classes arise, even among the workers; maintenance of equilibrium between wages and prices; the need to make goods and services accessible to the greatest number; elimination, or at least the restriction, of inequalities in the various branches of the economy—that is, between agriculture, industry and services; creation of a proper balance between economic expansion and the development of social services… the best possible adjustment of the means of production to the progress of science and technology; seeing to it that the benefits which make possible a more human way of life will be available not merely to the present generation but to the coming generations as well.
… The demands of the common good on the international level include: the avoidance of all forms of unfair competition between the economies of different countries; the fostering of mutual collaboration…
…[all of the above] must also be borne in mind when assessing the rate of return due as compensation to the company's management, and as interest or dividends to investors." (*Mater et Magistra*, 1961, par.79-81)

"Moreover, in recent years, as we have seen, the productive efficiency of many national economies has been increasing rapidly. Justice and fairness demand, therefore, that, within the limits of the common good, wages too shall increase." (*Mater et Magistra*, 1961, par.112)

"In economic enterprises it is persons who are joined together, that is, free and independent human beings created to the image of God. Therefore, with attention to the functions of each—owners or employers, management or labor—and without doing harm to the necessary unity of management, the active sharing of all in the administration and profits of these enterprises in ways to be properly determined is to be promoted." (*Gaudium et Spes*, 1965, par.68)

"In the context of the present there is no more important way for securing a just relationship between the worker and the employer than that constituted by remuneration for work... Hence, in every case, a just wage is the concrete means of verifying the justice of the whole socioeconomic system and, in any case, of checking that it is functioning justly. It is not the only means of checking, but it is a particularly important one and, in a sense, the key means. <u>This means of checking concerns above all the family... Such remuneration can be given either through what is called a family wage - that is, a single salary given to the head of the family for his work, sufficient for the needs of the family</u> without the other spouse having to take up gainful employment outside the home - or through other social measures such as family allowances or grants to mothers devoting themselves exclusively to their families. <u>These grants should correspond to the actual needs</u>, that is, to the number of dependents for as long as they are not in a position to assume proper responsibility for their own lives." (*Laborem Exercens*, 1981, par. 19)

"A workman's wages should be sufficient to enable him to support himself, his wife and his children. 'If through necessity or fear of a worse evil the workman accepts harder conditions because an employer or contractor will afford no better, he is made the victim of force and injustice'.
<u>Would that these words, written at a time when what has been called "unbridled capitalism" was pressing forward, should not have to be repeated today with the same severity.</u> Unfortunately, even today one finds instances of contracts between employers and employees which lack reference to the most elementary justice regarding the employment of children or women, working hours, the hygienic condition of the work-place and fair pay..." (*Centesimus annus*, 1991, par. 8)

"Furthermore, society and the State must ensure wage levels adequate for the maintenance of the worker and his family, including a <u>certain amount for savings</u>... The role of trade unions in negotiating minimum salaries and working conditions is decisive in this area." (*Centesimus annus*, 1991, par. 15)

"<u>The Church acknowledges the legitimate role of profit as an indication that a business is functioning well...</u>" (*Centesimus annus*, 1991, par. 35)

-See Capitalism *for related references. In short, profit is one of several important indicators that a business is functioning well and contributing to the common good – but it is not the only, or even primary, indicator. Such a stance would be a materialist perversion of the idea of business and the dignity of the person. Profit must ensue, not merely be pursued.*

"We recognize, therefore, that the Church had good reason to be concerned about the capacity of a purely technological society to set realistic goals and to make good use of the instruments at its disposal. Profit is useful if it serves as a means towards an end that provides a sense both of how to produce it and how to make good use of it. Once profit becomes the exclusive goal, if it is produced by improper means and without the common good as its ultimate end, it risks destroying wealth and creating poverty." (*Caritas in Veritatae*, 2009, par.21)

"…it would appear that the traditionally valid distinction between profit-based companies and non-profit organizations can no longer do full justice to reality, or offer practical direction for the future. In recent decades a broad intermediate area has emerged between the two types of enterprise… This is not merely a matter of a "third sector", but of a broad new composite reality embracing the private and public spheres, one which does not exclude profit, but instead considers it a means for achieving human and social ends. Whether such companies distribute dividends or not, whether their juridical structure corresponds to one or other of the established forms, becomes secondary in relation to their willingness to view profit as a means of achieving the goal of a more humane market and society…. *The very plurality of institutional forms of business gives rise to a market which is not only more civilized but also more competitive.*" (*Caritas in Veritatae*, 2009, par.46)

"When nature is viewed solely as a source of profit and gain, this has serious consequences for society. (*Laudato Si*, 2015, par 82)

"This does not mean being opposed to any technological innovations which can bring about an improvement in the quality of life. But it does mean that profit cannot be the sole criterion to be taken into account, and that, when significant new information comes to light, a reassessment should be made, with the involvement of all interested parties. The outcome may be a decision not to proceed with a given project, to modify it or to consider alternative proposals." (*Laudato Si*, 2015, par 187)

"The principle of the maximization of profits, frequently isolated from other considerations, reflects a misunderstanding of the very concept of the economy.

As long as production is increased, little concern is given to whether it is at the cost of future resources or the health of the environment; as long as the clearing of a forest increases production, no one calculates the losses entailed in the desertification of the land, the harm done to biodiversity or the increased pollution. In a word, businesses profit by calculating and paying only a fraction of the costs involved."

-Workplace-

"[of] things external and material, the first thing of all to secure is to save unfortunate working people from the cruelty of men of greed, who use human beings as mere instruments for money-making. It is neither just nor human so to grind men down with excessive labor as to stupefy their minds and wear out their bodies… Daily labor, therefore, should be so regulated as not to be protracted over longer hours than strength admits… work which is quite suitable for a strong man cannot rightly be required from a woman or a child… Women, again, are not suited for certain occupations; a woman is by nature fitted for home-work, and it is that which is best adapted at once to preserve her modesty and to promote the good bringing up of children and the well-being of the family. As a general principle it may be laid down that a workman ought to have leisure and rest proportionate to the wear and tear of his strength, for waste of strength must be repaired by cessation from hard work." (*Rerum Novarum*, 1891, par.42)

-In context: the judgment must be made given each particular case, but erring on the side of the workmen.

"The conditions in which a man works form a necessary corollary to these rights. They must not be such as to weaken his physical or moral fibre…" (*Pacem in Terris*, 1963, par.19)

"[Rerum Novarum] affirms just as clearly the right to the "limitation of working hours", the right to legitimate rest and the right of children and women to be treated differently with regard to the type and duration of work." (*Centesimus annus*, 1991, par. 7)

-Rest & Sunday Worship-

"The working man, too, has interests in which he should be protected by the State ... To consent to any treatment which is calculated to defeat the end and purpose of his being is beyond his right; he cannot give up his soul to servitude, for it is not man's own rights which are here in question, but the rights of God, the most sacred and inviolable of rights... From this follows the obligation of the cessation from work and labor on Sundays and certain holy days." (*Rerum Novarum*, 1891, par.40-41)

"To safeguard man's dignity as a creature of God endowed with a soul in the image and likeness of God, the Church has always demanded a diligent observance of the third Commandment: "Remember that thou keep holy the sabbath day." God certainly has the right and power to command man to devote one day a week to his duty of worshipping the eternal Majesty.
...Thus, religion and moral and physical well-being are one in demanding this periodic rest, and for many centuries now the Church has set aside Sunday as a special day of rest for the faithful, on which they participate in the Holy Sacrifice of the Mass, the memorial and application of Christ's redemptive work for souls.
Heavy in heart, We cannot but deplore the growing tendency in certain quarters to disregard this sacred law, if not to reject it outright. This attitude must inevitably impair the bodily and spiritual health of the workers, whose welfare We have so much at heart." (*Mater et Magistra*, 1961, par.249-252)

"[In regards to religious freedom] one may ask whether existing laws and the practice of industrialized societies effectively ensure in our own day the exercise of this basic right to Sunday rest." ." (*Centesimus annus*, 1991, par. 9)

"Sunday is the day of the Resurrection, the "first day" of the new creation, whose first fruits are the Lord's risen humanity, the pledge of the final transfiguration of all created reality. It also proclaims "man's eternal rest in God"... Rest opens our eyes to the larger picture and gives us renewed sensitivity to the rights of others. And so the day of rest, centred on the Eucharist, sheds it light on the whole week, and motivates us to greater concern for nature and the poor." (*Laudato Si*, 2015, par 237)

-Unemployment-

"[When we consider Worker's rights] we must first direct our attention to a *fundamental issue*: the question of finding work, or, in other words, <u>the issue of suitable employment for all who are capable of it</u>... The role of the agents included under the title of indirect employer [i.e. those who direct economic policy] is to act against unemployment, which in all cases is an evil, and which, when it reaches a certain level, can become a real social disaster. It is particularly painful when it especially affects young people, who after appropriate cultural, technical and professional preparation fail to find work, and see their sincere wish to work and their readiness to take on their own responsibility for the economic and social development of the community sadly frustrated." (*Laborem Exercens*, 1981, par. 18)

"Being out of work or dependent on public or private assistance for a prolonged period undermines the freedom and creativity of the person and his family and social relationships, causing great psychological and spiritual suffering." (*Caritas in Veritatae*, 2009, par.25)

"Business is a vocation, and a noble vocation, provided that those engaged in it see themselves challenged by a greater meaning in life; this will enable them truly to serve the common good by striving to increase the goods of this world and to make them more accessible to all.
... I am far from proposing an irresponsible populism, but the economy can no longer turn to remedies that are a new poison, <u>such as attempting to increase profits by reducing the work force and thereby adding to the ranks of the excluded.</u>" (*Evangelii Gaudium*, 2013, par.203-204)

-Unions & Non-Government Organizations-

"The most important of all are workingmen's unions... History attests what excellent results were brought about by the artificers' guilds of olden times." (*Rerum Novarum*, 1891, par.49)

-In context: Unions, like all other non-governmental societies, are an important expression in response to modern challenges. At the time of Leo XIII, they, above others, were of pre-eminent importance.

"In [evidently bad, unlawful, or dangerous] cases, public authority may justly forbid the formation of such associations, and may dissolve them if they already exist. But every precaution should be taken not to violate the rights of individuals and not to impose unreasonable regulations under pretense of public benefit.." (*Rerum Novarum*, 1891, par.52)

"For, to enter into a "society" of this kind is the natural right of man…" (*Rerum Novarum*, 1891, par.57)

"To sum up, then, We may lay it down as a general and lasting law that working men's associations should be so organized and governed … for helping each individual member to better his condition to the utmost in body, soul, and property." (*Rerum Novarum*, 1891, par.57)

"[Many men who have given up their religion] feel in most cases that they have been fooled by empty promises and deceived by false pretexts. They cannot but perceive that their grasping employers too often treat them with great inhumanity and hardly care for them outside the profit their labor brings; and if they belong to any union, it is probably one in which there exists, instead of charity and love, that intestine strife which ever accompanies poverty when unresigned and unsustained by religion… To such as these Catholic associations are of incalculable service, by helping them out of their difficulties…" (*Rerum Novarum*, 1891, par.61)

"For under nature's guidance it comes to pass that just as those who are joined together by nearness of habitation establish towns, so those who follow the same industry or profession - whether in the economic or other field - form guilds or associations, so that many are wont to consider these self-governing organizations, if not essential, at least natural to civil society." (*Quadragesimo Anno*, 1931, par 83)

"Moreover, We consider it altogether vital that the numerous intermediary bodies and corporate enterprises—which are, so to say, the main vehicle of this social growth—be really autonomous, and loyally collaborate in pursuit of their own specific interests and those of the common good." (*Mater et Magistra*, 1961, par.65)

-*See* Principle of Subsidiarity *for related references*

"Among the basic rights of the human person is to be numbered the right of freely founding unions for working people. These should be able truly to represent them and to contribute to the organizing of economic life in the right way. Included is the right of freely taking part in the activity of these unions without risk of reprisal.

... When, however, socio-economic disputes arise, efforts must be made to come to a peaceful settlement. Although recourse must always be had first to a sincere dialogue between the parties, a strike, nevertheless, can remain even in present-day circumstances a necessary, though ultimate, aid for the defense of the workers' own rights and the fulfillment of their just desires. As soon as possible, however, ways should be sought to resume negotiation and the discussion of reconciliation." (*Gaudium et Spes*, 1965, par.68)

"Every form of social action involves some doctrine; and the Christian rejects that which is based on a materialistic and atheistic philosophy, namely one which shows no respect for a religious outlook on life, for freedom or human dignity. So long as these higher values are preserved intact, however, the existence of a variety of professional organizations and trade unions is permissible. Variety may even help to preserve freedom and create friendly rivalry." (*Populorum Progresso*, 1967, par.39)

"The important role of union organizations must be admitted... Their activity, however, is not without its difficulties. Here and there the temptation can arise of profiting from a position of force to impose, particularly by strikes - the right to which as a final means of defense remains certainly recognized - conditions which are too burdensome for the overall economy and for the social body, or to desire to obtain in this way demands of a directly political nature." (*Octogesima Adveniens*, 1971, par.14)

"All these rights, together with the need for the workers themselves to secure them, give rise to yet another right: the right of association, that is to form associations for the purpose of defending the vital interests of those employed in the various professions. These associations are called labour or trade unions." (*Laborem Exercens*, 1981, par. 20)

"[Unions] are indeed a *mouthpiece for the struggle for social justice*, for the just rights of working people in accordance with their individual professions. However, this struggle should be seen as a normal endeavor "for" the just good: in the present case, for the good which corresponds to the needs and merits of working people associated by profession; but it is *not* a *struggle "against"* others. Even if in controversial questions the struggle takes on a character of opposition towards others, this is because it aims at the good of social justice, not for the sake of "struggle" or in order to eliminate the opponent. It is characteristic of work that it first and foremost unites people.

... Just efforts to secure the rights of workers who are united by the same profession should always take into account the limitations imposed by the general economic situation of the country. Union demands cannot be turned into a kind of *group* or *class "egoism"*....

... In this sense, union activity undoubtedly enters the field of *politics*, understood as *prudent concern for the common good.* However, the role of unions is not to "play politics" in the sense that the expression is commonly understood today. Unions do not have the character of political parties struggling for power; they should not be subjected to the decision of political parties or have too close links with them. In fact, in such a situation they easily lose contact with their specific role, which is to secure the just rights of workers within the framework of the common good of the whole of society; instead they become *an instrument used for other purposes.*

... The activity of union organizations opens up many possibilities in this respect, including their efforts to *instruct and educate* the workers and to *foster their self-education.*

... *One method* used by unions in pursuing the just rights of their members is the strike or work stoppage, as a kind of ultimatum to the competent bodies, especially the employers. This method is recognized by Catholic social teaching as legitimate in the proper conditions and within just limits. ... It must not be abused; it must not be abused especially for "political" purposes." (*Laborem Exercens*, 1981, par. 20)

"Here we find the reason for the Church's defense and approval of the establishment of what are commonly called trade unions: certainly not because of ideological prejudices or in order to surrender to a class mentality, but because the right of association is a natural right of the human being, which therefore precedes his or her incorporation into political society." (*Centesimus annus*, 1991, par. 7)

"[Labor Unions] - which have always been encouraged and supported by the Church - should be open to the new perspectives that are emerging in the world of work. Looking to wider concerns than the specific category of labor for which they were formed, union organizations are called to address some of the new questions arising in our society: I am thinking, for example, of the complex of issues that social scientists describe in terms of a conflict between worker and consumer. Without necessarily endorsing the thesis that the central focus on the worker has given way to a central focus on the consumer, this would still appear to constitute new ground for unions to explore creatively. The global context in which work takes place also demands that national labour unions, which tend to limit themselves to defending the interests of their registered members, should turn their attention to those outside their membership, and in particular to workers in developing countries where social rights are often violated." (*Caritas in Veritatae*, 2009, par.64)

-Liberalism-

-Once again, "Liberalism," despite being loosely used to identify with a given political current today in the U.S., simply means (even today, though few realize it) the <u>Philosophy of the Enlightenment</u>, which puts individual choice above all else (i.e. John Locke) as the social contract, where each pursued his own interest. The goal of society is not virtue, but material production; ergo, government is a necessary evil. Following the post-reformation wars associated with religion, Liberals sought to create as society structured purely on non-religious elements (i.e. economics) – God was recognized only as present in one's personal, private belief. This is a radical departure from Christian thought, which has always taught that the goal of society is virtue (hence, proper government is essentially a good thing) and that some recognition of God and right religion <u>must</u> be central to the public sphere. Cf. John 19:11. Liberalism's historical prodigy, in regards to economics and social thought, is Capitalism and especially Liberal Capitalism (a.k.a. "Manchester Liberals," or Libertarianism).

"And while the principles of Liberalism were tottering, which had long prevented effective action by those governing the State, the Encyclical [*Rerum Novarum*] in truth impelled peoples themselves to promote a social policy on truer grounds and with greater intensity…" (*Quadragesimo Anno*, 1931, par. 27)

"The introduction of industrialization, which is necessary for economic growth and human progress, is both a sign of development and a spur to it." (*Populorum Progresso*, 1967, par.25)

"These concepts present profit as the chief spur to economic progress, free competition as the guiding norm of economics, and private ownership of the means of production as an absolute right, having no limits nor concomitant social obligations…

This unbridled liberalism paves the way for a particular type of tyranny, rightly condemned by Our predecessor Pius XI, for it results in the "international imperialism of money."

Such improper manipulations of economic forces can never be condemned enough; let it be said once again that economics is supposed to be in the service of man.

But if it is true that a type of capitalism, as it is commonly called, has given rise to hardships, unjust practices, and fratricidal conflicts that persist to this day, it would be a mistake to attribute these evils to the rise of industrialization itself, for they really derive from the pernicious economic concepts that grew up along with it. We must in all fairness acknowledge the vital role played by labor systemization and industrial organization in the task of development." (*Populorum Progresso*, 1967, par.26)

"Then, the conviction that the economy must be autonomous, that it must be shielded from "influences" of a moral character, has led man to abuse the economic process in a thoroughly destructive way." (*Caritas in Veritatae*, 2009, par.34)

"Today everything comes under the laws of competition and the survival of the fittest, where the powerful feed upon the powerless.
… Human beings are themselves considered consumer goods to be used and then discarded. We have created a "throw away" culture which is now spreading." (*Evangelii Gaudium*, 2013, par.53)

-Capitalism-

See Prelude for an overview of Capitalism. In brief, Capitalism is the economic offshoot of Liberalism, which proposes that individual (i.e. private) efforts towards production and profit should be, to a greater or lesser degree, unrestricted, because maximum production is the objective of a society - hence the name "Free Market." Accordingly, society's relationships are assessed on the basis of economics, and God is only recognized pertaining to private individual preference. Capitalism is so named because the all-out efficiency that Capitalism seeks *requires a system which aggressively separates Capital from Labor, historically popularized as "division of labor" (which refers <u>both</u> to the labor process as well as Capital and Labor).*

"There remains to Us, after again calling to judgment the economic system now in force [in context "Capitalism"] and its most bitter accuser, Socialism, and passing explicit and just sentence upon them, to search out more thoroughly the root of these many evils and to point out that the first and most necessary remedy is a reform of morals.
Important indeed have the changes been which both the economic system [i.e. "Capitalism"] and Socialism have undergone since Leo XIII's time.
…With all his energy Leo XIII sought to adjust this economic system according to the norms of right order; hence, it is evident that this system is not to be condemned in itself. <u>And surely it is not of its own nature vicious. But it does violate right order when capital hires workers, that is, the non-owning working class, with a view to and under such terms that it directs business and even the whole economic system according to its own will and advantage, scorning the human dignity of the workers, the social character of economic activity and social justice itself, and the common good.</u>
… the "capitalist" economic regime has spread everywhere to such a degree… that it has invaded and pervaded the economic and social life of even those outside its orbit and is unquestionably impressing on it its advantages, disadvantages and vices, and, in a sense, is giving it its own shape and form.
…. In the first place, it is obvious that not only is wealth concentrated in our times but an immense power and despotic economic dictatorship is consolidated in the hands of a few, who often are not owners but only the trustees and managing directors of invested funds which they administer according to their own arbitrary will and pleasure."
… <u>This dictatorship is being most forcibly exercised by those who, since they hold the money and completely control it, control credit also and rule the lending of money. Hence they regulate the flow, so to speak, of the life-blood whereby the entire economic system lives, and have so firmly in their grasp the soul, as it were, of economic life that no one can breathe against their will.</u>
This concentration of power and might, the characteristic mark, as it were, of contemporary economic life, is the fruit that the unlimited freedom of struggle among competitors has of its own nature produced, and which lets only the strongest survive; and this is often the same as saying, those who fight the most violently, those who give least heed to their conscience.

This accumulation of might and of power generates in turn three kinds of conflict. First, there is the struggle for economic supremacy itself; then there is the bitter fight to gain supremacy over the State in order to use in economic struggles its resources and authority; finally there is conflict between States themselves, not only because countries employ their power and shape their policies to promote every economic advantage of their citizens, but also because they seek to decide political controversies that arise among nations through the use of their economic supremacy and strength.

The ultimate consequences of the individualist spirit in economic life are those which you yourselves, Venerable Brethren and Beloved Children, see and deplore: <u>Free competition has destroyed itself</u>; economic dictatorship has supplanted the free market; unbridled ambition for power has likewise succeeded greed for gain; all economic life has become tragically hard, inexorable, and cruel. To these are to be added the grave evils that have resulted from an intermingling and shameful confusion of the functions and duties of public authority with those of the economic sphere - such as, one of the worst, the virtual degradation of the majesty of the State, which although it ought to sit on high like a queen and supreme arbitress, free from all partiality and intent upon the one common good and justice, is become a slave, surrendered and delivered to the passions and greed of men. And as to international relations, two different streams have issued from the one fountain-head: On the one hand, economic nationalism or even economic imperialism; on the other, a no less deadly and accursed internationalism of finance or international imperialism whose country is where profit is." (*Quadragesimo Anno*, 1931, par 101-109)

-Unlike Socialism, it is more difficult to pin down "core" tenants of Capitalism — such as emphasizing individual property rights and holding production as the measure of success — because there is a broad spectrum of "Capitalism," ranging from traditional Capitalism to those who think it means being "not Socialist." Ergo, it is unclear what a universal condemnation or endorsement of "Capitalism" would be. Rather, "Capitalism" tends to refer to popular characteristics (i.e. the "Industrial Age" etc.) There are, however, assumptions or elements that appear, however quietly, in Capitalistic ideologies that are always condemned: proposing that economics is amoral or separable from God, unregulated "Free Market" where inequality is imbalanced, Individualist ideology, massive concentrations of wealth and power, utilization of the State for private economic interests (which is historically prevalent wherever Capitalism thrives), the excessive separation of ownership and Capital (hence the name "Capitalist"), etc. "Capitalism", inasmuch as it could be thought of as the division of labor and free trade amongst equal parties (yet regulated, for proper regulations do not inhibit, but

promote freedom – see Freedom), *is a very healthy thing. Industrialization, private enterprise, etc. are good and necessary things. One must always keep in mind the context of reality, over the ideological theories, however – the primacy of reality over ideas. For example, a truly "Free Market" may seem wonderful in theory when hypothetical numbers are calculated, but given fallen man, and "gunpoint" economics (i.e. strong parties leveraging "free choice" to exert their will over the weak), it behooves us to remember that man's needs are more than economic – mere number crunching cannot evaluate true progress. All empirical sciences are tempted with a myopic confusion of "can" with "ought," and economics is no exception.*

"The call to solidarity and common action addressed to the workers-especially to those engaged in narrowly specialized, monotonous and depersonalized work in industrial plants, when the machine tends to dominate man - was important and eloquent from the point of view of social ethics. It was the reaction against the degradation of man as the subject of work, and against the unheard-of accompanying exploitation in the field of wages, working conditions and social security for the worker.

… it must be frankly recognized that the reaction against the system of injustice and harm that cried to heaven for vengeance and that weighed heavily upon workers in that period of rapid industrialization was justified from the point of view of social morality. This state of affairs was favored by the liberal socio-political system, which, in accordance with its "economistic" premises, strengthened and safeguarded economic initiative by the possessors of capital alone, but did not pay sufficient attention to the rights of the workers, on the grounds that human work is solely an instrument of production, and that capital is the basis, efficient factor and purpose of production." (Laborem Exercens, 1981, par. 8)

"…*the antinomy* in which *labour was separated from capital and set up in opposition to it*…did not originate merely in the philosophy and economic theories of the eighteenth century; rather it originated in the whole of the *economic and social practice* of that time, the time of the birth and rapid development of industrialization, in which what was mainly seen was the possibility of vastly increasing material wealth, means, while the end, that is to say, man, who should be served by the means, was ignored. It was this practical error that *struck a blow* first and foremost against human labour, against *the working man*, and caused the ethically just social reaction already spoken of above. The same error, which is now part of history, and which was connected with the period of primitive capitalism and liberalism, can nevertheless be repeated in other circumstances of time and place, if people's thinking starts from the same theoretical or practical premises." (*Laborem Exercens*, 1981, par. 13)

"In the present document, which has human work as its main theme, it is right to confirm all the effort with which the Church's teaching has striven and continues to strive always to ensure the priority of work and, thereby, man's character as a subject in social life and, especially, in the dynamic structure of the whole economic process. <u>From this point of view the position of "rigid" capitalism continues to remain unacceptable, namely the position that defends the exclusive right to private ownership of the means of production as an untouchable "dogma" of economic life.</u>" (*Laborem Exercens*, 1981, par. 14)

"Another kind of response, practical in nature, is represented by the affluent society or the consumer society. <u>It seeks to defeat Marxism on the level of pure materialism by showing how a free-market society can achieve a greater satisfaction of material human needs than Communism, while equally excluding spiritual values. In reality, while on the one hand it is true that this social model shows the failure of Marxism to contribute to a humane and better society, on the other hand, insofar as it denies an autonomous existence and value to morality, law, culture and religion, it agrees with Marxism, in the sense that it totally reduces man to the sphere of economics and the satisfaction of material needs.</u>" (*Centesimus annus*, 1991, par. 19)

"In this sense, it is right to speak of a struggle against an economic system, if the latter is understood as a method of upholding the absolute predominance of capital, the possession of the means of production and of the land, in contrast to the free and personal nature of human work. In the struggle against such a system, what is being proposed as an alternative is not the socialist system, which in fact turns out to be State capitalism, but rather a society of free work, of enterprise and of participation. Such a society is not directed against the market, but demands that the market be appropriately controlled by the forces of society and by the State, so as to guarantee that the basic needs of the whole of society are satisfied.
The Church acknowledges the legitimate *role of profit* as an indication that a business is functioning well. When a firm makes a profit, this means that productive factors have been properly employed and corresponding human needs have been duly satisfied. But profitability is not the only indicator of a firm's condition. It is possible for the financial accounts to be in order, and yet

for the people — who make up the firm's most valuable asset — to be humiliated and their dignity offended. Besides being morally inadmissible, this will eventually have negative repercussions on the firm's economic efficiency. In fact, the purpose of a business firm is not simply to make a profit, but is to be found in its very existence as a *community of persons* who in various ways are endeavouring to satisfy their basic needs, and who form a particular group at the service of the whole of society. <u>Profit is a regulator of the life of a business, but it is not the only one;</u> *other human and moral factors* <u>must also be considered which, in the long term, are at least equally important for the life of a business."</u> (*Centesimus annus*, 1991, par. 35)

-Socialism-

See Prelude for an overview of Socialism. In brief, historically Socialism is a reaction against Liberal Capitalism, which denies the fundamental right to personal property. The State, or some synonymously powerful body, becomes arbiter of all property. Like Capitalism, Socialism also accepts the basic tenant of Liberalism that the objective of society is the maximum production of goods, and accordingly, that economics is the benchmark for social relationships.

"Socialists, therefore, by endeavoring to transfer the possessions of individuals to the community at large, strike at the interests of every wage-earner, since they would deprive him of the liberty of disposing of his wages…" (*Rerum Novarum*, 1891, par.5)

"<u>Hence, it is clear that the main tenet of socialism, community of goods, must be utterly rejected…</u>" (*Rerum Novarum*, 1891, par.15)

-an interesting note: the early Christian community did live in community and shared their goods (Acts 2:44) but not in repudiation of the right to private property; rather, it was freely shared much like a Monastic community is today.

"[In the context of evolving Socialism since Leo XIII] The other section [of Socialists], which has kept the name Socialism, is surely more moderate. It not only professes the rejection of violence but modifies and tempers to some degree, if it does not reject entirely, the class struggle and the abolition of private ownership. <u>One might say that, terrified by its own principles and by the conclusions drawn therefrom by Communism, Socialism inclines toward and in a certain measure approaches the truths which Christian tradition has always</u>

held sacred; for it cannot be denied that its demands at times come very near those that Christian reformers of society justly insist upon.

For if the class struggle abstains from enmities and mutual hatred, it gradually changes into an honest discussion of difference… and if this is not that blessed social peace which we all seek, it can and ought to be the point of departure from which to move forward… So also the war declared on private ownership, more and more abated, is being so restricted that now, finally, not the possession itself of the means of production is attacked but rather a kind of sovereignty over society which ownership has, contrary to all right, seized and usurped. For such sovereignty belongs in reality not to owners but to the public authority. If the foregoing happens, it can come even to the point that imperceptibly these ideas of the more moderate socialism will no longer differ from the desires and demands of those who are striving to remold human society on the basis of Christian principles.

… Such just demands and desire have nothing in them now which is inconsistent with Christian truth, and much less are they special to Socialism. Those who work solely toward such ends have, therefore, no reason to become socialists.

Yet let no one think that all the socialist groups or factions that are not communist have, without exception, recovered their senses to this extent either in fact or in name. For the most part they do not reject the class struggle or the abolition of ownership, but only in some degree modify them. Now…[the question] is raised without warrant by some, whether the principles of Christian truth cannot perhaps be also modified to some degree and be tempered so as to meet Socialism half-way and, as it were, by a middle course, come to agreement with it. There are some allured by the foolish hope that socialists in this way will be drawn to us. A vain hope! Those who want to be apostles among socialists ought to profess Christian truth whole and entire, openly and sincerely, and not connive at error in any way.

… We make this pronouncement: Whether considered as a doctrine, or an historical fact, or a movement, Socialism, if it remains truly Socialism, even after it has yielded to truth and justice on the points which we have mentioned, cannot be reconciled with the teachings of the Catholic Church because its concept of society itself is utterly foreign to Christian truth." (*Quadragesimo Anno*, 1931, par 112-117)

-In other words, if Socialists no longer hold class warfare, if they rescind Liberalism, and if they allow private property while holding that it is not ultimate, but is still answerable to the

common good – *these ideas are in line with Christian teaching. Therefore, they have no need to call themselves "Socialists." However, Socialism by definition repudiates the right to personal property. Catholic teaching, being the mediator, and not the creator, of Truth, cannot compromise.*

"Socialism, on the other hand, wholly ignoring and indifferent to this sublime end of both man and society, affirms that human association has been instituted for the sake of <u>material advantage alone.</u>

...If Socialism, like all errors, contains some truth (which, moreover, the Supreme Pontiffs have never denied), it is based nevertheless on a theory of human society peculiar to itself and irreconcilable with true Christianity. <u>Religious socialism, Christian socialism, are contradictory terms; no one can be at the same time a good Catholic and a true socialist.</u>" (*Quadragesimo Anno*, 1931, par 118-120)

"<u>Pope Pius XI… and made it clear that no Catholic could subscribe even to moderate Socialism.</u>" (*Mater et Magistra*, 1961, par.34)

"…but [the Government] may also carry [its duties] out badly by claiming for itself a *monopoly of the administration and* disposal of the means of production… merely converting the means of production into State property in the collectivist system is by no means equivalent to "socializing" that property." (*Laborem Exercens*, 1981, par. 14)

-In other words, "Socialism" is merely a concentration of private ownership in the hands of the central authority.

"Socialism likewise maintains that the good of the individual can be realized without reference to his free choice, to the unique and exclusive responsibility which he exercises in the face of good or evil. Man is thus reduced to a series of social relationships, and the concept of the person as the autonomous subject of moral decision disappears, the very subject whose decisions build the social order. From this mistaken conception of the person there arise both a distortion of law, which defines the sphere of the exercise of freedom, and an opposition to private property. A person who is deprived of something he can call "his own", and of the possibility of earning a living through his own initiative, comes to depend on the social machine and on those who control it. This makes it much more difficult for him to recognize his dignity as a person, and hinders progress towards the building up of an authentic human community." (*Centesimus annus*, 1991, par. 13)

"In the recent past, the sincere desire to be on the side of the oppressed and not to be cut off from the course of history has led many believers to seek in various ways an impossible compromise between Marxism and Christianity. Moving beyond all that was short-lived in these attempts, present circumstances are leading to a reaffirmation of the positive value of an authentic theology of integral human liberation." (*Centesimus annus*, 1991, par. 26)

-Communism & Marxism-

See Prelude for an introduction to Communism and Socialism. Communism is merely a brand of socialism which implements itself via violent uprising and class warfare.

"…We, therefore, deem it superfluous to warn upright and faithful children of the Church regarding the impious and iniquitous character of Communism…" (*Quadragesimo Anno*, 1931, par 112)

"Marxism thus ends up by affirming that only in a collective society can alienation be eliminated. However, the historical experience of socialist countries has sadly demonstrated that collectivism does not do away with alienation but rather increases it, adding to it a lack of basic necessities and economic inefficiency." (*Centesimus annus*, 1991, par. 41)

"Part of Marxist strategy is the theory of impoverishment: in a situation of unjust power, it is claimed, anyone who engages in charitable initiatives is actually serving that unjust system, making it appear at least to some extent tolerable. This in turn slows down a potential revolution and thus blocks the struggle for a better world. Seen in this way, charity is rejected and attacked as a means of preserving the status quo. What we have here, though, is really an inhuman philosophy. People of the present are sacrificed to the *moloch* of the future—a future whose effective realization is at best doubtful. One does not make the world more human by refusing to act humanely here and now." (*Deus Caritas Est*, 2005, par.31)

-Capitalism v. Socialism-

"Property, that is, "capital," has undoubtedly long been able to appropriate too much to itself. Whatever was produced, whatever returns accrued, capital claimed for itself, hardly leaving to the worker enough to restore and renew his strength. For the doctrine was preached that all accumulation of capital falls by an absolutely insuperable economic law to the rich, and that by the same law the workers are given over and bound to perpetual want, to the scantiest of livelihoods. It is true, indeed, that things have not always and everywhere corresponded with this sort of teaching of the so-called Manchesterian Liberals; yet it cannot be denied that economic social institutions have moved steadily in that direction. That these false ideas, these erroneous suppositions, have been vigorously assailed, and not by those alone who through them were being deprived of their innate right to obtain better conditions, will surprise no one. And therefore, to the harassed workers there have come "intellectuals," as they are called, setting up in opposition to a fictitious law the equally fictitious moral principle that all products and profits, save only enough to repair and renew capital, belong by very right to the workers. This error, much more specious than that of certain of the Socialists who hold that whatever serves to produce goods ought to be transferred to the State, or, as they say "socialized," is consequently all the more dangerous and the more apt to deceive the unwary. It is an alluring poison which many have eagerly drunk whom open Socialism had not been able to deceive.
Unquestionably, so as not to close against themselves the road to justice and peace through these false tenets, both parties ought to have been forewarned by the wise words of [Pope Leo XIII].." (*Quadragesimo Anno*, 1931, par 54-56)

-In Context: Pope Pius XI is describing the two opposing ideologies, both of which are harmful to society: first, "Manchesterian Liberals" i.e. Liberal Capitalists, which trace their intellectual lineage from Adam Smith's Wealth of Nations *(above hinted to as "the doctrine"); then Socialists, who are a reaction to them. See* Capitalism *and* Socialism *for further references.*

"Just as the unity of human society cannot be founded on an opposition of classes, so also the right ordering of economic life cannot be left to a free competition of forces." (*Quadragesimo Anno*, 1931, par 88)

"Because of the fact that goods are produced more efficiently by a suitable division of labor than by the scattered efforts of individuals, socialists infer that economic activity, only the material ends of which enter into their thinking, ought of necessity to be carried on socially. Because of this necessity, they hold that men are obliged, with respect to the producing of goods, to surrender and subject themselves entirely to society. Indeed, possession of the greatest possible supply of things that serve the advantages of this life is considered of such great importance that the higher goods of man, liberty not excepted, must take a secondary place and even be sacrificed to the demands of the most efficient production of goods." (*Quadragesimo Anno*, 1931, par 119)

-Socialists, then, as well as traditional "Capitalists", accept the <u>same</u> underlying principles, namely, that the goal of society is primarily the material production of as many goods as possible – referenced by the Popes as a materialistic goal of society. The best system, according to this assumption, is whichever can produce more. This is a danger not only to human society, but to nature, and thus the environment as well – i.e. how we relate to the world around us. Note that some make a distinction between "the market" and "society," as if human beings could bifurcate between the two: this dualistic portrayal of humanity is unrealistic at best, as if humans could flip a switch from "Human" and suddenly become a schizophrenic "Market Man." This dualistic view is condemned by the Popes, who insist that the subject of the economy is <u>man</u>, and that purchasing is not merely economic – it is a moral choice.

"<u>Unrestricted competition in the Liberal sense, and the Marxist creed of class warfare; are clearly contrary to Christian teaching and the nature of man.</u>" (*Mater et Magistra*, 1961, par.23)

-It is necessary to remember that Capitalism is, historically, the first child of Liberalism. See the introduction for a brief overview of Liberalism.

"Therefore the Christian who wishes to live his faith in a political activity which he thinks of as service cannot without contradicting himself adhere to ideological systems which radically or substantially go against his faith and his concept of man. He cannot adhere to the Marxist ideology, to its atheistic materialism... at the same time denying all transcendence to man and his personal and collective history; nor can be adhere to the liberal ideology which believes it exalts individual freedom by withdrawing it from every limitation, by stimulating it through exclusive seeking of interest and power, and by considering social solidarities as more or less automatic consequences of individual initiatives, not as an aim and a major criterion of the value of the social organization." (*Octogesima Adveniens*, 1971, par.26)

"Some Christians are today attracted by socialist currents and their various developments…Too often Christians attracted by socialism tend to idealize it in terms which, apart from anything else, are very general: a will for justice, solidarity and equality. They refuse to recognize the limitations of the historical socialist movements, which remain conditioned by the ideologies from which they originated.
…While, through the concrete existing form of Marxism, one can distinguish these various aspects and the questions they pose for the reflection and activity of Christians, it would be illusory and dangerous to reach a point of forgetting the intimate link which radically binds them together, to accept the elements of Marxist analysis without recognizing their relationships with ideology, and to enter into the practice of class struggle and its Marxist interpretations, while failing to note the kind of totalitarian and violent society to which this process leads.
On another side, we are witnessing a renewal of the liberal ideology. This current asserts itself both in the name of <u>economic efficiency</u>, and for the defense of the individual against the increasingly overwhelming hold of organizations, and as a reaction against the totalitarian tendencies of political powers. Certainly, personal initiative must be maintained and developed. But do not Christians who take this path tend to idealize liberalism in their turn, making it a proclamation in favor of freedom? They would like a new model, more adapted to present-day conditions, while easily forgetting that at the very root of philosophical liberalism is an erroneous affirmation of the autonomy of the individual in his activity, his motivation and the exercise of his liberty. Hence, the liberal ideology likewise calls for careful discernment on their part. In this renewed encounter of the various ideologies, the <u>Christian will draw from the sources of his faith and the Church's teaching the necessary principles and suitable criteria to avoid permitting himself to be first attracted by and then imprisoned within a system whose limitations and totalitarianism may well become evident to him too late, if he does nor perceive them in their roots.</u>" (*Octogesima Adveniens*, 1971, par.31-36)

"Everybody knows that capitalism has a definite historical meaning as a system, an economic and social system, opposed to "socialism" or "communism"… it should be recognized that the error of early capitalism can be repeated wherever man is in a way treated on the same level as the whole complex of the material means of production, as an instrument and not in accordance with the true dignity of his work-that is to say, where he is not treated as subject and maker, and for this very reason as the true purpose of the whole process of production." (*Laborem Exercens*, 1981, par. 7)

"[The Church's Official Teachings of] *the issue of ownership or property*... as it was then stated and as it is still taught by the Church, *diverges* radically from the programme of *collectivism* as proclaimed by Marxism and put into practice in various countries [after *Rerum Novarum*]. At the same time it differs from the programme of *capitalism* practiced by liberalism and by the political systems inspired by it. In the latter case, the difference consists in the way the right to ownership or property is understood. Christian tradition has never upheld this right as absolute and untouchable. On the contrary, it has always understood this right within the broader context of the right common to all to use the goods of the whole of creation: *the right to private property is subordinated to the right to common use*, to the fact that goods are meant for everyone." (*Laborem Exercens*, 1981, par. 14)

"If at this point we examine the reasons for this serious delay in the process of development... our attention is especially drawn to the political causes of today's situation.
... In the West there exists a system which is historically inspired by the principles of the liberal capitalism which developed with industrialization during the last century. In the East there exists a system inspired by the Marxist collectivism which sprang from an interpretation of the condition of the proletarian classes made in the light of a particular reading of history.
... It was inevitable that by developing antagonistic systems and centers of power, each with its own forms of propaganda and indoctrination... give rise to two blocs of armed forces... [which to some extent continues]
... This happens with particularly negative effects in the international relations which concern the developing countries.
... This is one of the reasons why the Church's social doctrine adopts a critical attitude towards both liberal capitalism and Marxist collectivism.
... Each of the two blocs harbors in its own way a tendency towards imperialism, as it is usually called, or towards forms of new - colonialism: an easy temptation to which they frequently succumb, as history, including recent history, teaches." (*Sollilicitudo Rei Socialis*, 1987, par.20-22)

"The Church's social doctrine is not a "third way" between liberal capitalism and Marxist collectivism, nor even a possible alternative to other solutions less radically opposed to one another: rather, it constitutes a category of its own. Nor is it an ideology, but rather the accurate formulation of the results of a careful reflection on the complex realities of human existence, in society and in the international order, in the light of faith and of the Church's tradition. Its main aim is to interpret these realities, determining their conformity with or divergence from the lines of the Gospel teaching on man and his vocation, a vocation which is at once earthly and transcendent; its aim is thus to guide Christian behavior. It therefore belongs to the field, not of ideology, but of theology and particularly of moral theology." (*Sollilicitudo Rei Socialis*, 1987, par.41)

"The Church is well aware that in the course of history conflicts of interest between different social groups inevitably arise, and that in the face of such conflicts Christians must often take a position, honestly and decisively. … However, what is condemned in class struggle is the idea that conflict is not restrained by ethical or juridical considerations, or by respect for the dignity of others (and consequently of oneself); a reasonable compromise is thus excluded, and what is pursued is not the general good of society, but a partisan interest which replaces the common good and sets out to destroy whatever stands in its way." (*Centesimus annus*, 1991, par.14)

"We have seen that it is unacceptable to say that the defeat of so-called "Real Socialism" leaves capitalism as the only model of economic organization. It is necessary to break down the barriers and monopolies which leave so many countries on the margins of development, and to provide all individuals and nations with the basic conditions which will enable them to share in development." (*Centesimus annus*, 1991, par. 35)

"Returning now to the initial question: can it perhaps be said that, after the failure of Communism, capitalism is the victorious social system, and that capitalism should be the goal of the countries now making efforts to rebuild their economy and society?
…The answer is obviously complex. If by "capitalism" is meant an economic system which recognizes the fundamental and positive role of business, the market, private property and the resulting responsibility for the means of

production, as well as free human creativity in the economic sector, then the answer is certainly in the affirmative, even though it would perhaps be more appropriate to speak of a "business economy", "market economy" or simply "free economy". But if by "capitalism" is meant a system in which freedom in the economic sector is not circumscribed within a strong juridical framework which places it at the service of human freedom in its totality, and which sees it as a particular aspect of that freedom, the core of which is ethical and religious, then the reply is certainly negative.

The collapse of the Communist system in so many countries certainly removes an obstacle to facing these problems in an appropriate and realistic way, but it is not enough to bring about their solution. Indeed, there is a risk that a radical capitalistic ideology could spread which refuses even to consider these problems, in the *a priori* belief that any attempt to solve them is doomed to failure, and which blindly entrusts their solution to the free development of market forces.

The Church has no models to present; models that are real and truly effective can only arise within the framework of different historical situations, through the efforts of all those who responsibly confront concrete problems in all their social, economic, political and cultural aspects, as these interact with one another. For such a task the Church offers her social teaching as an *indispensable and ideal orientation*, a teaching which, as already mentioned, recognizes the positive value of the market and of enterprise, but which at the same time points out that these need to be oriented towards the common good."
(*Centesimus annus*, 1991, par. 42)

-Reform-

"The root and font of this defection in economic and social life from the Christian law, …are the disordered passions of the soul, the sad result of original sin which has so destroyed the wonderful harmony of man's faculties that, easily led astray by his evil desires, he is strongly incited to prefer the passing goods of this world to the lasting goods of Heaven.

… Strict and watchful moral restraint enforced vigorously by governmental authority could have banished these enormous evils and even forestalled them; this restraint, however, has too often been sadly lacking.

… Thus it came to pass that many, much more than ever before, were solely concerned with increasing their wealth by any means whatsoever, and that in seeking their own selfish interests before everything else they had no conscience about committing even the gravest of crimes against others. Those first entering upon this broad way that leads to destruction easily found numerous imitators of their iniquity by the example of their manifest success, by their insolent display of wealth, by their ridiculing the conscience of others, who, as they said, were troubled by silly scruples, or lastly by crushing more conscientious competitors.

…No genuine cure can be furnished for this lamentable ruin of souls… unless men return openly and sincerely to the teaching of the Gospel, to the precepts of Him Who alone has the words of everlasting life, words which will never pass away, even if Heaven and earth will pass away. All experts in social problems are seeking eagerly a structure so fashioned in accordance with the norms of reason that it can lead economic life back to sound and right order. But this order, which We Ourselves ardently long for and with all Our efforts promote, will be wholly defective and incomplete unless all the activities of men harmoniously unite to imitate and attain, in so far as it lies within human strength, …that perfect order which the Church with great force and power preaches and which right human reason itself demands, that all things be directed to God as the first and supreme end of all created activity, and that all created good under God be considered as mere instruments to be used only in so far as they conduce to the attainment of the supreme end." (*Quadragesimo Anno*, 1931, par 132)

-Foreign Markets-

"Even in recent years it was thought that the poorest countries would develop by isolating themselves from the world market and by depending only on their own resources. Recent experience has shown that countries which did this have suffered stagnation and recession, while the countries which experienced development were those which succeeded in taking part in the general interrelated economic activities at the international level. <u>It seems therefore that the chief problem is that of gaining fair access to the international market, based not on the unilateral principle of the exploitation of the natural resources of these countries but on the proper use of human resources.</u>" (*Centesimus annus*, 1991, par. 33)

-Investments & Investing-

"Expending larger incomes so that opportunity for gainful work may be abundant, provided, however, that this work is applied to producing <u>really useful goods</u>, ought to be considered… an outstanding exemplification of the virtue of munificence and one particularly suited to the needs of the times." (*Quadragesimo Anno*, 1931, par 51)

-There is a temptation when discussing jobs to merely create meaningless jobs merely for the sake of employment, especially in the context of government jobs. This is of little benefit to society and ultimately is injurious to the dignity of the employed - see Unemployment *or* Proportional Ownership.

"Investments, for their part, must be directed toward procuring employment and sufficient income for the people both now and in the future. Whoever makes decisions concerning these investments and the planning of the economy—whether they be individuals or groups of public authorities—are bound to keep these objectives in mind and to recognize their serious obligation of watching, on the one hand, that provision be made for the necessities required for a decent life both of individuals and of the whole community and, on the other, of looking out for the future and of establishing a right balance between the needs of present-day consumption, both individual and collective, and the demands of investing for the generation to come. They should also always bear in mind the urgent needs of underdeveloped countries or regions. <u>In monetary matters they should beware of hurting the welfare of their own country or of other countries.</u> Care should also be taken lest the economically weak countries unjustly suffer any loss from a change in the value of money." (*Gaudium et Spes*, 1965, par.70)

"<u>I am referring to the fact that even the decision to invest in one place rather than another, in one productive sector rather than another, is always *a moral and cultural choice*.</u>" (*Centesimus annus*, 1991, par. 36)

-In context: Investing is <u>specifically</u> mentioned.

"Ownership of the means of production, whether in industry or agriculture, is just and legitimate if it serves useful work. <u>It becomes illegitimate, however, when it is not utilized or when it serves to impede the work of others, in an</u>

effort to gain a profit which is not the result of the overall expansion of work and the wealth of society, but rather is the result of curbing them or of illicit exploitation, speculation or the breaking of solidarity among working people. Ownership of this kind has no justification, and represents an abuse in the sight of God and man." (*Centesimus annus*, 1991, par. 43)

-Often, even companies that make good profit contribute no real or constructive value to society as a whole – many of these exist. The companies, by operating flimsy or even harmful business models, or, especially, "skimming" transactions, do make a profit, but are damaging society. These would be an example of the abuse mentioned above.
Especially in our "make money at all costs" world, this is a relative and much-needed (and, often ignored or ridiculed) voice. Again: products or services that generate money, but provide no real value, or even seek to prey on society by exploiting superficial "needs", are an abuse of property. An owner or investor should honestly ask: Does this <u>truly</u> contribute to society, or just generate profit?

"John Paul II taught that *investment always has moral, as well as economic significance.* All this — it should be stressed — is still valid today, despite the fact that the capital market has been significantly liberalized, and modern technological thinking can suggest that investment is merely a technical act, not a human and ethical one. There is no reason to deny that a certain amount of capital can do good, if invested abroad rather than at home. Yet the requirements of justice must be safeguarded, with due consideration for the way in which the capital was generated and the harm to individuals that will result if it is not used where it was produced. What should be avoided is a speculative *use of financial resources* that yields to the temptation of seeking only short-term profit, without regard for the long-term sustainability of the enterprise, its benefit to the real economy and attention to the advancement, in suitable and appropriate ways, of further economic initiatives in countries in need of development. It is true that the export of investments and skills can benefit the populations of the receiving country. Labour and technical knowledge are a universal good. Yet it is not right to export these things merely for the sake of obtaining advantageous conditions, or worse, for purposes of exploitation, without making a real contribution to local society by helping to bring about a robust productive and social system, an essential factor for stable development." (*Caritas in Veritatae*, 2009, par.40)

"One cause of this situation is found in our relationship with money, since we calmly accept its dominion over ourselves and our societies. The current financial crisis can make us overlook the fact that it originated in a profound human crisis: the denial of the primacy of the human person! We have created new idols. The worship of the ancient golden calf (cf. Ex 32:1-35) has returned in a new and ruthless guise in the idolatry of money and the dictatorship of an impersonal economy lacking a truly human purpose." (*Evangelii Gaudium*, 2013, par.55)

"<u>Money must serve, not rule!</u>" (*Evangelii Gaudium*, 2013, par.58)

"…economic powers continue to justify the current global system where priority tends to be given to speculation and the pursuit of financial gain, which fail to take the context into account, let alone the effects on human dignity and the natural environment. Here we see how environmental deterioration and human and ethical degradation are closely linked." (*Laudato Si*, 2015, par 56)

"The economy accepts every advance in technology with a view to profit, without concern for its potentially negative impact on human beings. Finance overwhelms the real economy. The lessons of the global financial crisis have not been assimilated, and we are learning all too slowly the lessons of environmental deterioration." (*Laudato Si*, 2015, par 109)

-Finance-

"<u>*Finance, therefore*</u> — through the renewed structures and operating methods that have to be designed after its misuse, which wreaked such havoc on the real economy — <u>now needs to go back to being an</u> *<u>instrument directed towards improved wealth creation and development</u>*… It is certainly useful, and in some circumstances imperative, to launch financial initiatives in which the humanitarian dimension predominates. However, this must not obscure the fact that the entire financial system has to be aimed at sustaining true development. Above all, the intention to do good must not be considered incompatible with the effective capacity to produce goods. <u>Financiers must rediscover the genuinely ethical foundation of their activity, so as not to abuse the sophisticated instruments which can serve to betray the interests of savers.</u> Right intention, transparency, and the search for positive results are mutually compatible and must never be detached from one another. If love is wise, it can find ways of working in accordance with provident and just expediency, as is illustrated in a significant way by much of the experience of credit unions.

Both the regulation of the financial sector, so as to safeguard weaker parties and discourage scandalous speculation, and experimentation with new forms of finance, designed to support development projects, are positive experiences that should be further explored and encouraged, *highlighting the responsibility of the investor*. Furthermore, the *experience of micro-finance* [i.e. services to low-income populations]... should be strengthened and fine-tuned... The weakest members of society should be helped to defend themselves against usury, just as poor peoples should be helped to derive real benefit from micro-credit, in order to discourage the exploitation that is possible in these two areas." (*Caritas in Veritatae*, 2009, par.65)

"Politics must not be subject to the economy, nor should the economy be subject to the dictates of an efficiency-driven paradigm of technocracy. Today... there is urgent need for politics and economics to enter into a frank dialogue in the service of life, especially human life. Saving banks at any cost, making the public pay the price, foregoing a firm commitment to reviewing and reforming the entire system, only reaffirms the absolute power of a financial system, a power which has no future and will only give rise to new crises after a slow, costly and only apparent recovery." (*Laudato Si*, 2015, par 189)

-Small Businesses & Co-operatives-

"The small and average sized undertakings in agriculture, in the arts and crafts, in commerce and industry, should be safeguarded and fostered. Moreover, they should join together in co-operative associations to gain for themselves the benefits and advantages that usually can be gained only from large organizations.
... Furthermore, these two categories of citizens—craftsmen and members of cooperatives—are fully entitled to these watchful measures of the State" (*Mater et Magistra*, 1961, par.84)

-Outsourcing-

"...there are some countries where there is an imbalance between the amount of arable land and the number of inhabitants; others where there is an imbalance between the richness of the resources and the instruments of agriculture available. It is imperative, therefore, that nations enter into collaboration with each other, and facilitate the circulation of goods, capital and manpower.
We advocate in such cases the policy of bringing the work to the workers, wherever possible, rather than bringing workers to the scene of the work. In

this way many people will be afforded an opportunity of increasing their resources without being exposed to the painful necessity of uprooting themselves from their own homes, settling in a strange environment, and forming new social contacts." (*Pacem in Terris*, 1963, par.101-102)

-This is not to be taken by any means as a justification for "comparative" abuse of workers of poorer countries – i.e. "compared to formerly, this treatment is less evil" etc. In other words, if a powerful, wealthy company enters a developing area, they still have a duty to treat their employees as human beings – not merely "better off than they were before" as a standard, which is essentially meaningless. See Obligations of Employers to Workers *for related references.*

"The global market has stimulated first and foremost, on the part of rich countries, a search for areas in which to outsource production at low cost with a view to reducing the prices of many goods, increasing purchasing power and thus accelerating the rate of development in terms of greater availability of consumer goods for the domestic market. Consequently, the market has prompted new forms of competition between States as they seek to attract foreign businesses to set up production centres, by means of a variety of instruments, including favourable fiscal regimes and deregulation of the labour market. These processes have led to a *downsizing of social security systems* as the price to be paid for seeking greater competitive advantage in the global market, with consequent grave danger for the rights of workers, for fundamental human rights and for the solidarity associated with the traditional forms of the social State." (*Caritas in Veritatae*, 2009, par.25)

"Without doubt, one of the greatest risks for businesses is that they are almost exclusively answerable to their investors, thereby limiting their social value… Moreover, the so-called outsourcing of production can weaken the company's sense of responsibility towards the stakeholders — namely the workers, the suppliers, the consumers, the natural environment and broader society — in favor of the shareholders, who are not tied to a specific geographical area and who therefore enjoy extraordinary mobility. Today's international capital market offers great freedom of action. Yet there is also increasing awareness of the need for greater social responsibility on the part of business." (*Caritas in Veritatae*, 2009, par.40)

-Tariffs-

"It is significant that some of the causes of this situation were identified in *Populorum Progressio*, such as the high tariffs imposed by economically developed countries, which still make it difficult for the products of poor countries to gain a foothold in the markets of rich countries." (*Caritas in Veritatae*, 2009, par.33)

-Monopolies-

"… the hiring of labor and the conduct of trade are concentrated in the hands of comparatively few; so that a small number of very rich men have been able to lay upon the teeming masses of the laboring poor a yoke little better than that of slavery itself." (*Rerum Novarum*, 1891, par.3)

"Now, there is a good deal of evidence in favor of the opinion that many of these societies are in the hands of secret leaders, and are managed on principles ill - according with Christianity and the public well-being; and that they do their utmost to get within their grasp the whole field of labor, and force working men either to join them or to starve." (*Rerum Novarum*, 1891, par.54)

"Such a system of mutual dependence is in itself normal. However, it can easily become an occasion for various forms of exploitation or injustice and as a result influence the labour policy of individual States; and finally it can influence the individual worker, who is the proper subject of labour. For instance the highly industrialized countries, and even more the businesses that direct on a large scale the means of industrial production (the companies referred to as multinational or transnational), fix the highest possible prices for their products, while trying at the same time to fix the lowest possible prices for raw materials or semi-manufactured goods. This is one of the causes of an ever increasing disproportion between national incomes." (*Laborem Exercens*, 1981, par. 17)

"It is necessary to break down the barriers and monopolies which leave so many countries on the margins of development, and to provide all individuals and nations with the basic conditions which will enable them to share in development." (*Centesimus annus*, 1991, par. 35)

"The State has the further right to intervene when particular monopolies create delays or obstacles to development." (*Centesimus annus*, 1991, par. 48)

-International Trade-

"There is a need to establish a greater justice in the sharing of goods, both within national communities and on the international level.
…Under the driving force of new systems of production, national frontiers are breaking down, and we can see new economic powers emerging, the multinational enterprise, which by the concentration and flexibility of their means can conduct autonomous strategies which are largely independent of the national political powers and therefore not subject to control from the point of view of the common good. By extending their activities, these private organizations can lead to a new and abusive form of economic domination on the social, cultural and even political level. The excessive concentration of means and powers that Pope Pius XI already condemned on the fortieth anniversary of Rerum Novarum is taking on a new and very real image." (*Octogesima Adveniens*, 1971, par.43-44)

"In [regards to the Poor] I wish to mention specifically: the reform of the international trade system, which is mortgaged to protectionism and increasing bilateralism; the reform of the world monetary and financial system, today recognized as inadequate; the question of technological exchanges and their proper use; the need for a review of the structure of the existing international organizations, in the framework of an international juridical order.
The international trade system today frequently discriminates against the products of the young industries of the developing countries and discourages the producers of raw materials. There exists, too, a kind of international division of labor, whereby the low-cost products of certain countries which lack effective labor laws or which are too weak to apply them are sold in other parts of the world at considerable profit for the companies engaged in this form of production, which knows no frontiers.
The world monetary and financial system is marked by an excessive fluctuation of exchange rates and interest rates, to the detriment of the balance of payments and the debt situation of the poorer countries.
Forms of technology and their transfer constitute today one of the major problems of international exchange and of the grave damage deriving therefrom. There are quite frequent cases of developing countries being denied

needed forms of technology or sent useless ones." (*Sollilicitudo Rei Socialis*, 1987, par.43)

"Lowering the level of protection accorded to the rights of workers, or abandoning mechanisms of wealth redistribution in order to increase the country's international competitiveness, hinder the achievement of lasting development. Moreover, the human consequences of current tendencies towards a short-term economy — sometimes very short-term — need to be carefully evaluated." (*Caritas in Veritatae*, 2009, par.32)

"Without doubt, one of the greatest risks for businesses is that they are almost exclusively answerable to their investors, thereby limiting their social value... Even if the ethical considerations that currently inform debate on the social responsibility of the corporate world are not all acceptable from the perspective of the Church's social doctrine, there is nevertheless a growing conviction that *business management cannot concern itself only with the interests of the proprietors, but must also assume responsibility for all the other stakeholders who contribute to the life of the business.*" (*Caritas in Veritatae*, 2009, par.40)

-The above is mentioned in an international context, but applies to a domestic and even sometimes local context as well.

-World Fund & International Debt-

"A further step must be taken... We asked world leaders to set aside part of their military expenditures for a world fund to relieve the needs of impoverished peoples." (*Populorum Progresso*, 1967, par.51)

"All nations must initiate the dialogue [to] permit a well-balanced assessment of the support to be provided, taking into consideration not only the generosity and the available wealth of the donor nations, but also the real needs of the receiving countries ... Developing countries will thus no longer risk being overwhelmed by debts whose repayment swallows up the greater part of their gains. Rates of interest and time for repayment of the loan could be so arranged as not to be too great a burden on either party, taking into account free gifts, interest-free or low-interest loans, and the time needed for liquidating the debts. The donors could certainly ask for assurances as to how the money will be used. It should be used for some mutually acceptable purpose and with reasonable hope of success, <u>for there is no question of backing idlers and parasites</u>. On the other hand, the recipients would certainly have the right to demand that no one interfere in the internal affairs of their government or disrupt their social order. <u>As sovereign nations, they are entitled to manage their own affairs, to fashion their own policies, and to choose their own form of government.</u> In other words, what is needed is mutual cooperation among nations, freely undertaken, where each enjoys equal dignity and can help to shape a world community truly worthy of man." (*Populorum Progresso*, 1967, par.54)

"[A specific sign of underdevelopment] is the question of the international debt, concerning which the Pontifical Commission *Iustitia et Pax* has issued a document.
... The reason which prompted the developing peoples to accept the offer of abundantly available capital was the hope of being able to invest it in development projects. Thus the availability of capital and the fact of accepting it as a loan can be considered a contribution to development, something desirable and legitimate in itself, even though perhaps imprudent and occasionally hasty. <u>Circumstances have changed, both within the debtor nations and in the international financial market; the instrument chosen to make a contribution to development has turned into a counterproductive mechanism. This is because the debtor nations, in order to service their debt, find themselves obliged to export the capital needed for improving or at least maintaining their standard of living. It is also because, for the same reason, they are unable to obtain new and equally essential financing.</u>
Through this mechanism, the means intended for the development of peoples has turned into a brake upon development instead, and indeed in some cases has even aggravated underdevelopment." (*Sollilicitudo Rei Socialis*, 1987, par.19)

"At present, the positive efforts which have been made along these lines are being affected by the still largely unsolved problem of the foreign debt of the poorer countries. <u>The principle that debts must be paid is certainly just. However, it is not right to demand or expect payment when the effect would be the imposition of political choices leading to hunger and despair for entire peoples. It cannot be expected that the debts which have been contracted should be paid at the price of unbearable sacrifices. In such cases it is necessary to find — as in fact is partly happening — ways to lighten, defer or even cancel the debt, compatible with the fundamental right of peoples to subsistence and progress.</u>" (*Centesimus annus*, 1991, par. 35)

6. One Human Body (Solidarity)

-Solidarity & Human Dignity-

"According to the almost unanimous opinion of believers and unbelievers alike, all things on earth should be related to man as their center and crown." (*Gaudium et Spes*, 1965, par. 12)

"The root reason for human dignity lies in man's call to communion with God... Thus atheism must be accounted among the most serious problems of this age, and is deserving of closer examination." (*Gaudium et Spes*, 1965, par. 19)

"In our times a special obligation binds us to make ourselves the neighbor of every person without exception and of actively helping him when he comes across our path, whether he be an old person abandoned by all, a foreign laborer unjustly looked down upon, a refugee, <u>a child born of an unlawful union and wrongly suffering for a sin he did not commit,</u> or a hungry person who disturbs our conscience by recalling the voice of the Lord, "As long as you did it for one of these the least of my brethren, you did it for me" (Matt. 25:40)" (*Gaudium et Spes*, 1965, par. 27)

"The duty of promoting human solidarity also falls upon the shoulders of nations...<u>While it is proper that a nation be the first to enjoy the God-given fruits of its own labor, no nation may dare to hoard its riches for its own use alone.</u>
...Considering the mounting indigence of less developed countries, it is only fitting that a prosperous nation set aside some of the goods it has produced in order to alleviate their needs; and that it train educators, engineers, technicians and scholars who will contribute their knowledge and their skill to these less fortunate countries." (*Populorum Progresso*, 1967, par.48)

"Solidarity helps us to see the "other" - whether a person, people or nation-not just as some kind of instrument, with a work capacity and physical strength to be exploited at low cost and then discarded when no longer useful, but as our "neighbor," a "helper" (cf. Gen 2:18-20), to be made a sharer, on a par with ourselves, in the banquet of life to which all are equally invited by God." (*Sollilicitudo Rei Socialis*, 1987, par.39)

"Solidarity is first and foremost a sense of responsibility on the part of everyone with regard to everyone, and it cannot therefore be merely delegated to the State." (*Caritas in Veritatae*, 2009, par.38)

"Consequently, projects for integral human development cannot ignore coming generations, but need to be *marked by solidarity and inter-generational justice*, while taking into account a variety of contexts: ecological, juridical, economic, political and cultural." (*Caritas in Veritatae*, 2009, par.48)

"Thinking of this kind requires *a deeper critical evaluation of the category of relation.* … It is not by isolation that man establishes his worth, but by placing himself in relation with others and with God. Hence these relations take on fundamental importance. The same holds true for peoples as well… In this regard, reason finds inspiration and direction in Christian revelation, according to which the human community does not absorb the individual, annihilating his autonomy, as happens in the various forms of totalitarianism, but rather values him all the more because the relation between individual and community is a relation between one totality and another. Just as a family does not submerge the identities of its individual members, just as the Church rejoices in each "new creation" (Gal 6:15; 2 Cor 5:17) incorporated by Baptism into her living Body, so too the unity of the human family does not submerge the identities of individuals, peoples and cultures, but makes them more transparent to each other and links them more closely in their legitimate diversity." (*Caritas in Veritatae*, 2009, par.53)

"The word "solidarity" is a little worn and at times poorly understood, but it refers to something more than a few sporadic acts of generosity. It presumes the creation of a new mindset which thinks in terms of community and the priority of the life of all over the appropriation of goods by a few." (*Evangelii Gaudium*, 2013, par.188)

-Equality & Inequality-

"...that ideal equality about which [the Socialists] entertain pleasant dreams would be in reality the levelling down of all to a like condition of misery and degradation." (*Rerum Novarum*, 1891, par.15)

"It must be first of all recognized that the condition of things inherent in human affairs must be borne with, for it is impossible to reduce civil society to one dead level. Socialists may in that intent do their utmost, but all striving against nature is in vain... Such inequality is far from being disadvantageous either to individuals or to the community.
To suffer and to endure, therefore, is the lot of humanity; let them strive as they may, no strength and no artifice will ever succeed in banishing from human life the ills and troubles which beset it. If any there are who pretend differently... they delude the people..." (*Rerum Novarum*, 1891, par.17-18)

"As regards the State, the interests of all, whether high or low, are equal." (*Rerum Novarum*, 1891, par.33)

"Among citizens of the same political community there is often a marked degree of economic and social inequality. The main reason for this is the fact that they are living and working in different areas, some of which are more economically developed than others.
Where this situation obtains, justice and equity demand that public authority try to eliminate or reduce such imbalances.
... In short, [A balanced internal economy should have] a policy designed to promote useful employment, enterprising initiative, and the exploitation of local resources." (*Mater et Magistra*, 1961, par.150)

"Therefore, although rightful differences exist between men, the equal dignity of persons demands that a more humane and just condition of life be brought about." (*Gaudium et Spes*, 1965, par. 29)

-In context: This includes material well-being as well.

"...how can one justify the fact that huge sums of money, which could and should be used for increasing the development of peoples, are instead utilized for the enrichment of individuals or groups, or assigned to the increase of stockpiles of weapons, both in developed countries and in the developing ones, thereby upsetting the real priorities?" (*Sollilicitudo Rei Socialis*, 1987, par.10)

"In fact, just as social inequalities down to the level of poverty exist in rich countries, so, in parallel fashion, in the less developed countries one often sees manifestations of selfishness and a flaunting of wealth which is as disconcerting, as it is scandalous.
... We must also add the differences of culture and value systems between the various population groups, differences which do not always match the degree of economic development, but which help to create distances.
... It should be noted that in today's world, among other rights, the right of economic initiative is often suppressed. Yet it is a right which is important not only for the individual but also for the common good. Experience shows us that the denial of this right, or its limitation in the name of an alleged "equality" of everyone in society, diminishes, or in practice absolutely destroys the spirit of initiative, that is to say the creative subjectivity of the citizen. <u>As a consequence, there arises, not so much a true equality as a "leveling down."</u> In the place of creative initiative there appears passivity, dependence and submission to the bureaucratic apparatus which, as the only "ordering" and "decision-making" body - if not also the "owner"- of the entire totality of goods and the means of production, puts everyone in a position of almost absolute dependence, which is similar to the traditional dependence of the worker-proletarian in capitalism. This provokes a sense of frustration or desperation and predisposes people to opt out of national life, impelling many to emigrate and also favoring a form of <u>"psychological" emigration</u>." (*Sollilicitudo Rei Socialis*, 1987, par.14-15)

"One of the greatest injustices in the contemporary world consists precisely in this: that the ones who possess much are relatively few and those who possess almost nothing are many. It is the injustice of the poor distribution of the goods and services originally intended for all.
... The evil does not consist in "having" as such, but in possessing without regard for the quality and the ordered hierarchy of the goods one has."
(*Sollilicitudo Rei Socialis*, 1987, par.28)

"<u>The world's wealth is growing in absolute terms, but inequalities are on the increase.</u> In rich countries, new sectors of society are succumbing to poverty and new forms of poverty are emerging. In poorer areas some groups enjoy a sort of "superdevelopment" of a wasteful and consumerist kind which forms an unacceptable contrast with the ongoing situations of dehumanizing deprivation." (*Caritas in Veritatae*, 2009, par.22)

"The dignity of the individual and the demands of justice require, particularly today, that economic choices do not cause disparities in wealth to increase in an excessive and morally unacceptable manner, and that we continue to *prioritize the goal of access to steady employment for everyone*. All things considered, this is also required by "economic logic"." (Caritas in Veritatae, 2009, par.32)

"Can we continue to stand by when food is thrown away while people are starving? This is a case of inequality." (*Evangelii Gaudium*, 2013, par.53)

-Immigration & Emigration-

"When there are just reasons in favor of it, he must be permitted to emigrate to other countries and take up residence there. The fact that he is a citizen of a particular State does not deprive him of membership in the human family, nor of citizenship in that universal society, the common, world-wide fellowship of men." (*Pacem in Terris*, 1963, par. 25)

"And among man's personal rights we must include his right to enter a country in which he hopes to be able to provide more fittingly for himself and his dependents. It is therefore the duty of State officials to accept such immigrants and—so far as the good of their own community, rightly understood, permits— to further the aims of those who may wish to become members of a new society." (*Pacem in Terris*, 1963, par. 106)

"When workers come from another country or district and contribute to the economic advancement of a nation or region by their labor, all discrimination as regards wages and working conditions must be carefully avoided. All the people, moreover, above all the public authorities, must treat them not as mere tools of production but as persons, and must help them to bring their families to live with them and to provide themselves with a decent dwelling; they must also see to it that these workers are incorporated into the social life of the country or region that receives them. Employment opportunities, however, should be created in their own areas as far as possible." (*Gaudium et Spes*, 1965, par.66)

"<u>Emigrant workers should also be given a warm welcome.</u> Their living conditions are often inhuman, and they must scrimp on their earnings in order to send help to their families who have remained behind in their native land in poverty." (*Populorum Progresso*, 1967, par.69)

"We are thinking of the precarious situation of a great number of emigrant workers whose condition as foreigners makes it all the more difficult for them to make any sort of social vindication, in spite of their real participation in the economic effort of the country that receives them. It is urgently necessary for people to go beyond a narrowly nationalist attitude in their regard and to give them a charter which will assure them a right to emigrate, favor their integration, facilitate their professional advancement and give them access to decent housing where, if such is the case, their families can join them.
Linked to this category are the people who, to find work, or to escape a disaster or a hostile climate, leave their regions and find themselves without roots among other people.
<u>It is everyone's duty, but especially that of Christians, to work with energy for the establishment of universal brotherhood, the indispensable basis for authentic justice and the condition for enduring peace: 'We cannot in truthfulness call upon that God who is the Father of all if we refuse to act in a brotherly way toward certain men, created to God's image.'"</u> (*Octogesima Adveniens*, 1971, par.17)

"Finally, we must say at least a few words on the subject of *emigration in search of work*... Man has the right to leave his native land for various motives-and also the right to return-in order to seek better conditions of life in another country. This fact is certainly not without difficulties of various kinds.
... Everything should be done... to prevent this material evil from causing greater *moral harm*; indeed every possible effort should be made to ensure that it may bring benefit to the emigrant's personal, family and social life, both for the country to which he goes and the country which he leaves. In this area much depends on just legislation, in particular with regard to the rights of workers.
... The most important thing is that the person working away from his native land, whether as a permanent emigrant or as a seasonal worker, should not be *placed at a disadvantage* in comparison with the other workers in that society in the matter of working rights. Emigration in search of work must in no way become an opportunity for financial or social exploitation... The value of work should be measured by the same standard and not according to the difference in

nationality, religion or race. For even greater reason the *situation of constraint* in which the emigrant may find himself *should not be exploited*... Once more the fundamental principle must be repeated: the hierarchy of values and the profound meaning of work itself require that capital should be at the service of labour and not labour at the service of capital." (*Laborem Exercens*, 1981, par. 23)

"We can say that we are facing a social phenomenon of epoch-making proportions that requires bold, forward-looking policies of international cooperation if it is to be handled effectively... No country can be expected to address today's problems of migration by itself. We are all witnesses of the burden of suffering, the dislocation and the aspirations that accompany the flow of migrants. The phenomenon, as everyone knows, is difficult to manage; but there is no doubt that foreign workers, despite any difficulties concerning integration, make a significant contribution to the economic development of the host country through their labor, besides that which they make to their country of origin through the money they send home. Obviously, these laborers cannot be considered as a commodity or a mere workforce... Every migrant is a human person who, as such, possesses fundamental, inalienable rights that must be respected by everyone and in every circumstance." (*Caritas in Veritatae*, 2009, par.62)

"Migrants present a particular challenge for me, since I am the pastor of a Church without frontiers, a Church which considers herself mother to all. For this reason, I exhort all countries to a generous openness which, rather than fearing the loss of local identity, will prove capable of creating new forms of cultural synthesis. How beautiful are those cities which overcome paralyzing mistrust, integrate those who are different and make this very integration a new factor of development!" (*Evangelii Gaudium*, 2013, par.210)

-Revolution-

"Everyone knows, however, that revolutionary uprisings—except where there is manifest, longstanding tyranny which would do great damage to fundamental personal rights and dangerous harm to the common good of the country—engender new injustices, introduce new inequities and bring new disasters. <u>The evil situation that exists, and it surely is evil, may not be dealt with in such a way that an even worse situation results.</u>" (*Populorum Progresso*, 1967, par.31)

-The Arms Race & Disarmament-

"We are deeply distressed to see the enormous stocks of armaments that have been, and continue to be, manufactured...
...<u>There is a common belief that under modern conditions peace cannot be assured except on the basis of an equal balance of armaments and that this factor is the probable cause of this stockpiling of armaments.</u>
... Consequently people are living in the grip of constant fear... While it is difficult to believe that anyone would dare to assume responsibility for initiating the appalling slaughter and destruction that war would bring in its wake, there is no denying that the conflagration could be started by some chance and unforeseen circumstance.
... <u>Hence justice, right reason, and the recognition of man's dignity cry out insistently for a cessation to the arms race.</u> The stock-piles of armaments which have been built up in various countries must be <u>reduced all round</u> and <u>simultaneously by the parties concerned.</u> <u>Nuclear weapons must be banned.</u>
... Everyone, however, must realize that, unless this process of disarmament be thoroughgoing and complete, and reach men's very souls, ...—and this is the main thing—ultimately to abolish them entirely... But this requires that the fundamental principles upon which peace is based in today's world be replaced by an altogether different one, namely, the realization that true and lasting peace among nations cannot consist in the possession of an equal supply of armaments but only in mutual trust." (*Pacem in Terris*, 1963, par.109-113)

"To be sure, scientific weapons are not amassed solely for use in war. Since the defensive strength of any nation is considered to be dependent upon its capacity for immediate retaliation, this accumulation of arms, which increases each year, likewise serves, in a way heretofore unknown, as deterrent to possible enemy attack. Many regard this procedure as the most effective way by which peace of a sort can be maintained between nations at the present time.
Whatever be the facts about this method of deterrence, men should be convinced that the arms race in which an already considerable number of countries are engaged is not a safe way to preserve a steady peace, nor is the so-called balance resulting from this race a sure and authentic peace. Rather than being eliminated thereby, the causes of war are in danger of being gradually aggravated.

"... Therefore, we say it again: the arms race is an utterly treacherous trap for humanity, and one which ensnares the poor to an intolerable degree. It is much to be feared that if this race persists, it will eventually spawn all the lethal ruin whose path it is now making ready." (*Gaudium et Spes*, 1965, par. 81)

"If "development is the new name for peace," war and military preparations are the major enemy of the integral development of peoples." (*Sollilicitudo Rei Socialis*, 1987, par. 10)

"If arms production is a serious disorder in the present world with regard to true human needs and the employment of the means capable of satisfying those needs, the arms trade is equally to blame.
...If to all this we add the tremendous and universally acknowledged danger represented by atomic weapons stockpiled on an incredible scale, the logical conclusion seems to be this: in today's world, including the world of economics, the prevailing picture is one destined to lead us more quickly towards death rather than one of concern for true development which would lead all towards a "more human" life..." (*Sollilicitudo Rei Socialis*, 1987, par.24)

"This need, however, must not lead to a slackening of efforts to sustain and assist the countries of the Third World, which often suffer even more serious conditions of poverty and want. What is called for is a special effort to mobilize resources, which are not lacking in the world as a whole, for the purpose of economic growth and common development, redefining the priorities and hierarchies of values on the basis of which economic and political choices are made. Enormous resources can be made available by disarming the huge military machines which were constructed for the conflict between East and West. These resources could become even more abundant if, in place of war, reliable procedures for the resolution of conflicts could be set up, with the resulting spread of the principle of arms control and arms reduction, also in the countries of the Third World, through the adoption of appropriate measures against the arms trade." (*Centesimus annus*, 1991, par. 28)

-Global Cooperation & Foreign Policy-

-In context: This "global authority" is not a "World Government," as some would inaccurately portray of Pope John XXIII – and his predecessors – rather, it is a collection of separate nations, working in tandem and peaceful cooperation, to achieve such ends as the

avoidance of war, regulation of abusive trade, "gunpoint economics," etc. Hence the phrase "consent of all nations" as opposed to one governance. See par. 141 of Pacem in Terris (below). See Forms of Government. The Church specifically declares that she does not, and will not, speak on the best form of government; rather, the principles by which governments operate. I note this because I have seen these quotes monstrously distorted out of context.

"Men's common interests make it imperative that at long last a world-wide community of nations be established." (*Pacem in Terris*, 1963, par.7)

"…it is clear that no State can fittingly pursue its own interests in isolation from the rest, nor, under such circumstances, can it develop itself as it should." (*Pacem in Terris*, 1963, par.131)

"But this general authority equipped with world-wide power and adequate means for achieving the universal common good cannot be imposed by force. It must be set up with the consent of all nations." (*Pacem in Terris*, 1963, par.138)

"But it is no part of the duty of universal authority to limit the sphere of action of the public authority of individual States, or to arrogate any of their functions to itself. On the contrary, its essential purpose is to create world conditions in which the public authorities of each nation, its citizens and intermediate groups, can carry out their tasks, fullfill their duties and claim their rights with greater security." (*Pacem in Terris*, 1963, par.141)

"…it is absolutely necessary for countries to cooperate more advantageously and more closely together and to organize together international bodies and to work tirelessly for the creation of organizations which will foster peace. In view of the increasingly close ties of mutual dependence today between all the inhabitants and peoples of the earth, [pursuit] of the universal common good now require of the community of nations that it organize itself in a manner suited to its present responsibilities, especially toward the many parts of the world which are still suffering from unbearable want." (*Gaudium et Spes*, 1965, par. 83-84)

"If an authentic economic order is to be established on a world-wide basis, an end will have to be put to profiteering, to national ambitions, to the appetite for political supremacy, to militaristic calculations, and to machinations for the sake of spreading and imposing ideologies." (*Gaudium et Spes*, 1965, par. 85)

"It is timely to mention - and it is no exaggeration — that a leadership role among nations can only be justified by the possibility and willingness to contribute widely and generously to the common good." (*Sollilicitudo Rei Socialis*, 1987, par.23)

"At the same time, in a world divided and beset by every type of conflict, the conviction is growing of a radical interdependence and consequently of the need for a solidarity which will take up interdependence and transfer it to the moral plane." (*Sollilicitudo Rei Socialis*, 1987, par.26)

"When interdependence becomes recognized in this way, the correlative response as a moral and social attitude, as a "virtue," is solidarity. This then is not a feeling of vague compassion or shallow distress at the misfortunes of so many people, both near and far. On the contrary, it is a firm and persevering determination to commit oneself to the common good; that is to say to the good of all and of each individual, because we are all really responsible for all." (*Sollilicitudo Rei Socialis*, 1987, par.38)

"Surmounting every type of imperialism and determination to preserve their own hegemony, the stronger and richer nations must have a sense of moral responsibility for the other nations, so that a real international system may be established which will rest on the foundation of the equality of all peoples and on the necessary respect for their legitimate differences. The economically weaker countries, or those still at subsistence level, must be enabled, with the assistance of other peoples and of the international community, to make a contribution of their own to the common good with their treasures of humanity and culture, which otherwise would be lost forever." (*Sollilicitudo Rei Socialis*, 1987, par.39)

"The existing institutions and organizations have worked well for the benefit of peoples. Nevertheless, humanity today is in a new and more difficult phase of its genuine development. It needs a greater degree of international ordering, at the service of the societies, economies and cultures of the whole world." (*Sollilicitudo Rei Socialis*, 1987, par.43)

"What is needed are concrete steps to create or consolidate international structures capable of intervening through appropriate arbitration in the conflicts which arise between nations, so that each nation can uphold its own rights and reach a just agreement and peaceful settlement vis-à-vis the rights of others. …Peace and prosperity, in fact, are goods which belong to the whole human race: it is not possible to enjoy them in a proper and lasting way if they are achieved and maintained at the cost of other peoples and nations, by violating their rights or excluding them from the sources of well-being." (*Centesimus annus*, 1991, par. 27)

"<u>Stronger nations must offer weaker ones opportunities for taking their place in international life</u>, and the latter must learn how to use these opportunities by making the necessary efforts and sacrifices and by ensuring political and economic stability, the certainty of better prospects for the future, the improvement of workers' skills, and the training of competent business leaders who are conscious of their responsibilities." (*Centesimus annus*, 1991, par. 35)

"This duty [of responsibility for *all* humanity] is not limited to one's own family, nation or State, but extends progressively to all mankind, since no one can consider himself extraneous or indifferent to the lot of another member of the human family." (*Centesimus annus*, 1991, par. 51)

"Creating such conditions [of peace and development] calls for a concerted worldwide effort to promote development, an effort which also involves sacrificing the positions of income and of power enjoyed by the more developed economies." (*Centesimus annus*, 1991, par. 52)

"<u>It is not merely a matter of "giving from one's surplus", but of helping entire peoples which are presently excluded or marginalized to enter into the sphere of economic and human development.</u> For this to happen, it is not enough to draw on the surplus goods which in fact our world abundantly produces; it requires above all a change of life-styles, of models of production and consumption, and of the established structures of power which today govern societies…Today we are facing the so-called "globalization" of the economy, a phenomenon which is not to be dismissed, since it can create unusual opportunities for greater prosperity. There is a growing feeling, however, that this increasing internationalization of the economy ought to be accompanied by effective international agencies which will oversee and direct the economy to the common good, something that an individual State, even if it were the most powerful on earth, would not be in a position to do. In order to achieve this result, it is necessary that there be increased coordination among the more powerful countries, and that in international agencies the interests of the whole human family be equally represented...Much remains to be done in this area." (*Centesimus annus*, 1991, par. 58)

"As society becomes ever more globalized, it makes us neighbors but does not make us brothers. Reason, by itself, is capable of grasping the equality between men and of giving stability to their civic coexistence, but it cannot establish fraternity. This originates in a transcendent vocation from God the Father, who loved us first, teaching us through the Son what fraternal charity is." (*Caritas in Veritatae*, 2009, par.19)

"Moreover, the elimination of world hunger has also, in the global era, become a requirement for safeguarding the peace and stability of the planet. Hunger is not so much dependent on lack of material things as on shortage of social resources, the most important of which are institutional. What is missing, in other words, is a network of economic institutions capable of guaranteeing regular access to sufficient food and water for nutritional needs, and also capable of addressing the primary needs and necessities ensuing from genuine food crises, whether due to natural causes or political irresponsibility, nationally and internationally. The problem of food insecurity needs to be addressed within a long-term perspective, eliminating the structural causes that give rise to it and promoting the agricultural development of poorer countries. This can be done by investing in rural infrastructures, irrigation systems, transport, organization of markets, and in the development and dissemination of agricultural technology that can make the best use of the human, natural and socio-economic resources that are more readily available at the local level, while guaranteeing their sustainability over the long term as well... It is therefore necessary to cultivate a public conscience that considers *food and access to water as universal rights of all human beings, without distinction or discrimination.*" (*Caritas in Veritatae*, 2009, par.27)

"The integrated economy of the present day does not make the role of States redundant, but rather it commits governments to greater collaboration with one another. Both wisdom and prudence suggest not being too precipitous in declaring the demise of the State...The focus of *international aid*, within a solidarity-based plan to resolve today's economic problems, should rather be on consolidating constitutional, juridical and administrative systems in countries that do not yet fully enjoy these goods. Alongside economic aid, there needs to be aid directed towards reinforcing the guarantees proper to the State of law: a system of public order and effective imprisonment that respects human rights, truly democratic institutions. The State does not need to have identical characteristics everywhere" (*Caritas in Veritatae*, 2009, par.41)

- *"Globalization" does not mean "World Government." Rather, it means that different, local, subdivided (see* **Principle of Subsidiarity***) communities and governments working together for the good of all, and especially with an increased sense of responsibility towards all.*

"Sometimes *globalization* is viewed in fatalistic terms, as if the dynamics involved were the product of anonymous impersonal forces or structures independent of the human will. In this regard it is useful to remember that while globalization should certainly be understood as a socio-economic process, this is not its only dimension. Underneath the more visible process, humanity itself is becoming increasingly interconnected; it is made up of individuals and peoples to whom this process should offer benefits and development, as they assume their respective responsibilities, singly and collectively. The breaking-down of borders is not simply a material fact: it is also a cultural event both in its causes and its effects. If globalization is viewed from a deterministic standpoint, the criteria with which to evaluate and direct it are lost… Hence a sustained commitment is needed so as to *promote a person-based and community-oriented cultural process of world-wide integration that is open to transcendence.*

Despite some of its structural elements, which should neither be denied nor exaggerated, "globalization, a priori, is neither good nor bad. It will be what people make of it". We should not be its victims, but rather its protagonists, acting in the light of reason, guided by charity and truth. Blind opposition would be a mistaken and prejudiced attitude, incapable of recognizing the positive aspects of the process, with the consequent risk of missing the chance to take advantage of its many opportunities for development. The processes of globalization, suitably understood and directed, open up the unprecedented possibility of large-scale redistribution of wealth on a world-wide scale; if badly directed, however, they can lead to an increase in poverty and inequality, and could even trigger a global crisis… Globalization is a multifaceted and complex phenomenon which must be grasped in the diversity and unity of all its different dimensions, including the theological dimension. In this way it will be possible to experience and to *steer the globalization of humanity in relational terms, in terms of communion and the sharing of goods.*" (*Caritas in Veritatae*, 2009, par.42)

"In order not to produce a dangerous universal power of a tyrannical nature, the governance of globalization must be marked by subsidiarity, articulated into several layers and involving different levels that can work together. Globalization certainly requires authority, insofar as it poses the problem of a global common good that needs to be pursued. This authority, however, must be organized in a subsidiary and stratified way, if it is not to infringe upon freedom and if it is to yield effective results in practice." (*Caritas in Veritatae*, 2009, par.58)

"To manage the global economy; to revive economies hit by the crisis; to avoid any deterioration of the present crisis and the greater imbalances that would result; to bring about integral and timely disarmament, food security and peace; to guarantee the protection of the environment and to regulate migration: for all this, there is urgent need of a true world political authority, as my predecessor Blessed John XXIII indicated some years ago. Such an authority would need to be regulated by law, to observe consistently the principles of subsidiarity and solidarity, to seek to establish the common good, *and to make a commitment to securing authentic integral human development inspired by the values of charity in truth.* Furthermore, such an authority would need to be universally recognized and to be vested with the effective power to ensure security for all, regard for justice, and respect for rights. Obviously it would have to have the authority to ensure compliance with its decisions from all parties, and also with the coordinated measures adopted in various international forums. Without this, despite the great progress accomplished in various sectors, international law would risk being conditioned by the balance of power among the strongest nations." (Caritas in Veritatae, 2009, par.67)

-Again… it is not a world government, but a cooperation, a working together to create a World Authority, that is necessary to guarantee protection of those who cannot protect themselves, rather than a global "Wild West" where the most powerful force prevails.

"… recent World Summits on the environment have not lived up to expectations because, due to lack of political will, they were unable to reach truly meaningful and effective global agreements on the environment." (*Laudato Si*, 2015, par 166)

"Enforceable international agreements are urgently needed, since local authorities are not always capable of effective intervention. Relations between states must be respectful of each other's sovereignty, but must also lay down mutually agreed means of averting regional disasters which would eventually affect everyone. Global regulatory norms are needed to impose obligations and prevent unacceptable actions, for example, when powerful companies or countries dump contaminated waste or offshore polluting industries in other countries." (*Laudato Si*, 2015, par 173)

"As Benedict XVI has affirmed in continuity with the social teaching of the Church: 'To manage the global economy; to revive economies hit by the crisis; to avoid any deterioration of the present crisis and the greater imbalances that would result; to bring about integral and timely disarmament, food security and peace; to guarantee the protection of the environment and to regulate migration: for all this, there is urgent need of a true world political authority, as my predecessor Blessed John XXIII indicated some years ago'." (*Laudato Si*, 2015, par 175)

-United Nations-

"A clear proof of the farsightedness of this organization is provided by the Universal Declaration of Human Rights passed by the United Nations General Assembly on December 10, 1948.
…We are, of course, aware that some of the points in the declaration did not meet with unqualified approval in some quarters; and there was justification for this. Nevertheless, We think the document should be considered a step in the right direction…" (*Pacem in Terris*, 1963, par.142-143)

"At this level one must acknowledge the influence exercised by the Declaration of Human Rights, promulgated some forty years ago by the United Nations Organization. Its very existence and gradual acceptance by the international community are signs of a growing awareness." (*Sollilicitudo Rei Socialis*, 1987, par.26)

"While noting this process with satisfaction, nevertheless one cannot ignore the fact that the overall balance of the various policies of aid for development has not always been positive. The United Nations, moreover, has not yet succeeded in establishing, as alternatives to war, effective means for the resolution of international conflicts. This seems to be the most urgent problem which the international community has yet to resolve." (*Centesimus annus*, 1991, par. 21)

"In the face of the unrelenting growth of global interdependence, there is a strongly felt need, even in the midst of a global recession, for a reform of the

United Nations Organization, and likewise of economic institutions and international finance, so that the concept of the family of nations can acquire real teeth." (*Caritas in Veritatae*, 2009, par.67)

-Population Expansion-

"How can economic development and the supply of food keep pace with the continual rise in population?
...we are told, if nothing is done… the world will be faced in the not too distant future with an increasing shortage in the necessities of life.
… Truth to tell, we do not seem to be faced with any immediate or imminent world problem arising from the disproportion between the increase of population and the supply of food. Arguments to this effect are based on such unreliable and controversial data that they can only be of very uncertain validity. [Because of God's design of Nature & Man's ingenuity], the real solution of the problem is not to be found in expedients which offend against the divinely established moral order and which attack human life at its very source, but in a renewed scientific and technical effort on man's part to deepen and extend his dominion over Nature.
… As for the problems which face the poorer nations in various parts of the world, We realize, of course, that these are very real. They are caused, more often than not, by a deficient economic and social organization, which does not offer living conditions proportionate to the increase in population. They are caused, also, by the lack of effective solidarity among such peoples.
But granting this, We must nevertheless state most emphatically that no statement of the problem and no solution to it is acceptable which does violence to man's essential dignity; those who propose such solutions base them on an utterly materialistic conception of man himself and his life.
… The only possible solution to this question is one which envisages the social and economic progress both of individuals and of the whole of human society, and which respects and promotes true human values." (*Mater et Magistra*, 1961, par.185-192)

"But there are many today who maintain that the increase in world population, or at least the population increase in some countries, must be radically curbed by every means possible and by any kind of intervention on the part of public authority. In view of this contention, the council urges everyone to guard against solutions, whether publicly or privately supported, or at times even imposed, which are contrary to the moral law.

… Men should discreetly be informed, furthermore, of scientific advances in exploring methods whereby spouses can be helped in regulating the number of their children and whose safeness has been well proven and whose harmony with the moral order has been ascertained." (*Gaudium et Spes*, 1965, par. 87)

-See Life *for related references. The "scientific advances" that the above refers to is Natural Family Planning (NFP), which does not involve contraception. Example of the opposite "solutions" are contraception, sterilization, abortion, euthanasia, etc., which progressively lead to one another – given any one, all logically follow.*

"There is no denying that the accelerated rate of population growth brings many added difficulties to the problems of development where the size of the population grows more rapidly than the quantity of available resources to such a degree that things seem to have reached an impasse. In such circumstances people are inclined to apply drastic remedies to reduce the birth rate.
There is no doubt that public authorities can intervene in this matter, within the bounds of their competence. They can instruct citizens on this subject and adopt appropriate measures, so long as these are in conformity with the dictates of the moral law and the rightful freedom of married couples is preserved completely intact. <u>When the inalienable right of marriage and of procreation is taken away, so is human dignity.</u>
<u>Finally, it is for parents to take a thorough look at the matter and decide upon the number of their children.</u> This is an obligation they take upon themselves, before their children already born, and before the community to which they belong—following the dictates of their own consciences informed by God's law authentically interpreted, and bolstered by their trust in Him." (*Populorum Progresso*, 1967, par.37)

-Having children must be done responsibly. If there is risk to the Mother's life, uncertainty of the ability to support them, or other serious reasons, it could be wrong to have more children – only as many as you can <u>love</u> and <u>provide for</u>, it might be said. However, the well-intentioned good end (of responsibility) never justifies destruction of life or the separation of sex from its life-giving potency.

"And now We wish to speak to rulers of nations. To you most of all is committed the responsibility of safeguarding the common good. You can contribute so much to the preservation of morals. We beg of you, never allow the morals of your peoples to be undermined. The family is the primary unit in the state; do not tolerate any legislation which would introduce into the family those practices which are opposed to the natural law of God. For there are other ways by which a government can and should solve the population problem—that is to say by enacting laws which will assist families and by educating the people wisely so that the moral law and the freedom of the citizens are both safeguarded." (*Humanae Vitae*,1968, par.23)

"Today an important part of policies which favor life is the issue of population growth. Certainly public authorities have a responsibility to "intervene to orient the demography of the population". But such interventions must always take into account and respect the primary and inalienable responsibility of married couples and families, and cannot employ methods which fail to respect the person and fundamental human rights, beginning with the right to life of every innocent human being. <u>It is therefore morally unacceptable to encourage, let alone impose, the use of methods such as contraception, sterilization and abortion in order to regulate births.</u> The ways of solving the population problem are quite different." (*Evangelium Vitae*, 1995, par.91)

"<u>To consider population increase as the primary cause of underdevelopment is mistaken, even from an economic point of view.</u> Suffice it to consider, on the one hand, the significant reduction in infant mortality and the rise in average life expectancy found in economically developed countries, and on the other hand, the signs of crisis observable in societies that are registering an alarming decline in their birth rate." (*Caritas in Veritatae*, 2009, par.44)

"At times, developing countries face forms of international pressure which make economic assistance contingent on certain policies of "reproductive health"… To blame population growth instead of extreme and selective consumerism on the part of some, is one way of refusing to face the issues. It is an attempt to legitimize the present model of distribution, where a minority believes that it has the right to consume in a way which can never be universalized, since the planet could not even contain the waste products of such consumption." (*Laudato Si*, 2015, par 50)

7. Creation, Ecological Issues, and the Environment

-Science & Technology-

"It has been claimed that in an era of scientific and technical triumphs such as ours man can well afford to rely on his own powers, and construct a very good civilization without God. But the truth is that these very advances in science and technology frequently involve the whole human race in such difficulties as can only be solved in the light of a sincere faith in God, the Creator and Ruler of man and his world." (*Mater et Magistra*, 1961, par.209)

"Let men make all the technical and economic progress they can, there will be no peace nor justice in the world until they return to a sense of their dignity as creatures and sons of God…" (*Mater et Magistra*, 1961, par.215)

"One of the salient features of the modern world is the growing interdependence of men one on the other, a development promoted chiefly by modern technical advances. Nevertheless brotherly dialogue among men does not reach its perfection on the level of technical progress, but on the deeper level of interpersonal relationships." (Gaudium et Spes, 1965, par. 23)

"Now many of our contemporaries seem to fear that a closer bond between human activity and religion will work against the independence of men, of societies, or of the sciences.
… Therefore if methodical investigation within every branch of learning is carried out in a genuinely scientific manner and in accord with moral norms, it never truly conflicts with faith, for earthly matters and the concerns of faith derive from the same God.
… Consequently, we cannot but deplore certain habits of mind, which are sometimes found too among Christians, which do not sufficiently attend to the rightful independence of science and which, from the arguments and controversies they spark, lead many minds to conclude that faith and science are mutually opposed." (*Gaudium et Spes*, 1965, par. 36)

"Indeed today's progress in science and technology can foster a certain exclusive emphasis on observable data, and an agnosticism about everything else. For the methods of investigation which these sciences use can be wrongly

considered as the supreme rule of seeking the whole truth. By virtue of their methods these sciences cannot penetrate to the intimate notion of things. Indeed the danger is present that man, confiding too much in the discoveries of today, may think that he is sufficient unto himself and no longer seek the higher things.
<u>Those unfortunate results, however, do not necessarily follow from the culture of today, nor should they lead us into the temptation of not acknowledging its positive values.</u>" (*Gaudium et Spes*, 1965, par. 57)

"Let them blend new sciences and theories and the understanding of the most recent discoveries with Christian morality and the teaching of Christian doctrine, so that their religious culture and morality may keep pace with scientific knowledge and with the constantly progressing technology." (*Gaudium et Spes*, 1965, par. 62)

"Therefore, technical progress, an inventive spirit, an eagerness to create and to expand enterprises, the application of methods of production, and the strenuous efforts of all who engage in production—in a word, all the elements making for such development—must be promoted. The fundamental finality of this production is not the mere increase of products nor profit or control but rather the service of man…" (Gaudium et Spes, 1965, par. 64)

"It may also be… a new positivism: universalized technology as the dominant form of activity, as the overwhelming pattern of existence, even as a language, without the question of its meaning being really asked." (*Octogesima Adveniens*, 1971, par.29)

"Having subdued nature by using his reason, man now finds that he himself is as it were imprisoned within his own rationality; he in turn becomes the object of science. The "human sciences" are today enjoying a significant flowering. On the one hand they are subjecting to critical and radical examination the hitherto accepted knowledge about man, on the grounds that this knowledge seems either too empirical or too theoretical. On the other hand, methodological necessity and ideological presuppositions too often lead the human sciences to isolate, in the various situations, certain aspects of man, and yet to give these an explanation which claims to be complete or at least an interpretation which is meant to be all-embracing from a purely quantitative or phenomenological point of view. This scientific reduction betrays a dangerous presupposition. To give a privileged position in this way to such an aspect of analysis is to mutilate man and, under the pretext of a scientific procedure, to make it impossible to understand man in his totality.

One must be no less attentive to the action which the human sciences can instigate, giving rise to the elaboration of models of society to be subsequently imposed on men as scientifically tested types of behavior. Man can then become the object of manipulations directing his desires and needs and modifying his behavior and even his system of values.

Should the Church in its turn contest the proceedings of the human sciences, and condemn their pretentions? As in the case of the natural sciences, the Church has confidence in this research also and urges Christians to play an active part in it. Prompted by the same scientific demands and the desire to know man better, but at the same time enlightened by their faith, Christians who devote themselves to the human sciences will begin a dialogue between the Church and this new field of discovery, a dialogue which promises to be fruitful. Of course, each individual scientific discipline will be able, in its own particular sphere, to grasp only a partial-yet true-aspect of man; the complete picture and the full meaning will escape it. But within these limits the human sciences give promise of a positive function that the Church willingly recognizes.

These sciences are a condition at once indispensable and inadequate for a better discovery of what is human. They are a language which becomes more and more complex, yet one that deepens rather than solves the mystery of the heart of man; nor does it provide the complete and definitive answer to the desire which springs from his innermost being." (*Octogesima Adveniens*, 1971, par 38-40)

"Understood in this case not as a capacity or aptitude for work, but rather *as a whole set of instruments* which man uses in his work, technology is undoubtedly man's ally... However, it is also a fact that, in some instances, technology can cease to be man's ally and become almost his enemy, as when the mechanization of work "supplants" him, taking away all personal satisfaction and the incentive to creativity and responsibility, when it deprives many workers of their previous employment, or when, through exalting the machine, it reduces man to the status of its slave.

... The recent stage of human history, especially that of certain societies, brings a correct affirmation of technology as a basic coefficient of economic progress; but, at the same time, this affirmation has been accompanied by and continues to be accompanied by the raising of essential questions concerning human work in relationship to its subject, which is man. These questions are particularly

charged with *content and tension of an ethical and an ethical and social character.*"
(*Laborem Exercens*, 1981, par. 5)

"It is therefore a serious mistake to undervalue human capacity to exercise control over the deviations of development or to overlook the fact that man is constitutionally oriented towards "being more". <u>Idealizing technical progress, or contemplating the utopia of a return to humanity's original natural state, are two contrasting ways of detaching progress from its moral evaluation and hence from our responsibility.</u>" (*Caritas in Veritatae*, 2009, par.14)

"This means that moral evaluation and scientific research must go hand in hand, and that charity must animate them in a harmonious interdisciplinary whole, marked by unity and distinction. The Church's social doctrine, which has "*an important interdisciplinary dimension*", can exercise, in this perspective, a function of extraordinary effectiveness. It allows faith, theology, metaphysics and science to come together in a collaborative effort in the service of humanity." (*Caritas in Veritatae*, 2009, par.31)

"The challenge of development today is closely linked to *technological progress*, with its astounding applications in the field of biology... Technology enables us to exercise dominion over matter, to reduce risks, to save labour, to improve our conditions of life... Technology is the objective side of human action whose origin and *raison d'etre* is found in the subjective element: the worker himself. For this reason, technology is never merely technology... <u>Technology, in this sense, is a response to God's command to till and to keep the land</u> (cf. Gen 2:15). ... Technological development can give rise to the idea that technology is self-sufficient when too much attention is given to the "*how*" questions, and not enough to the many "*why*" questions underlying human activity... The process of globalization could replace ideologies with technology, allowing the latter to become an ideological power that threatens to confine us within an *a priori* that holds us back from encountering being and truth... But when the sole criterion of truth is efficiency and utility, development is automatically denied. True development does not consist primarily in "doing". The key to development is a mind capable of thinking in technological terms and grasping the fully human meaning of human activities, within the context of the holistic meaning of the individual's being. Even when we work through satellites or through remote electronic impulses, our actions always remain human, an expression of our responsible freedom... But when the sole criterion of truth is efficiency and utility, development is automatically denied. True development does not consist primarily in "doing". The key to development is a mind capable of thinking in technological terms and grasping the fully human meaning of human activities, within the context of the holistic meaning of the individual's being. Even when we work through satellites or through remote electronic impulses, our actions always remain human, an expression of our responsible freedom." (*Caritas in Veritatae*, 2009, par.69-70)

"The supremacy of technology tends to prevent people from recognizing anything that cannot be explained in terms of matter alone. Yet everyone experiences the many immaterial and spiritual dimensions of life. Knowing is not simply a material act, since the object that is known always conceals something beyond the empirical datum. All our knowledge, even the most simple, is always a minor miracle, since it can never be fully explained by the material instruments that we apply to it…[the development of individuals and peoples] requires new eyes and a new heart, capable of rising above a materialistic vision of human events, capable of glimpsing in development the "beyond" that technology cannot give." (*Caritas in Veritatae*, 2009, par.77)

"Whereas positivism and scientism "refuse to admit the validity of forms of knowledge other than those of the positive sciences", the Church proposes another path, which calls for a synthesis between the responsible use of methods proper to the empirical sciences and other areas of knowledge such as philosophy, theology, as well as faith itself, which elevates us to the mystery transcending nature and human intelligence. <u>Faith is not fearful of reason; on the contrary, it seeks and trusts reason, since "the light of reason and the light of faith both come from God" and cannot contradict each other.</u>
… Whenever the sciences – rigorously focused on their specific field of inquiry – arrive at a conclusion which reason cannot refute, faith does not contradict it. Neither can believers claim that a scientific opinion which is attractive but not sufficiently verified has the same weight as a dogma of faith. <u>At times some scientists have exceeded the limits of their scientific competence by making certain statements or claims. But here the problem is not with reason itself, but with the promotion of a particular ideology which blocks the path to authentic, serene and productive dialogue.</u>" (*Evangelii Gaudium*, 2013, par.242-243)

"Human beings, even if we postulate a process of evolution, also possess a uniqueness which cannot be fully explained by the evolution of other open systems. Each of us has his or her own personal identity and is capable of entering into dialogue with others and with God himself." (*Laudato Si*, 2015, par 81)

"Never has humanity had such power over itself, yet nothing ensures that it will be used wisely, particularly when we consider how it is currently being used... There is a tendency to believe that every increase in power means "an increase of 'progress' itself", an advance in "security, usefulness, welfare and vigour; ...an assimilation of new values into the stream of culture", as if reality, goodness and truth automatically flow from technological and economic power as such. The fact is that "contemporary man has not been trained to use power well", because our immense technological development has not been accompanied by a development in human responsibility, values and conscience." (*Laudato Si*, 2015, par 104-105)

"The basic problem goes even deeper: it is the way that humanity has taken up technology and its development according to an undifferentiated and one-dimensional paradigm. This paradigm exalts the concept of a subject who, using logical and rational procedures, progressively approaches and gains control over an external object. This subject makes every effort to establish the scientific and experimental method, which in itself is already a technique of possession, mastery and transformation. It is as if the subject were to find itself in the presence of something formless, completely open to manipulation. Men and women have constantly intervened in nature, but for a long time this meant being in tune with and respecting the possibilities offered by the things themselves. It was a matter of receiving what nature itself allowed, as if from its own hand. Now, by contrast, we are the ones to lay our hands on things, attempting to extract everything possible from them while frequently ignoring or forgetting the reality in front of us." (*Laudato Si*, 2015, par 106)

This statement is deeper than first glance; headier than we are perhaps used to. Pope Francis is calling for the world to move beyond Bacon's New Organon, *and to recognize that things are inseparably related, as a whole, instead of a myopic examination and mastery of parts – dissecting a frog is useful, but a frog is not a collection of muscles and organs. Nuclear science is useful – it can tell us how – but it cannot tell us "should." Science is an ineffective instrument for deciding whether something is good or bad – it tells us about the force of a hammer, not whether that force should be used on someone's head. Science is not progress; learning to use well the results of study, including scientific results, is progress.*

"Decisions which may seem purely instrumental are in reality decisions about the kind of society we want to build." (*Laudato Si*, 2015, par 107)

i.e. especially in our science-saturated society, we can think through the "how," but seem unable to think through the "why" and therefore the "should or should not."

"While human intervention on plants and animals is permissible when it pertains to the necessities of human life, the Catechism of the Catholic Church teaches that experimentation on animals is morally acceptable only "if it remains within reasonable limits [and] contributes to caring for or saving human lives". The Catechism firmly states that human power has limits and that "it is contrary to human dignity to cause animals to suffer or die needlessly". All such use and experimentation "requires a religious respect for the integrity of creation"." (*Laudato Si*, 2015, par 130)

"There are certain environmental issues where it is not easy to achieve a broad consensus. Here I would state once more that the Church does not presume to settle scientific questions or to replace politics. But I am concerned to encourage an honest and open debate so that particular interests or ideologies will not prejudice the common good." (*Laudato Si*, 2015, par 188)

"It cannot be maintained that empirical science provides a complete explanation of life, the interplay of all creatures and the whole of reality. This would be to breach the limits imposed by its own methodology. If we reason only within the confines of the latter, little room would be left for aesthetic sensibility, poetry, or even reason's ability to grasp the ultimate meaning and purpose of things." (*Laudato Si*, 2015, par 199)

When one considers this in context: we merely know the material makeup and arc of the planets and stars. A group of ancient wise men once determined, by only looking at the heavens, that (1) there was a child born (2) who was King of the Jews, (3) who was to be worshipped, (4) the child was priest, prophet, and king (gold, frankincense, and myrrh). Matthew 2:1-12. Whose knowledge, ours or theirs, is more "enlightened?"

"Any technical solution which science claims to offer will be powerless to solve the serious problems of our world if humanity loses its compass…" (*Laudato Si*, 2015, par 200)

Merely knowing "that" does not tell us "why." People justify themselves "because XYZ weakness is in my DNA." Technical science affirms this; however, it fails to convey reality: we are <u>all</u> weak in our DNA. Human excellence has always, and will always be, a struggle against our animal weaknesses and deficiencies; it is not capitulating to them.

-Ecological & Environmental Concerns-

"According to the almost unanimous opinion of believers and unbelievers alike, all things on earth should be related to man as their center and crown.
… when [man] recognizes in himself a spiritual and immortal soul, he is not being mocked by a fantasy born only of physical or social influences, but is

rather laying hold of the proper truth of the matter." (*Gaudium et Spes*, 1965, par. 12-14)

-The above is not merely a declaration of Man's prominence, but also an acknowledgement of Man's responsibilities therein.

"In the very first pages of Scripture we read these words: "Fill the earth and subdue it." This teaches us that the whole of creation is for man, that he has been charged to give it meaning by his intelligent activity, to complete and perfect it by his own efforts and to his own advantage" (*Populorum Progresso*, 1967, par.22).

"<u>Man is suddenly becoming aware that by an ill-considered exploitation of nature he risks destroying it and becoming in his turn the victim of this degradation.</u> Not only is the material environment becoming a permanent menace - pollution and refuse, new illness and absolute destructive capacity - but the human framework is no longer under man's control, thus creating an environment for tomorrow which may well be intolerable. This is a wide-ranging social problem which concerns the entire human family.
<u>The Christian must turn to these new perceptions in order to take on responsibility, together with the rest of men, for a destiny which from now on is shared by all.</u>" (*Octogesima Adveniens*, 1971, par.21)

"Among today's positive signs we must also mention a greater realization of the limits of available resources, and of the need to respect the integrity and the cycles of nature and to take them into account when planning for development, rather than sacrificing them to certain demagogic ideas about the latter. Today this is called ecological concern." (*Sollilicitudo Rei Socialis*, 1987, par.26)

"<u>Nor can the moral character of development exclude respect for the beings which constitute the natural world…</u>
<u>… The first consideration is the appropriateness of acquiring a growing awareness of the fact that one cannot use with impunity the different categories of beings, whether living or inanimate - animals, plants, the natural elements - simply as one wishes, according to one's own economic needs.</u>
<u>… The second consideration is based on the realization - which is perhaps more urgent - that natural resources are limited; some are not, as it is said, renewable.</u>

"… The third consideration refers directly to the consequences of a certain type of development on the quality of life in the industrialized zones. We all know that the direct or indirect result of industrialization is, ever more frequently, the pollution of the environment, with serious consequences for the health of the population." (*Sollilicitudo Rei Socialis*, 1987, par. 34)

"Equally worrying is *the ecological question* which accompanies the problem of consumerism and which is closely connected to it. In his desire to have and to enjoy rather than to be and to grow, man consumes the resources of the earth and his own life in an excessive and disordered way. At the root of the senseless destruction of the natural environment lies an anthropological error, which unfortunately is widespread in our day. Man, who discovers his capacity to transform and in a certain sense create the world through his own work, forgets that this is always based on God's prior and original gift of the things that are. Man thinks that he can make arbitrary use of the earth, subjecting it without restraint to his will, as though it did not have its own requisites and a prior God-given purpose, which man can indeed develop but must not betray. Instead of carrying out his role as a co-operator with God in the work of creation, man sets himself up in place of God and thus ends up provoking a rebellion on the part of nature, which is more tyrannized than governed by him.

…In addition to the irrational destruction of the natural environment, we must also mention the more serious destruction of the *human environment*, something which is by no means receiving the attention it deserves. Although people are rightly worried — though much less than they should be — about preserving the natural habitats of the various animal species threatened with extinction, because they realize that each of these species makes its particular contribution to the balance of nature in general, too little effort is made to *safeguard the moral conditions for an authentic "human ecology"*. Not only has God given the earth to man, who must use it with respect for the original good purpose for which it was given to him, but man too is God's gift to man. He must therefore respect the natural and moral structure with which he has been endowed. In this context, mention should be made of the serious problems of modern urbanization, of the need for urban planning which is concerned with how people are to live, and of the attention which should be given to a "social ecology" of work." (*Centesimus annus*, 1991, par. 37-38)

"In nature, the believer recognizes the wonderful result of God's creative activity, which we may use responsibly to satisfy our legitimate needs, material or otherwise, while respecting the intrinsic balance of creation. If this vision is lost, we end up either considering nature an untouchable taboo or, on the contrary, abusing it. Neither attitude is consonant with the Christian vision of nature as the fruit of God's creation.

…But it should also be stressed that it is contrary to authentic development to view nature as something more important than the human person. This position leads to attitudes of neo-paganism or a new pantheism [i.e. worship of nature]… This having been said, it is also necessary to reject the opposite position, which aims at total technical dominion over nature, because the natural environment is more than raw material to be manipulated at our pleasure; it is a wondrous work of the Creator containing a "grammar" which sets forth ends and criteria for its wise use, not its reckless exploitation. Today much harm is done to development precisely as a result of these distorted notions. Reducing nature merely to a collection of contingent data ends up doing violence to the environment and even encouraging activity that fails to respect human nature itself." (*Caritas in Veritatae*, 2009, par.48)

"It is likewise incumbent upon the competent authorities to make every effort to ensure that the economic and social costs of using up shared environmental resources are recognized with transparency and fully borne by those who incur them, not by other peoples or future generations: the protection of the environment, of resources and of the climate obliges all international leaders to act jointly and to show a readiness to work in good faith, respecting the law and promoting solidarity with the weakest regions of the planet. One of the greatest challenges facing the economy is to achieve the most efficient use — not abuse — of natural resources, based on a realization that the notion of "efficiency" is not value-free.

The way humanity treats the environment influences the way it treats itself, and vice versa.
This invites contemporary society to a serious review of its life-style, which, in many parts of the world, is prone to hedonism and consumerism, regardless of their harmful consequences. What is needed is an effective shift in mentality which can lead to the adoption of new life-styles "in which the quest for truth, beauty, goodness and communion with others for the sake of common growth are the factors which determine consumer choices, savings and investments"… When incentives are offered for their economic and cultural development, nature itself is protected. Moreover, how many natural resources are squandered by wars! …The hoarding of resources, especially water, can generate serious conflicts among the peoples involved.

... In order to protect nature, it is not enough to intervene with economic incentives or deterrents; not even an apposite education is sufficient. These are important steps, but the *decisive issue is the overall moral tenor of society*. If there is a lack of respect for the right to life and to a natural death, if human conception, gestation and birth are made artificial, if human embryos are sacrificed to research, the conscience of society ends up losing the concept of human ecology and, along with it, that of environmental ecology. It is contradictory to insist that future generations respect the natural environment when our educational systems and laws do not help them to respect themselves... It would be wrong to uphold one set of duties while trampling on the other. Herein lies a grave contradiction in our mentality and practice today: one which demeans the person, disrupts the environment and damages society." (*Caritas in Veritatae*, 2009, par.50-51)

-This principle of conferring the costs of the destruction of the environment to those who incur them, is in legal speak called "internalizing the externalities," that is to say, making sure that those who do the harm to the environment – or other such harm – are the ones who pay for it, not an innocent or helpless third party.

"<u>There are other weak and defenseless beings who are frequently at the mercy of economic interests or indiscriminate exploitation. I am speaking of creation as a whole… Let us not leave in our wake a swath of destruction and death which will affect our own lives and those of future generations.</u>" (*Evangelii Gaudium*, 2013, par.215)

"Regrettably, many efforts to seek concrete solutions to the environmental crisis have proved ineffective, not only because of powerful opposition but also <u>because of a more general lack of interest</u>… It is my hope that this Encyclical Letter, which is now added to the body of the Church's social teaching, can help us to acknowledge the appeal, immensity and urgency of the challenge we face." (Laudato Si, 2015, par 14-15)

"Because of us, thousands of species will no longer give glory to God by their very existence, nor convey their message to us. We have no such right… Because all creatures are connected, each must be cherished with love and respect, for all of us as living creatures are dependent on one another." (*Laudato Si*, 2015, par 33, 42)

"We were not meant to be inundated by cement, asphalt, glass and metal, and deprived of physical contact with nature." (*Laudato Si*, 2015, par 44)

"At one extreme, we find those who doggedly uphold the myth of progress and tell us that ecological problems will solve themselves simply with the application of new technology and without any need for ethical considerations or deep change. At the other extreme are those who view men and women and all their interventions as no more than a threat, jeopardizing the global ecosystem, and consequently the presence of human beings on the planet should be reduced and all forms of intervention prohibited. Viable future scenarios will have to be generated between these extremes, since there is no one path to a solution." (*Laudato Si*, 2015, par 60)

"On many concrete questions, the Church has no reason to offer a definitive opinion; she knows that honest debate must be encouraged among experts, while respecting divergent views. But we need only take a frank look at the facts to see that our common home is falling into serious disrepair." (*Laudato Si*, 2015, par 61)

"The creation accounts in the book of Genesis… suggest[s] that human life is grounded in three fundamental and closely intertwined relationships: with God, with our neighbour and with the earth itself. According to the Bible, these three vital relationships have been broken, both outwardly and within us. This rupture is sin." (*Laudato Si*, 2015, par 66)

"[Some claim that] the Genesis account which grants man "dominion" over the earth (cf. Gen 1:28), has encouraged the unbridled exploitation of nature by painting him as domineering and destructive by nature. This is not a correct interpretation of the Bible as understood by the Church." (*Laudato Si*, 2015, par 67)

"[Historically] Judaeo-Christian thought demythologized nature. While continuing to admire its grandeur and immensity, it no longer saw nature as divine. In doing so, it emphasizes all the more our human responsibility for nature." (*Laudato Si*, 2015, par 78)

"This is not to put all living beings on the same level nor to deprive human beings of their unique worth and the tremendous responsibility it entails. Nor does it imply a divinization of the earth which would prevent us from working on it and protecting it in its fragility. Such notions would end up creating new imbalances which would deflect us from the reality which challenges us." (*Laudato Si*, 2015, par 90)

"It is clearly inconsistent to combat trafficking in endangered species while remaining completely indifferent to human trafficking, unconcerned about the poor, or undertaking to destroy another human being deemed unwanted." (*Laudato Si*, 2015, par 91)

"It follows that our indifference or cruelty towards fellow creatures of this world sooner or later affects the treatment we mete out to other human beings." (*Laudato Si*, 2015, par 92)

"[Quoting John Paul II] 'we cannot interfere in one area of the ecosystem without paying due attention to the consequences of such interference in other areas'." (*Laudato Si*, 2015, par 131)

"It cannot be emphasized enough how everything is interconnected." (*Laudato Si*, 2015, par 138)

"When we speak of the "environment", what we really mean is a relationship existing between nature and the society which lives in it… We are faced not with two separate crises, one environmental and the other social, but rather with one complex crisis which is both social and environmental. Strategies for a solution demand an integrated approach to combating poverty, restoring dignity to the excluded, and at the same time protecting nature."" (*Laudato Si*, 2015, par 139)

-This is the key to understanding (or misunderstanding) the Catholic position on the Environment, Pope Francis, and Laudato Si. The "Environment" is not just the green stuff and animals; it is our relationship to the world at large, encompassing time, space, and the hierarchy of living things.

"With regard to climate change, the advances have been regrettably few. Reducing greenhouse gases requires honesty, courage and responsibility, above all on the part of those countries which are more powerful and pollute the most." (*Laudato Si*, 2015, par 169)

"The strategy of buying and selling "carbon credits" can lead to a new form of speculation which would not help reduce the emission of polluting gases worldwide. This system seems to provide a quick and easy solution under the guise of a certain commitment to the environment, but in no way does it allow for the radical change which present circumstances require. Rather, it may simply become a ploy which permits maintaining the excessive consumption of some countries and sectors." (*Laudato Si*, 2015, par 171)

"Education in environmental responsibility can encourage ways of acting which directly and significantly affect the world around us, such as avoiding the use of plastic and paper, reducing water consumption, separating refuse, cooking only what can reasonably be consumed, showing care for other living beings, using public transport or car-pooling, planting trees, turning off unnecessary lights, or any number of other practices... Reusing something instead of immediately discarding it, when done for the right reasons, can be an act of love which expresses our own dignity. We must not think that these efforts are not going to change the world. They benefit society, often unbeknown to us, for they call forth a goodness which, albeit unseen, inevitably tends to spread." (*Laudato Si*, 2015, par 211, 212)

"We do not understand our superiority [in the hierarchy of living things] as a reason for personal glory or irresponsible dominion, but rather as a different capacity which, in its turn, entails a serious responsibility stemming from our faith." (*Laudato Si*, 2015, par 220)

"Mary, the Mother who cared for Jesus, now cares with maternal affection and pain for this wounded world. Just as her pierced heart mourned the death of Jesus, so now she grieves for the sufferings of the crucified poor and for the creatures of this world laid waste by human power... She treasures the entire life of Jesus in her heart (cf. Lk 2:19,51), and now understands the meaning of all things. Hence, we can ask her to enable us to look at this world with eyes of wisdom." (*Laudato Si*, 2015, par 241)

-Energy-

"The fact that some States, power groups and companies hoard non-renewable energy resources represents a grave obstacle to development in poor countries. Those countries lack the economic means either to gain access to existing sources of non-renewable energy or to finance research into new alternatives. The stockpiling of natural resources, which in many cases are found in the poor countries themselves, gives rise to exploitation and frequent conflicts between and within nations. These conflicts are often fought on the soil of those same countries, with a heavy toll of death, destruction and further decay. The international community has an urgent duty to find institutional means of regulating the exploitation of non-renewable resources, involving poor countries in the process, in order to plan together for the future.
… The technologically advanced societies can and must lower their domestic energy consumption, either through an evolution in manufacturing methods or through greater ecological sensitivity among their citizens… What is also

needed, though, is a worldwide redistribution of energy resources, so that countries lacking those resources can have access to them. The fate of those countries cannot be left in the hands of whoever is first to claim the spoils, or whoever is able to prevail over the rest." (*Caritas in Veritatae*, 2009, par.49)

"We know that technology based on the use of highly polluting fossil fuels – especially coal, but also oil and, to a lesser degree, gas – needs to be progressively replaced without delay." (*Laudato Si*, 2015, par 165)

"Benedict XVI has said that 'technologically advanced societies must be prepared to encourage more sober lifestyles, while reducing their energy consumption and improving its efficiency'." (*Laudato Si*, 2015, par 193)

"It is in the Eucharist that all that has been created finds its greatest exaltation. Grace, which tends to manifest itself tangibly, found unsurpassable expression when God himself became man and gave himself as food for his creatures. The Lord, in the culmination of the mystery of the Incarnation, chose to reach our intimate depths through a fragment of matter… Thus, the Eucharist is also a source of light and motivation for our concerns for the environment, directing us to be stewards of all creation." (*Laudato Si*, 2015, par 236)

-Agriculture-

"We know that as an economy develops, the number of people engaged in agriculture decreases, while the percentage employed in industry and the various services rises.
… Nearly every country, therefore, is faced with this fundamental problem: What can be done to reduce the disproportion in productive efficiency between agriculture on the one hand, and industry and services on the other; and to ensure that agricultural living standards approximate as closely as possible those enjoyed by city dwellers who draw their resources either from industry or from the services in which they are engaged?
… In the first place, considerable thought must be given, especially by public authorities, to the suitable development of essential facilities in country areas— such as roads; transportation; means of communication; drinking water; housing; health services; elementary, technical and professional education; religious and recreational facilities; and the supply of modern installations and furnishings for the farm residence.
…If a country is to develop economically, it must do so gradually, maintaining an even balance between all sectors of the economy. Agriculture, therefore,

must be allowed to make use of the same reforms in the method and type of production and in the conduct of the business side of the venture as are permitted or required in the economic system as a whole.

… In addition, a sound agricultural program is needed if public authority is to maintain an evenly balanced progress in the various branches of the economy. This must take into account tax policies, credit, social insurance, prices, the fostering of ancillary industries and the adjustment of the structure of farming as a business enterprise.

… In a system of taxation based on justice and equity it is fundamental that the burdens be proportioned to the capacity of the people contributing.

But the common good also requires the public authorities, in assessing the amount of tax payable, take cognizance of the peculiar difficulties of farmers. They have to wait longer than most people for their returns, and these are exposed to greater hazards.

… <u>Farmers are unable to pay high rates of interest.</u> Indeed, they cannot as a rule make the trading profit necessary to furnish capital for the conduct and development of their own business. It is therefore necessary, for reasons of the common good, for public authorities to evolve a special credit policy and to form credit banks which will guarantee such capital to farmers at a moderate rate of interest.

… We realize that agricultural workers earn less per capita than workers in industry and the services, but that is no reason why it should be considered socially just and equitable to set up systems of social insurance in which the allowances granted to farm workers and their families are substantially lower than those payable to other classes of workers. Insurance programs that are established for the general public should not differ markedly whatever be the economic sector in which the individuals work or the source of their income.

… <u>Given the special nature of agricultural produce, modern economists must devise a suitable means of price protection.</u> Ideally, such price protection should be enforced by the interested parties themselves, though supervision by the public authority cannot be altogether dispensed with.

On this subject it must not be forgotten that the price of agricultural produce represents, for the most part, the reward of the farmer's labor rather than a return on invested capital.

… <u>While it is true that farm produce is mainly intended for the satisfaction of man's primary needs, and the price should therefore be within the means of all consumers, this cannot be used as an argument for keeping a section of the population—farm workers—in a permanent state of economic and social</u>

inferiority, depriving them of the wherewithal for a decent standard of living. This would be diametrically opposed to the common good.

… We are bound above all to consider as an ideal the kind of farm which is owned and managed by the family. Every effort must be made in the prevailing circumstances to give effective encouragement to farming enterprises of this nature.

To ensure [success], farmers must be given up-to-date instruction on the latest methods of cultivation, and the assistance of experts must be put at their disposal. They should also form a flourishing system of cooperative undertakings, and organize themselves professionally to take an effective part in public life, both on the administrative and the political level.

…We are convinced that the farming community must take an active part in its own economic advancement, social progress and cultural betterment.

… Theirs is a work which carries with it a dignity all its own.

… Rural workers should feel a sense of solidarity with one another, and should unite to form co-operatives and professional associations… The lone voice is not likely to command much of a hearing in times such as ours.

In using their various organizations, agricultural workers—as indeed all other classes of workers—must always be guided by moral principles and respect for the civil law. They must try to reconcile their rights and interests with those of other classes of workers, and even subordinate the one to the other if the common good demands it." (*Mater et Magistra*, 1961, par.124-147)

"The world of agriculture, which provides society with the goods it needs for its daily sustenance, is of *fundamental importance*.

… Agricultural work involves considerable difficulties… to the point of making agricultural people feel that they are social outcasts and of speeding up the phenomenon of their mass exodus from the countryside to the cities and unfortunately to still more dehumanizing living conditions. Added to this are the lack of adequate professional training and of proper equipment, the spread of a certain individualism, and also *objectively unjust situations*. In certain developing countries, millions of people are forced to cultivate the land belonging to others and are exploited by the big landowners, without any hope of ever being able to gain possession of even a small piece of land of their own. There is a lack of forms of legal protection for the agricultural workers themselves and for their families in case of old age, sickness or unemployment. Long days of hard physical work are paid miserably. Land which could be cultivated is left abandoned by the owners. Legal titles to possession of a small portion of land that someone has personally cultivated for years are disregarded or left defenseless against the "land hunger" of more powerful individuals or groups. But even in the economically developed countries, where scientific research, technological achievements and State policy have brought agriculture to a very advanced level, the right to work can be infringed when the farm workers are denied the possibility of sharing in decisions concerning their services, or when they are denied the right to free association with a view to their just advancement socially, culturally and economically.

… <u>Thus it is necessary to proclaim and promote the dignity of work, of all work but especially of agricultural work…</u>" (*Laborem Exercens*, 1981, par. 21)

-The above was written long before the GMO/Gene Patenting system and subsequent controversies were a widespread issue. These issues, as well as the growing blemishes of land speculation from the Financial Sector and other powerful centres, makes St. John Paul II's words especially relevant.

"[St. John Paul II] made it clear that the Church values the benefits which result "from the study and applications of molecular biology, supplemented by other disciplines such as genetics, and its technological application in agriculture and industry". But he also pointed out that this should not lead to "indiscriminate genetic manipulation" which ignores the negative effects of such interventions… It is difficult to make a general judgement about genetic modification (GM), whether vegetable or animal, medical or agricultural, since these vary greatly among themselves and call for specific considerations. The risks involved are not always due to the techniques used, but rather to their improper or excessive application. Genetic mutations, in fact, have often been, and continue to be, caused by nature itself. Nor are mutations caused by human intervention a modern phenomenon. The domestication of animals, the crossbreeding of species and other older and universally accepted practices can be mentioned as examples. We need but recall that scientific developments in GM cereals began with the observation of natural bacteria which spontaneously modified plant genomes. In nature, however, this process is slow and cannot be compared to the fast pace induced by contemporary technological advances, even when the latter build upon several centuries of scientific progress. Although no conclusive proof exists that GM cereals may be harmful to human beings, and in some regions their use has brought about economic growth which has helped to resolve problems, there remain a number of significant difficulties which should not be underestimated [including creating dependency of smaller farmers on powerful rights-holders]." (*Laudato Si*, 2015, par 131-134

INDEX OF PAPAL DOCUMENTS

All Encyclicals and documents are sourced from Vatican.va, where they can be found and read free of charge.

Encyclicals:

Rerum Novarum, 1891 - Pope Leo XIII

Quadragesimo Anno, 1931 - Pope Pius XI

Mater et Magistra, 1961 - Pope John XXIII

Pacem in Terris, 1963 - Pope John XXIII

Gaudium et Spes, 1965 - Pope Paul VI

Populorum Progresso, 1967 - Pope Paul VI

Humanae Vitae, 1968 - Pope Paul VI

Laborem Exercens, 1981 - Pope John Paull II

Sollilicitudo Rei Socialis, 1987 - Pope John Paull II

Centesimus annus, 1991 -Pope John Paull II

Evangelium Vitae, 1995 - Pope John Paull II

Deus Caritas Est, 2005 - Pope Benedict XVI

Caritas in Veritatae, 2009 - Pope Benedict XVI

Laudato Si, 2015 - Pope Francis

Apostolic Letter:

Octogesima Adveniens, 1971 - Pope Paul VI

Apostolic Exhortation:

Evangelii Gaudium, 2013 - Pope Francis

Alphabetized Table of Contents

1. Life & Human Nature	1
2. Family, Community, and Government	14
3. Rights & Responsibilities	102
4. Poor and Vulnerable	111
5. Work & the Economy	123
6. One Human Body (Solidarity)	181
7. Creation, Ecological Issues, and the Environment	200
Abortion – see "Contraception, Sterilization, and Abortion"	
Adoption	19
Advertising & Consumerism	70
Agriculture	214
Anarchy	36
Atheism	98
Bioethics	11
Capital Punishment	12
Capitalism	156
Capitalism v. Socialism	165
Catholic Social Teaching	48
Charity (Caritas)	102
Class Warfare	66
Communism & Marxism	164
Consumers	71

Contraception, Sterilization, & Abortion	5
Contracts	139
Culture	95
Democracy	88
Development	116
Dialogue & Differences in Opinion	81
Discrimination	87
Divorce	17
Ecological & Environmental Concerns	206
Economics	123
Education	74
Elderly & Disabled	8
Energy	213
Equality & Inequality	183
Ethics	10
Euthanasia	9
Evangelization	81
Family	14
Finance	174
Foreign Aid	112
Foreign Markets	171
Foreign Policy	94
Form of Government	88
Free Consent	138

Alphabetized Table of Contents

1. Life & Human Nature	1
2. Family, Community, and Government	14
3. Rights & Responsibilities	102
4. Poor and Vulnerable	111
5. Work & the Economy	123
6. One Human Body (Solidarity)	181
7. Creation, Ecological Issues, and the Environment	200
Abortion – see "Contraception, Sterilization, and Abortion"	
Adoption	19
Advertising & Consumerism	70
Agriculture	214
Anarchy	36
Atheism	98
Bioethics	11
Capital Punishment	12
Capitalism	156
Capitalism v. Socialism	165
Catholic Social Teaching	48
Charity (Caritas)	102
Class Warfare	66
Communism & Marxism	164
Consumers	71

Contraception, Sterilization, & Abortion	5
Contracts	139
Culture	95
Democracy	88
Development	116
Dialogue & Differences in Opinion	81
Discrimination	87
Divorce	17
Ecological & Environmental Concerns	206
Economics	123
Education	74
Elderly & Disabled	8
Energy	213
Equality & Inequality	183
Ethics	10
Euthanasia	9
Evangelization	81
Family	14
Finance	174
Foreign Aid	112
Foreign Markets	171
Foreign Policy	94
Form of Government	88
Free Consent	138

Free Market or Laissez Faire Market	131
Freedom	106
Freedom of Press & Freedom of Speech	66
Freedom of Religion and Conscience	108
Global and Foreign Relationships	93
Global Cooperation & Foreign Policy	189
Guns – see "The Arms Race & Disarmament"	
Healthcare	64
Human Trafficking	13
Immigration & Emigration	185
Inheritance	19
International Trade	178
Investments & Investing	172
Labor	127
Legislation & Practical Application of Social Principles	56
Liberalism	155
Liberation Theology	121
Life	1
Marriage	17
Media, Social Media, & the News	67
Minorities	87
Monopolies	177
NonViolent Resistance	122
Obligations of Employers to Workers	141

Obligations of Workers to Employers	141
Outsourcing	175
Patriotism	100
Peace	90
Politics & Public Activity	46
Poor	111
Population Expansion	197
Pornography & Drugs	12
Principle of Subsidiarity	37
Private Property	19
Production	139
Progress & Reform	51
Propaganda	70
Proportional Ownership for All –or – Promotion of Ownership	24
Public Authority	89
Public versus Private	72
Racism	87
Reform	170
Regulation	60
Rest & Sunday Worship	150
Revolution	187
Right to Life	106
Rights	103
Role of Catholics in Public Activity	45

Role of the Church in Society & Politics	38
Role of the State	28
Science & Technology	200
Self-Interest – see "Free Consent" or "Free Market"	
Separation of Church and State or Church and Public Life	48
Small Businesses & Cooperatives	175
Socialism	161
Solidarity & Human Dignity	181
Sterilization – see "Contraception, Sterilization, and Abortion"	
Strikes	141
Tariffs	177
Taxes & Tax Evasion	65
Terrorism	100
The Arms Race & Disarmament	188
The Market	130
Tourism	101
Unemployment	151
Unions & NonGovernment Organizations	151
United Nations	196
Urbanization	96
Utopias & Ideologies	79
Volunteer Aid	116
Voting	100
Wages & Profit	143

War	92
Welfare & State Subsidies	61
Women & Women in the Workplace	86
Workplace	149
World Fund & International Debt	179
Youth	78

© Christopher Jay, 2016

Author is an Alumnus of Wyoming Catholic College, and of Ave Maria School of Law.

www.whywesingatmass.org
music@whywesingatmass.org

www.ingramcontent.com/pod-product-compliance
Lightning Source LLC
Chambersburg PA
CBHW061318040426
42444CB00011B/2697